Across Seven Seas
and
Thirteen Rivers

Caroline Adams

Caroline Adams was born in Britain in 1949. Both her grandfathers had experience of being migrant workers – one coming to this country from Hungary, the other going from Britain to Mauritius.

Brought up in Somerset, she travelled extensively in South Asia. In 1971 she became involved in the Bangladesh struggle for independence and worked as a volunteer with children in the refugee camps.

Her interests include travelling, history, politics and mountain walking. She lives in South London.

Her first book – **'They Sell Cheaper And They Live Very Odd'** a study of immigrant groups coming to the East End – was published by the British Council of Churches in 1977. **'Across Seven Seas and Thirteen Rivers'** is her second publication.

Eastside is a member of the Federation of Worker Writers and Community Publishers **(FWWCP)**, a national federation whose member groups seek to promote the creative writings of ordinary people working through writers workshops and community publishing projects.

Eastside Books

In memory of my friend
Md. Jafar Khan
who died too soon.

আমরা এসেছি সুদূরের ডাক শুনে
সাত সাগরের অচেনা ঢেউ গুণে
নব জীবনের আশায়

We were called from a distant land,
Counting the waves of
Thirteen rivers and seven seas
With hopes for a better life.

'Trades Union' by Abdus Salique

Across Seven Seas
and
Thirteen Rivers

Life Stories of
pioneer Sylheti settlers
in
Britain

edited by
Caroline Adams

Foreword by
Tassaduq Ahmed

Drawings by
Dan Jones

Eastside Books

First published 1987 by THAP Books
2nd edition November 1994 by Eastside Books
With thanks to Bethnal Green City Challenge for
financial support

Photoset in Century Schoolbook 10 on 11 point.
Typeset and printed by
Expression Printers Ltd, 49 Corsica Street, London N5 1JT.

Eastside is a member of the Federation of Worker Writers and
Community Publishers.

British Library Cataloguing in Publication Data

Across Seven Seas and Thirteen Rivers: life
    stories of pioneer Sylheti settlers in Britain.
    1. Bangladeshis——England——Social
    life and customs
    I. Adams, Caroline
    942'.00491412   DA125.S57

ISBN: 0 906698 22 7 paperback

cover illustration: Ahmed Hossain, Dhaka.
production: Denise Jones, Roger Mills, John Wallett
EASTSIDE BOOKS: 178 Whitechapel Road, London E1 1BJ

Contents

Acknowledgements

There are many people to be thanked for their help and support, which has enabled this book to be produced.

The most important are those who gave so much of their time and their memories, the men whose life stories are written here: Haji Nawab Ali; the late Haji Shirajul Islam; the late Mr Abdul Malik; Haji Kona Miah; Shah Abdul Majid Qureshi; Syed Rasul; Mr Attar Ullah; Mr Hasmat Ullah; Mr Abdul Wahab and their families.

Much valuable information and inspiration were also given by: Mrs Aysha Ali; Haji Taslim Ali; Mr Ijad Ali; Haji Kolondor Ali; Haji Nesar Ali; the late Haji Abdul Gafur; Mr Ashraf Hussain; Mr Nurul Islam; Mr Abdul Mannan M.L.A.; Haji Kotu Miah, and the late Mr Tayibur Rahman and family.

From the beginning of the research to publication, the project owes its existence to the enthusiasm and guidance tirelessly given by Tassaduq Ahmed; the late Ahmed Fakhruddin; Shahjehan Lutfur Rahman, and Shah Abdul Majid Qureshi.

The following friends have given all kinds of help, from practical tasks to encouragement to author and publishers: Kamal Ahmed; Ruhul Amin; Liz Anderton; Phil Ballard; Vanessa Chadwick; John Eversley; Bill Fishman; Sandy Hedderwick; Rajan Uddin Jalal; Dan Jones; Tom Learmonth; Ken Leech; Shwasti Mitter; Clare Murphy; David Slack and Abbas Uddin.

Help with research is gratefully acknowledged from the staffs of various libraries and museums; notably those of the India Office Library and Records; National Maritime Museum; School of Oriental and African Studies and the

Imperial War Museum. Particular thanks are due to individuals within these and other institutions: Bob Aspinall of the Port of London Collection; Howard Bloch at Newham Local Studies Library; Tony Farrington (Marine Records Dept.) and Pat Katterhorn (Prints and Drawings Dept.) at the India Office Library; Chris Lloyd at Tower Hamlets Local History Library, and Tanya Morgan at the Church Missionary Society. Special thanks to Campbell McMurray of the National Maritime Museum (now Director of the Scottish Maritime Museum) and Stephen Rabson, Libraries of the P&O Group.

Finally, I would like to thank Denise Jones and John Wallett of Tower Hamlets Arts Project for their imagination, commitment and hard work, which have brought this history into print.

Caroline Adams

Foreword

At long last the book is out – the book for which some of us were anxiously waiting for several years – the book which tries to tell the personal tales of a few Bengali-speaking (Banglabhashi) settlers in the UK from among the first three hundred or so who came to this island during the early part of the century. They are the fore-runners of the 35,000 who are now living in East London, and of the thousands more who live throughout this country.

This is a book for which Caroline and her husband David had to travel extensively here and abroad . . . throughout this country, Sylhet and Assam . . . seeking out Bangladeshis who had migrated to Britain in the 20's, 30's and 40's, and collecting much documentary material to complement the illuminating life-stories which they told.

Most of these men had come by sea routes as ship crews. In those days it could take three or four weeks to travel by passenger boat, now of course from Dhaka to London, airport to airport, it takes barely nine and a half hours by direct flight. They used to be on the high seas for months together, before they could leave the ships to settle here – in a country which was alien and whose climate was uninviting. Nevertheless this country offered them the opportunity to escape from the poverty of their own country – the 'Golden Bengal' of Tagore – which was then a British Colony.

The story tellers in this book are all ex-seamen who served on the British Merchant Navy ships in peace and in war. There are not many of them left alive to tell their stories of adventure, endurance and hardships encountered in crossing the mythical *Seven Seas and Thirteen Rivers* related with

Rickshaw painting by Ahmed Hossain   *Tom Learmonth*

such eloquence in Bengali folk tales. Overcoming all the hurdles, they at long last managed to reach the shores of the 'promised land' where it was said that '. . . leaves of gold drop from the trees.' How many golden leaves our fore-runners were able to collect Caroline has not been able to tell us. But we know that she has faithfully recorded their stories of trials and tribulations, tragedies and pathos . . . their sense of fulfilment and their successes. These are stories of living human beings, narrated by those who were themselves on the stage. They are stories of immense human interest, and as such are more exciting than any thriller or fiction.

But alas! Some of the narrators are not with us to see their stories in print because of the delay in getting a publisher. To the commercial publishers there was no money in such a project because not enough sensational ammunition was packed in the book – they are plain facts, told by ordinary people. And to most of us of course this is the main strength of the book.

It is a book that will tell the story of why and how the fore-runners of the present generations of Banglabhashi settlers came to this country. In those not very far off days there were only a few households – mostly boarding houses scattered around the ports of call of the shipping lines . . . London, Liverpool, Cardiff, Portsmouth etc. – they could be counted on one hand. Today there are over 250,000 Banglabhashi settlers from Bangladesh alone, not taking into account those from the Indian State of West Bengal . . .

their number could be another sixty to seventy-thousand. In Tower Hamlets, the borough in East London where most of the Banglabhashis settled, they constitute the largest single group among the ethnic and Black communities here, and represent nearly sixty per cent of the non-European residents. For some it has become their second home . . . whilst for many others it is the only home they will ever know. Here also many of the schools are saturated with Banglabhashi children – nearly 9000 children in all, and in more than a dozen schools something like ninety per cent of the student population come from Bengali or Sylheti speaking backgrounds.

Taking all this into account we are hopeful that this small book will provide some much needed background information on this community which has settled in Tower Hamlets. This area incidentally, has the highest concentration of Banglabhashis in the UK (indeed in the world if we exclude only the Bengali-speaking regions of the South Asian subcontinent). Besides this there are many indications that the area may develop as a meeting place for Bengalis worldwide – they constitute the sixth largest linguistic group in the world with nearly 180 million voices pledging loyalty to one language and one culture, though differing in religious faiths and separated by political boundaries.

This is a book which has been brought together by one who has been a friend of the Bengali Community for over fifteen years – she was the Secretary of the Bengali Action Group which in 1974 focused attention on the need for a community centre in the Spitalfields area – where nearly seventy per cent of the population are Banglabhashi. Named after the 'Rebel Poet of Bengal' (Quazi Nazrul Islam), the Nazrul Centre was formally inaugurated in 1982 by Lord Fenner Brockway – that venerable statesman of British politics (who was himself born in Calcutta). An event of great significance and potential, the opening of this centre was followed by a combination of unfortunate circumstances, and it was forced to close only nine months later . . . the building is still unoccupied today, waiting for a new generation of Banglabhashis to make proper use of the premises.

But the involvement of the author with the Banglabhashi Community has been responsible for the weak spot of the book. Her attachment to the Community, and her cautious tread (so as not to offend the susceptibilities of a community under heavy attack from the racists, both overt and covert) has held her back from offering criticism where such criticisms were warranted for the betterment of the Community. I would not consider this to be her fault – maybe this unpleasant but necessary task will have to be undertaken by members of our own community, who feel that their credentials of service give them the right to criticize. This might open the door for the Community to play more fully the role which history has written for it. That role is to be at the vanguard of the multiracial mobilisation of all the anti-racist forces of British society. Banglabhashis are of course the worst victims of British racism – they are the most disadvantaged and underprivileged of all the racial minority groups. And it is the law of social development that the victims must be the vanguard in the struggle for emancipation, not only of themselves but also of others who are victims of similar social injustice and discrimination. Events following the racist killing of Altab Ali in 1978 have shown that they can play that role with honour if they can can develop correct political orientation and flexibility in their style of work.

When asked to write the foreword to this book I was at first hesitant. But then I thought that it is an opportunity for an activist member of the Banglabhashi Community to introduce a few introspective points, and that I should not miss the opportunity offered by the publishers. It is my very sincere hope that the book will work as a catalyst to provoke other community activists to come forward with their contributions and criticisms so that the failures that led to the closure of the Nazrul Centre and similar painful incidents, could be corrected.

Let us hope that this book will help us to look back and reflect on the past, not for the purposes of recrimination but in order to learn from its mistakes.

A first step was taken through the formation of the Bengali Action Group in 1974, and was followed by the 'Arts of Bengal' Exhibition in 1978. Later work (in the area of youth activities and with youth organisations) led to the establishment of the education campaign 'Bengali Educational Needs in Tower Hamlets' (BENTH) and was further consolidated through the 'International Tagore Festival' in 1986. Perhaps these developments can now be taken to their logical conclusion, so that together we will be able to make Tower Hamlets the centrepiece for the promotion of Bengali language, literature and culture in the world forum.

May luck favour us as it did in 1971 . . . when the creation of Bangladesh as a new sovereign state and the homeland of the Banglabhashi people for the first time in their two thousand year history gave the language of the land – the Bengali language – the status of the state language.

May we be lucky to be the worthy creators of a staging post for the projection of the new Bengali identity in the world . . . and add another chapter to the glorious history of Tower Hamlets as the haven of persecuted minorities like the Huguenots and the Jews, and the provider of jobs and homes to the deprived ones like the Irish and Banglabhashis.

Through reading these life stories we can enable our forerunners to speak to us . . . It is now up to us and the coming generations to listen, and to complete the works which they began . . .

Tassaduq Ahmed
Spitalfields
March 1987

Preface

The men whose life stories are told in this book were born early this century, the sons of peasants in villages in Sylhet District in what is now Bangladesh but was then Assam, in the north-eastern part of British India.

They were driven by poverty and drawn by ambition to leave their homes at an early age and to work in the merchant ships of the Raj, which took them all over the world.

With the outbreak of the Second World War, their services, and those of the thousands of Indian seamen who died in that conflict, were vital to Britain's survival.

After leaving the ships, they settled in the cities of Britain, where their presence was the stimulus for the migration from Sylhet which has established dynamic new communities in areas such as East London.

Some of the pioneers have flourished, particularly in the Indian restaurant business which they created. Others have barely survived, but in their survival were great adventures. Some are famous in their own community, heroes of songs and legends, others are unknown to any but their own families, to whom they are all heroes. In the wider community however, in Britain where they have made their homes, they are all unknown, just anonymous 'Asians'. But for every white-bearded elderly Bangladeshi gentleman strolling with dignity to the mosque, or beleaguered by racist attacks in a decrepit council flat, there is a life history: a tale of magic and mystery in Assam, adventure in the North Atlantic, romance in the Blitz, or simply the unfolding of a long life and all its lessons.

This, then, is why these life stories have been recorded. It would also perhaps by useful to explain how it happened.

In 1971, while travelling in India, I worked for a time as a volunteer with the Cathedral Relief Service of Calcutta, in the camps set up in West Bengal for refugees from the Bangladesh liberation struggle. Following the victory of Bangladesh, I went from India across the border to see the new nation, and to visit some of my friends from the camps in their village homes in Faridpur District. My love for Bangladesh began at its birth, and has continued and grown ever since.

On returning to England, I was lucky enough to get a perfect opportunity to get to know the Bangladeshi community in Britain, when I was appointed in 1974 as a youth and community worker at Avenues Unlimited, the YWCA/ILEA neighbourhood youth project in Tower Hamlets. My job for the next six years was to assist the Bangladeshi community in developing provision for young people.

During those years I was in contact mainly with children, young people and women, but just occasionally I would meet a father, grandfather, or uncle who would tell me that he was a 'navy man', or casually mention the Malta convoys, or wartime journeys to Australia. There was, however, never time to pursue these conversations.

Then in 1980, having left my job, I returned with my husband to Bangladesh, where we were entertained with overwhelming hospitality by some of our close friends from London, in their village homes in Sylhet district. We had many remarkable and surprising experiences in Sylhet but none more exciting than the encounters with gracious and charming old men, sitting with their hookahs, draped in shawls against the winter chill, outside simple village houses where they told us long leisurely tales of their days in the ships and in East London in the 1920's. From tin trunks they would produce creased and dog-eared 'continuous discharge certificates' identifying them (by a thumb print or the faded photograph of a bright-eyed boy) and detailing their journeys around the world. From these men I learned for the first time the stories of household names like Aftab Ali, and Ayub Ali Master (who was then in his last illness), and I realised how very little I knew about the origins of Bangladeshi settlement in Britain.

Back in London, I found that many people, even within the community, shared my ignorance of a piece of history which was about to disappear. With the guidance and encouragement of Bangladeshi friends who shared my enthusiasm, and without whose support and introductions the project would have been impossible, I began to tape-record conversations with men in London and Birmingham. Some of these men are still somewhat active in the community, others have left their careers behind them and lead a quiet and meditative life. Meeting and talking with these people was a fascinating and humbling experience, sometimes sad, often joyful.

Most of the people I talked to wished their story, and the story of their community to be written down 'because when I am dead, this will still be left, and I think it is important to tell the history of people like us.'

Some readers will certainly feel that it is inappropriate for these stories to have been recorded by a white person. I have always felt that a Bangladeshi person would have done it better, and was only anxious to catch the stories before it was too late. In one way however it was useful for an outsider to record the stories: to me they were fresh and exciting and, as a Bangladeshi friend put it: 'they talked to you because you wanted to know, but we've heard it all before and we don't listen.'

In order to 'tell the history' I have transcribed and edited the tapes, which are presented here, with an introductory commentary which is intended to put them into context and make them easier to follow, but is certainly not to be taken as a definitive historical background.

It is my hope and the hope of those who encouraged me in this work, that the history of the later generations of Bangladeshi settlement will be written by those who made it, and that fresh insights will be added to this first attempt.

Caroline Adams
March 1987

A Haji's Story

'I'm sorry, my dear, but I'm afraid you have come too late. If you had come before I went for Haj, I could have told you a lot of things, but now I can't talk about those things any more. You see, in our religion when you are this age and you have been for Haj, you have finished with the things of the world. So I won't tell you anything, because also, if I told you anything, I couldn't say anything bad now, only that this country is very nice, and the people are very good. There are some other things I would have liked to say, to the National Front, but I can't say those things now, so I won't say anything.

But I think what you are doing is very fine, because people don't understand why we are here. I say that this is my country, not just because I have been here a long time, but because when we came, it was one nation. We were born under British rule, and we were the citizens of this country. I didn't come here as an immigrant, I came here because I was asked to come. I have been here since 1926. I was a merchant seaman, I came here because I was asked to come, it was the mother country.

Do you know that forty-eight countries fought for Britain in the war? Without the Indians, West Indians, and all the others, Britain wouldn't have lasted more than a few days. I would like to ask the racists where they were in 1939, why they didn't say then that we shouldn't be here. Now, you know, my children get called black bastards, and knocked over in the street. Why didn't they say then that we were black bastards?

I have been here a long time, I have done many things. I don't think I have done anything bad, I was always a religious kind of person. If any of my friends wanted to do bad things, I said, 'Well, you please yourself, but I won't do it.' I never made any trouble, and I was never around when there was trouble.

Now if somebody calls me an effing B . . ., I won't say anything, I have finished with all that, let them say what they like. I hope you understand why I can't speak about the past.'

Home

'The people of Sylhet are seafaring people, because it is in their blood'[1]

The district of Sylhet forms the north-east corner of Bangladesh, some three hundred miles from the Chinese border, from which it is separated by the mountainous lands of the Indian hill-tribes. Across the river which forms the northern border of Sylhet, the high plateau of Meghalaya – 'the abode of the clouds' – is raised on a wall of mountains and cliffs, down which torrential waterfalls pour. Parts of Sylhet too are hilly in the east, where tea estates cover the slopes of hills whose tops are thick luxuriant jungle, swathed in mist and where perhaps a stray tiger lingers still. Most of the land however is flat: a patchwork of electric green ricefields with clusters of artificial hillocks, on which stand simple and beautiful village houses by ponds fringed with bamboo and banana trees and tall slender betel-nut palms; and for every village a tiny domed mosque, gleaming with whitewash like icing sugar.

In the rainy season the hillocks become islands, as the great waters of the annual floods turn the low lying areas into seas twelve or fifteen feet deep and hundreds of miles wide. Then, all transport is by boat, the songs of the boatmen echo across the expanse of water, and waterlilies and mosquitoes flourish in the villages. Cherrapunji, the wettest place in the world, is a few miles away in the mountains of Meghalaya, and Sylhet's share of rain is augmented by the bursting rivers. The floods are both a blessing, bringing immense fertility to the plains and for a time making communication

*Then ... the songs of the boatmen echo across
the expanse of water ...*

between remote villages possible, and a curse, destroying life
and property in bad years and roads and bridges every year.
Thus, within twenty miles of the modern town of Sylhet,
there are villages so remote from services and communica-
tions that the pace and style of life has changed little for
centuries.

The main town of the district is Sylhet, a fast growing and
developing town, with its own airport, well stocked bazaars
and shops, good schools and colleges, a fine new hospital and a
large number of travel agencies. The other major towns are
Chhatok and Maulvi Bazar and there are dozens of smaller
towns and bazaars, surrounded by hundreds of villages.

Although the language and culture of the people is
Bengali, the district of Sylhet has for large parts of its history
been administratively a part of Assam, rather than Bengal.
As Srihat, it was an important city of the ancient Assamese
kingdom of Kamrupa. According to the histories of those
days, the depressions around Sylhet were then a permanent
sea and the kings of Kamrupa kept their navy on them. The
navy consisted of the *Navadingas*, nine ships, each propelled
by one hundred and twenty oarsmen. In the twelfth century,
a great earthquake transformed the country, raising the

level of the sealike areas and forming a deep channel near the port town, Srihat. This new river was named Surma, after the queen of Kamrupa.

Sylhet then became two warring kingdoms of north and south, until both were united under the thirteenth century Hindu king, Rajah Gauda Govinda, who built a 'seven storied palace' in the town of Sylhet. The stage was now set for the greatest event in the history of Sylhet: the arrival of Shah Jalal, the bringer of Islam.

Since the coming of the Aryans, (probably via Assam, rather than Bengal), the people of Sylhet had been by turns Buddhists and Hindus, with a fair admixture of pagan survivals woven into their theology. But by the early thirteenth century the religion of the Moghuls had begun to penetrate even this remote corner of the subcontinent and there were already some practising Muslims. In about 1304 one of them, Burhan Uddin, of the village of Tulutikar near Sylhet town, 'took it into his head to secure the longevity of his newly born son by sacrificing the life of a calf in honour of his God. Unfortunately a foolish hawk carried a hoof of the sacrificed calf to the house of a fanatical Brahmin,' where it dropped into the courtyard.[2] The enraged Brahmin rushed to the king, who ordered that in punishment for this blasphemous killing of a cow, Burhan Uddin's right hand should be cut off, and his baby be cast adrift and helpless on a raft in the river.

Burhan Uddin fled to Muslim Bengal to appeal to the ruling Sultan, Firoz Shah, 'against the whims of the Kaffir ruler of this Godforsaken country'.[3] Firoz Shah responded by sending an army, which was routed by Gauda Govinda. Burhan Uddin's next appeal was to the Emperor in Delhi, who sent his nephew, Sikander Ghazi, to avenge the baby – it seems most likely that he was on his way in any case, coming to spread Islam, and the Moghul rule, by the sword. Ghazi's army was thrice vanquished by Gauda Govinda's secret weapon, bows and arrows (adopted, perhaps from the hill tribes), which they took to be witchcraft, and retreated to Bengal to await reinforcements.

Meanwhile, Burhan Uddin, setting out on pilgrimage to Mecca, 'to lodge a last complaint with the Almighty', met the great *Pir*, or Muslim saint, Shah Jalal from Konya in Yemen, proceeding from Delhi to Bengal on a mission of conversion, with his three hundred and sixty missionary followers.[4] Shah Jalal agreed to accompany Burhan Uddin to the stronghold of Hindu resistance and, on the banks of the Surma, he and his saints joined forces with Ghazi and his army for a final assault. Legend has it that Shah Jalal and his followers spread out their shawls and flew on them across the river to the attack, which naturally so demoralised Gauda Govinda's troops that they were forced to surrender. Shah Jalal then completed his victory by circumambulating the seven storied palace and magically causing it to fall, floor by floor from below.

Before commencing his missionary travels. Shah Jalal had been given a handful of earth by his uncle and told to wander the globe in search of a land where the earth was similar in colour and smell. Sylhet was that land and Shah Jalal accordingly settled there and continued his ministry until his death in 1356, at the age of one hundred and fifty. Ever since then he has been the patron saint of Sylhet and the mosque and *mazar* on the spot where he lived, taught and died, are the great centre of pilgrimage in Sylhet.

Meanwhile, the three hundred and sixty saints were despatched to various corners of the district, where they established themselves as teachers and were venerated by their converts, and in their turn commemorated by well tended shrines. The saints gave their names to the villages where they settled and many married and are proudly remembered by their descendants:

I am a direct descendant of Shah Kamal, who came to Sylhet with Shah Jalal.[5]

Shah Jalal came from Yemen with his three hundred and sixty followers. We originated from Shah Mustapha. He had two sons. One son's name was Shah Abdul Latif, they put him in our village as a teacher and there he settled and married.[6]

Shah Jalal and his followers were *Sufis*, mystics whose path to union with God was through meditation, devotional songs and poetry, rather than strict adherence to the austere laws of Islamic orthodoxy. The *Sufi* approach, called *'Maripathi'* in

Bengal, was similar in style to Hindu *Vedantism* (of which one of the leading proponents, the Vishnaivite mystic Chaitanya, came from Sylhet). It found great favour with the poor cultivators of Sylhet, who were ready to be liberated from the caste oppression they suffered under Hinduism and to receive the enlightened teachings of Islam, when they came in this gentle and loving form. Thus, where the swords of the Moghuls failed to conquer Sylhet, the example of the *Sufis* (who were, at their best, 'universality and liberality personified') prevailed and Sylhet became (and remains) a

Shah Jalal's Tomb

stronghold of Islam.[7] The mystical traditions of *Vedanta* and *Sufism* merged in the devotional songs, in celebration of Shah Jalal, which are still sung, by Hindu and Muslim musicians alike in the villages of Sylhet and the recording studios of East London.

As well as these spiritual traditions, Sylhet has retained the magical beliefs common in Assam, held in awe throughout India as a land of witches and magicians. These ancient spinechillers have been woven into Islam and even today *Pirs* are invested, by villagers, with superhuman powers. Ghosts and demons go abroad at night and must be treated with respect.

After the coming of the saints to liberate the peasants of Sylhet the next arrivals were the British who came, none too subtly, to exploit them, and their land. As Sir William Hunter put it, in his *Annals of Rural Bengal*, 'Bengal was regarded by the British public in the light of a vast warehouse, in which a number of adventurous Englishmen carried on business with great profit and on an enormous scale. That a numerous native population existed they were aware, but this they considered an accidental circumstance.'[8]

The exploitation of Bengal as a whole was a complex operation: the suppression of the exquisite Dacca muslin industry, to be replaced by inferior British made goods; the virtual enslavement of cultivators by indigo merchants; the wholesale planting and exporting of jute. In Sylhet, in those early days, however, it was all quite straightforward. When, in 1777, Robert Lindsay was appointed by the East India Company as the second Resident and Collector of the dangerous frontier province of Sylhet (the first having been William Makepeace Thackeray, grandfather of the novelist) he hailed the posting as 'the summit of my ambition'.[9] Arriving after seven days journey by boat from Dacca, he 'contemplated with delight the wide field of commercial speculation opening before (him)'.[10]

Having surveyed the possibilities, he recognised quickly that the greatest source of profit would be in the deposits of *chunam* (lime) in the hills above Chhatok. 'This branch of commerce became a large source of wealth to me, and in fact became the foundation of my fortune.'[11]

There is still, today, a cement factory in Chhatok, the only source of lime in Bangladesh. The lime trade when Lindsay arrived was carried on by 'low Europeans, Armenians, and Greeks', whom the Collector quickly used his official position to dispossess.[12] He then arranged a meeting with the chief of the Kashi hill tribe, in whose territory the lime was to be found. This fierce person, 'accompanied by other wildlooking demons', came to meet Lindsay by the river at Pondua, 'a region of paradise', and a deal was struck.[13] Lindsay appointed agents in Calcutta, a workforce of five hundred men began to extract the *chunam* and carry it by boat to Calcutta, and Lindsay returned to his 'monotonous life' in Sylhet, while keeping his eyes open for other ways to make money.[14]

In the meantime, he had to continue to collect the land revenues for the East India Company, which was after all what he was there for. The revenue was collected in cowrie shells, which were the normal commercial tender in Sylhet, and the large fleet of boats required to carry them to Dacca cost ten per cent of the revenue. Despite his eager attention to his own profits, Lindsay was not always as assiduous as the Company would have liked in collecting their revenue, being too prone to be moved by the plight of the people, particularly in times of flood and famine. In September 1784 he wrote:

Nothing can equal the distress experienced by the inhabitants for these three months past, crops destroyed and two thirds of the cattle dead from starvation, and not a tuft of grass or a spot of verdure to be seen . . . for at least one hundred miles. This country . . . exhibits the appearance of an open sea, in the midst of which a few islands appear scattered.[15]

In reply to his request that the demand for revenues might not be enforced in the circumstances, the Company wrote:

. . . every precaution should be used . . . to prevent any unfair advantage being taken of this indulgence by the *zemindars* . . . whilst every indulgence is made for real distress, we trust to you your endeavours to break a combination which has for its object the total loss of revenue in the Sylhet Province.[16]

There were other hazards too which threatened the Revenue. From time to time there were raids by the hill tribes, especially the Kuki Nagas from the East, who would swoop down into the plains and seize cattle, grain and human heads, forcing Lindsay to lead rather halfhearted punitive attacks. The other despoilers of the region interested him far more – the elephants. 'Most fortunately for the population of the country,' he wrote, 'they delight in the sequestered range of the mountain; did they prefer the plain, whole kingdoms would be laid waste.'[17] However, they did come and lay it waste sufficiently often for action to be needed against them and Lindsay was delighted to learn from the local *zemindars* the method of catching the elephants. Seven or eight hundred men would be sent into the hills to find a herd and surround them with stockades and ditches, until they were secured, and with the help of tame elephants, brought in:

> This practice is pursued by the *zemindars* who have for these fifty years paid them as Royal Revenue, but they have often complained of its taking their *raiyats* (peasants) away from cultivation and made it an excuse for their revenue falling short.[18]

So to defend the Revenue, Lindsay took upon himself the task of chief elephant hunter, despite the protests of the *zemindars*, who wished to retain the privilege. Like the Greek *chunam* quarriers before them, they vainly petitioned the Company against the Collector. Over the twelve years that Lindsay was in Sylhet, five hundred elephants were taken annually and, having been tamed, sold for his profit for forty to fifty pounds a head all around India: 'Few people have caught as many, or are more conversant with their natural history than myself', nor indeed, made so much money out of them. Lindsay was impressed by the integrity of the *peon*, one Manoo, who was sent to deliver the elephants around India, and dutifully brought back sums of three and four thousand pounds to Lindsay, although his own pay was only thirty shillings a month.[19]

As well as the elephants, there were plenty of tigers about. 'Tigers are in no part of the world more numerous than at Sylhet', but as they fed so freely on cattle, they hardly ever attacked people and were not particularly dreaded.[20] The tigers however had reason to fear Lindsay, who was liberally rewarded by the government for the fifty or sixty he killed every year, presumably because they threatened the Revenue. He shot them 'in perfect safety', from a platform, with

. . . few people have caught as many as I . . .

elephants as beaters, or 'causing them to be trapped into a tube twelve feet long and eighteen inches wide, where they were completely helpless and I have repeatedly taken them by the whiskers with impunity', and they could be carried to the town and tossed to death by buffalo.[21] The odd rhino which made its way to the plains was treated with no more respect, being killed by a shower of musket balls and chopped up for charms by the villagers.

By 1782, Lindsay was well on his way to having made his fortune, having amassed fifteen thousand pounds, 'acquired through my own industry' (to say nothing of that of Manoo and the elephant trappers).[22] He was able to write to his mother to purchase for him an estate in Scotland, to which he retired in 1789, after twenty years in India where, 'my affairs had been more prosperous than I imagined'.[23]

Many years after Lindsay's retirement there came an odd postscript to his years in Sylhet. There had been, in 1782, a communal disturbance at the mosque of Shah Jalal and Lindsay, going there with thirty sepoys, ordered the Muslims to lay down their arms. The *Pir Zada* (the priest of the mosque) then transformed the riot into a revolt against the British (the first of several in Sylhet), shouting: 'This is the day to kill or die; the reign of the British is at an end'.[24] In the ensuing struggle, Lindsay shot and killed the venerable *Pir*, after which he was far from popular amongst the Muslims. He described the occasion when a *fakir* came to try to kill him at dinner and remarked, 'instances such as I have described frequently occurred to me, owing to the annual assemblage of fanatics at the shrine of the tutelary saint'.[25]

It was another of these 'fanatics', Syed Ullah, the son of a follower of the *Pir* Zada, who came to Britain in search of Lindsay, as the servant to the son of a local vicar returning from India. Lindsay met the man in the village street and on finding that he was from Sylhet, invited him into his home, where he entertained his family with tales of the homeland. Lindsay then flattered Syed Ullah into cooking a chicken, telling him that Sylhetti cooks had 'long been famed for dressing the best curry in the world'.[26] Despite the fore-bodings of the governess, who dreamed 'that a black man came from the extremities of the East and killed Mr Lindsay and his family', they enjoyed their dinner and survived.[27] 'Never was a dish better dressed, and never did I make a better dinner.'[28] Whatever his motive for visiting the ex-Collector, Syed Ullah had the distinction of being the first named Sylhetti man to visit Britain, as well as the first to serve curry to English diners.

In 1856, tea was discovered growing wild in Sylhet and the tea planting mania spread from Upper Assam and with it the next phase in the exploitation of Sylhet. In the early 1860's in the first flush of enthusiasm, 'New gardens were commenced on impossible sites and by men as managers who did not know a tea plant from a cabbage . . . It seems to have been thought that any fool could run a tea garden. People who had failed in everything else were recruited as managers.'[29] In 1866 the boom crashed, and some at least of the fortune hunters were ruined. The industry then proceeded more sedately, and was well established by the 1890's, with wealth being acquired more discreetly but very steadily, by the tea firms and shipping lines which expanded to service them.

The early planters were notoriously badly behaved – drunkards who mismanaged estates and cheated and ill-used the workers. These were mainly tribal people and labourers from other parts of India, whose poverty was so great that they allowed themselves to be enticed by the 'coolie catchers' – the *sirdars* or recruiting foreman – who earned so much a head for each unfortunate worker they tricked with their tales of a life of ease and plenty in the 'gardens'. Then as now, the tea estate workers in Sylhet were overworked, badly housed and paid a pittance, out of all proportion to the profits of the British estate owners.

It was a source of grievance to the planters that the local people could not be induced to work on the estates and they even suggested that land revenues should be increased to force them to leave their crops and become wage labourers. Assam had escaped the *zemindari* system established by the British in the Permanent Settlement of 1793, whereby a class of landlords were created, whose sole job was to farm land revenues for the government from the peasants, who lost the title to their land and became labourers on their own property. The system in Assam was the *'Ryotwari Settlement'* or Independent Single Tenure, whereby the *Ryots* or peasants paid their taxes directly to the Government and retained the nominal ownership of their land, in theory at least, although in practice they were often forced to mortgage their land to moneylenders and become day labourers under them. This liberty of the peasantry infuriated the planters:

Each occupies a small plot of land . . .

'In this enlightened country, every man is his own master. Each Assamese occupies a small plot of land which he, with the assistance of his family, cultivates and the life of a *Ryot* is inconceivably, supremely, happy . . . Can one truly expect that this trueborn Freeman will work for the planters in their gardens?'[30]

There are those who believe that the Independent Single Tenure system was one of the direct causes of the tradition of men of Sylhet leaving home to work abroad. Having no money, but the dignity of owning land and also in some cases the status of descent from the Arab saints, the sons of the peasant aristocracy could not descend to labouring, which was the only work available locally:

Why did Sylhettis become seamen, although they live so far from the sea? This is what I think. Because Sylhet was not affected by the Permanent Settlement, so the land-holdings remained invested in those who worked them, therefore there was a class of relatively well off small landowners. They were petty bourgeois in the village context, and they had a lot of pride, because they were landowners, and also because they were descended from the saints, and were not original sons of the soil. This meant that they were not willing to do manual work there, where they would be seen and shamed, so they went away to a foreign place, where nobody would see them. It was not that they were afraid of hard work, here in England they would do anything, but they didn't want to be seen by known people. The reason the farmers needed to go away and work was partly because their lands were subdivided between brothers and also because the economic situation was ruining them. They couldn't get a proper price for their rice and sometimes the merchants cheated them so that they didn't get paid at all. They had to sell their rice at harvest time, when there was plenty of rice and the price was low and then the merchants would keep it and sell it in time of shortage for a high price. Some of the families were quite desperate, and of course they weren't educated enough to get office jobs, even if there were any, so the ships were the only thing.[31]

Whether or not the land tenure system had any particular bearing on the matter, it was and is common in rural India for breadwinners to be forced by poverty and the moneylenders to leave their land and families and struggle to earn a living in a city or a richer part of the country.

Thus the prosperous farmers of the Punjab recruit their labourers in Orissa, and the rickshaw pullers who sleep on the streets of Calcutta are poor peasants from Bihar. It is true

the rickshaw pullers of Calcutta

however, that the seafarers from Sylhet were not from the poorest families, and they may well have been influenced by the need to maintain their positions: 'We were very down and out, although we had some education, we couldn't do much, we had no income.'[32] There were also, perhaps, the stirrings of their Arab blood:

> The people of Sylhet, they claim, a good number of them, that they are the descendants of the Arabs. Arab people used to like travelling . . . that is why the Sylhet people, the muslims especially, they like to travel, it is in their blood.[33]

Whatever the reasons: the watery landscape of Sylhet, the blood of the wandering Arabs, or just the desperate need to earn a living, the tradition was there, and the *serangs*, the foremen, were available in Calcutta to help young men to find jobs and the example of those who had been away and returned with untold wealth was there to spur them on:

The Sylhet people were in the ship because these people follow each other, and some went there and others saw them, and they thought they could get jobs too. It all started before we were born.[34]

Sometimes a man might have been away for six months or a year, and everybody would come to see him, and everybody would enjoy . . . looking into his face, asking him all kind of questions. And the young people used to think, 'Oh, if I go there, people will come and look at me too and ask me things', so that was why they went, for money too of course, that was the most important thing.[35]

As well as the money, which would lift the family above bare survival, there was the adventure:

For poor people, it was beyond their dreams to go for a holiday, or anything like that, or spend money to go, by taking a journey like that, but it was usual for people to go to the ship. It wasn't thought wrong for a person from an educated family to go, it was quite the fashion at that time, the fashion.[36]

The more ambitious even looked beyond the ship:

Some when they came to America . . . managed to escape and somehow settle . . . they always used to send big money orders . . . and that gave me the idea . . . if I could manage to go to America, somehow or other I could earn enough money, that was my ambition.[37]

The first stage on the journey to riches was to get to Calcutta, with or without parental consent, walking across the paddy-fields away from the village, in the early morning sun . . .

My parents wouldn't agree, so I ran away, pinched my mother's savings and came to Calcutta with some other people who were going. The train fare was seven rupees 5 annas. My town had no railway station, so I had to walk 14 miles to the railway station at Sri Mangal. When I came to Calcutta, no money, I wrote to my mother, 'Please forgive me, I pinched your money, to earn money.'[38]

Going to the Ship

'They say, in the navy you see the world, but not true, you only see down inside the ship and the water and you can't get out'.[1]

The tradition of Indian peasants leaving their villages to work on foreign ships goes back to the time of Vasco da Gama and grew with the increasing requirements of the various colonial powers in India in the seventeenth and eighteenth centuries. By that time and up to 1947, Asian seamen were normally referred to as *'lascars'*. There are two possible derivations for this term: the rather fanciful suggestion that it comes from a combination of the Persian *'khalasi'*, a sailor, and the Tamil *'kara'*, a worker, hence *khalasikara-lasikara-lascar*, a labouring sailor. The more accepted version is that it comes from the Persian and Urdu word *'lashkar'*, an army, and that the word 'gun-lascar' was coined to describe Indian artillerymen on British and Portuguese ships in the eighteenth century. (From the same root, *'askari'* became the coast Swahili term in East Africa for a soldier.)

In the early days Indian seamen were used for the 'country ships', trading from India to Burma, China, the Malay Archipelago and East Africa. Indeed they were only officially allowed to be engaged for voyages east of the Cape of Good Hope, as a measure of employment protection for European sailors. Even in the seventeenth century, however, they were used for the return voyage to Britain for ships whose crews had been decimated by disease and desertion; the demands of the war with the French having led to a relaxation of the policy.

From then on the East India Company increasingly crewed its trading vessels with men recruited in Calcutta and the other Indian ports, and later with the demise of the Company the practice was continued by the shipping lines, so that the heyday of steam shipping, the 1850's to the 1950's, was also the heyday of the *lascar* seamen.

The Hooghly River, Calcutta   *National Maritime Museum*

Life for the early *lascars* was very hard, both at sea and on shore. On the ships they lived in cramped, overcrowded conditions, without exercise, fresh air, or fresh food and without suitable clothing or bedding for cold climates. In 1804, a ship's surgeon of the East Indian Company wrote of:

> the ravages of disease (among) a class of men whose labours have been employed, to a greater extent than ever before, for the advantage of the British nation and of the Honourable East India Company . . . the natives of India, retracing the route of the adventurous Gama and conducting ships into the Tagus, the Thames and the Baltic. The great change of climate and manner of life, to which they

have been exposed on such a voyage, might naturally be expected to produce distemper and accordingly experience has shown that it often prevails with fatal violence.[2]

He described graphically the sickness and deaths, from scurvy, beri-beri, etc. of the unfortunate *lascars* (for example twenty-four deaths on one voyage) and recommended improvements in diet, clothing and accommodation and 'a musician or two, of their own caste.' This physician's case was proved by the result of his recommendations on the next ship under his care:

The *Shah Byramore* has exhibited an instance perhaps unprecedented, of a voyage to England and back to Bengal, without the loss of a man by disease.[3]

In general, however, the premise that the deaths of *lascars* were the fault of the shipowners and masters was not accepted, but instead there persisted, right up until the First World War the myth that Indian sailors were:

just not suitable for service in colder climates. This opinion . . . of course complemented beautifully the equally erroneous belief that white sailors could not stand working conditions in the tropics.[4]

Conditions were perhaps even worse in East London, where *lascars* were often left stranded after their voyages in the East India Company's ships. At first, the Honourable Company ignored the problem of sailors adrift, homeless and penniless in a cold foreign land. But in 1782 a letter went from head office to the President and Council in Madras, grumbling that *lascars* were finding their way to Leadenhall Street, 'having been reduced to great distress and applying to us for relief'.[5] After 1795 the Company began to provide accommodation for the *lascars* in rock-bottom lodging houses in Kingsland Road. In 1802, following complaints from magistrates, the home for *lascars* was moved to Shoreditch, and later to a barracks on the Ratcliffe Highway. By the end of the Napoleonic wars there were as many as 1,100 *lascars* in London at any one time and they were allocated a barracks at

Gravesend. The death rate in winter in the barracks became known to the Asiatic Society and an angry letter to *The Times* led to a Parliamentary enquiry. 'Members of the Committee made an unannounced visit to the Gravesend barracks and found that *lascars* were sleeping on bare boards with a blanket apiece, in buildings that were devoid of any furniture and unheated' (lacking even hammocks for the sick).[6] With the decline of the East India Company, which was theoretically responsible under the Lascar Act of 1832 for the accommodation and repatriation of *lascars*, even these minimal provisions were dispensed with and the men were housed, if anywhere, in dockside sheds or left to fend for themselves on the streets.

By the 1840's the situation had become so scandalous that the Reverend Henry Venn, and Joseph Salter, of the Church Missionary Society, felt moved to undertake an investigation into the condition of the destitute seamen and ex-seamen living in lodging houses and hovels around Cable Street and the Ratcliffe Highway, which were full of brothels and gambling and opium establishments. Here the 'son of honest toil' would arrive, 'Queen Victoria's golden coins hidden in a corner of his gaudy *puggree*, enough . . . to supply him with the scanty wants of Oriental life, till he finds another ship that will take him back to family and friends rejoicing', but would soon, resorting to some house of ill-repute for lodging and companionship, be robbed and cheated of his wages and end up begging on the streets in rags, or joining the robbers and cheats.[7]

Some of these were very well set up enjoying their lives with congenial common-law wives, like 'Lascar Sally', 'Calcutta Louisa', and 'Chinese Emma', and their children of various races (some of these ladies 'have lived so long in this element that they use the Oriental vernacular'); running gambling and opium houses; travelling the country in circuses, or begging. There were:

> Two hundred and fifty Asiatics, like birds of passage from a foreign land, regularly visiting the provincial towns, and especially the autumn retreats at the sea-side, to come into contact with the English *sahib*, and extract a *backshish* from the friend of the black man.[8]

The less fortunate were 'herded like cattle', six or eight in a cellar, without bedding or furniture, or 'confined in boxes by the head *lascar*' in Wapping, or even sleeping on the streets.'[9] In the early 1850's, forty 'sons of India' were found dead of cold and hunger on the streets of East London. As Salter wrote:

> Strange, indeed, in the midst of so many merchant princes made rich with Indian gold, that the stranger who brought us the precious things of the torrid zone should die uncared for on a winter night on one of our London streets.[10]

'The Strangers Home'   *LBTH Local History Collection*

Venn and Salter followed their researches with an appeal for funds:

> You may have given liberally for the spread of the Gospel in foreign lands, but have you ever done anything for the furtherance of the temporal or spiritual welfare of the Oriental strangers residing in our midst? . . . You may have amassed a fortune in India; or have been an Employer of

Orientals who have assisted you in bringing merchandise to this Christian country, have you done anything to rescue them from the harpies that infest our seaports, or used means to prevent their being robbed of their money and stripped of their clothes?[11]

In 1858, with donations from India-enriched merchants and even Indian princes, the Strangers' Home for Asiatics, Africans and South Sea Islanders was opened, with 200 beds, in the West India Dock Road. Up to the time of publication of Salter's book *The Asiatic in England* in 1872, the Home had provided '6,400 Orientals with lodging', enabled 1300 'destitutes' to be sheltered, fed, clothed and 'rehabilitated' (taken on as crews or repatriated, or in some cases settled in Britain) and taken care of £10,000 cash and £6,000 in jewellery for the sailors passing through. Doubtless however, there were still some who preferred the company of Lascar Sally to the ministrations of the reverend gentlemen.

Back in Calcutta, the *lascars* faced difficulties largely through the recruitment system set up under Warren Hastings, Governor General of Bengal in 1783, and persisting unchanged until the 1940's. This system followed the Indian tradition of indirect access to paid employment, which was, and often still is, 'obtained through a combination of family contacts and professional intermediaries, with the jobber, or *sirdar*, a familiar figure in society.'[12] To get a job on the ship involved two intermediaries. One was the *serang* who acted as bosun for the deck or (later) engine room hands on the ship and was directly responsible for recruiting them and for their organisation and discipline on the ship. The other was the *ghat* (port) *serang*, a very powerful figure who was a combination of labour agent, money lender and lodging house keeper. Both of these middlemen had to be heavily bribed by any prospective sailor, or rather, as he had no money he would have to promise to pay them out of his future earnings. The *ghat serang* in turn was to be bribed by would-be *serangs*, whom he was in a position to recommend for appointments. (In 1945, evidence was given to the International Labour Organisation's investigation into seafarers' conditions by a '*tindal*' (bosun's mate) aged sixty, who had a record of forty-four voyages, each one with 'Very Good' in his

Serangs on deck   *PLA Collection, Museum in Docklands*

record book. Asked why he had never become a *serang*, he explained that he could never afford to pay the two hundred to five hundred rupees it would have taken to get the job).

The sole advantage of this system to aspiring *lascars* was that a *serang* would recruit a crew from his own area and this was undoubtedly one reason for the persistence of the seafaring tradition in Sylhet. Once the *serangs* became established with the shipping companies, the crewing of those lines became the birthright of the men of Sylhet, as long as they paid the *serang* his cut.

The close relationship between the seafarers of Bengal and the new capitalist class of Britain grew in the nineteenth century as the Empire settled down to trading in earnest. Crews were recruited in Calcutta to carry Assamese tea (some of it, of course, from Sylhet) to Tilbury, jute to Dundee, and fortunes to the merchants and shipowners, such as Charles Cayzer, founder of the Clan Line: 'Tea from Calcutta was to be one of the foundations of the Clan Line.'[13]

With the introduction of steam, the companies came to rely still more on Indian seamen who were held to be more suitable as engine-room crews than British seamen as they were used to high temperatures and could therefore withstand the appalling heat suffered by firemen stoking furnaces under a steel deck on the Arabian sea. In fact, of course Indian firemen got hot just like Europeans:

Stokers (from P&O Pencillings')   *P&O Group*

I was called a bunkerman, in the coal bunker . . . it was hot, oh yes, it was hot. We put coal in the boiler, and then it gets heat, and then the ship runs. It is a most difficult job, very hard and very hot too, many people died in that heat. In my sea life, I knew hundreds of people who died.[14]

Some men died of heat stroke and exhaustion, others, overcome with heat, threw themselves overboard in desperation. The truth of the matter probably was that the superior ability of the Indian firemen to withstand heat was simply a matter of his inferior economic position, and his desperate need to earn a few rupees, even at the risk of his life and health. Whatever the reason, the tradition became established with the shipping lines that *firemen-agwallahs* for Bombay crews were Pathans and Mirpuris and for Calcutta crews the majority of engine-room hands were from Sylhet, with some also from Noakhali and Chittagong. The other parts of the crew were also recruited on a regional basis, by *serangs* who collected men from their own districts. Thus, in Calcutta deck crews were from Noakhali and saloon crews were from Calcutta district, while in Bombay the deck crews came from Gujarat and Ratnagiri, and the stewards from Goa.

The importance of *lascar* crews in the big shipping lines was finally recognised after the First World War when 3,427 Indian crew members in British merchant ships were killed and 1,200 taken prisoner. As Lord Inchcape, the Chairman of the P & O put it:

> The *lascar*'s sobriety and his calm demeanour in emergency and philosophic endurance of catastrophe were beyond praise.[15]

The memoirs of P & O captains are full of praise for *lascar* seamen – for their discipline, sobriety, industry, cleanliness, loyalty and other useful virtues – and the general verdict was that 'Asians make useful and accomplished seamen, they are respectful, obedient and, if well led, they can keep the ship in excellent condition . . . I must say that I prefer to sail with Asian crews.[16] Some captains even recognised, albeit rather hazily, that their Indian crews have private lives:

> I have often found it fascinating to speculate on the strangeness of their lives, divided between their primitive villages many hundreds of miles inland, and the vast, humming engine-room of a modern ship, where they move about unconcernedly in a maze of complicated machinery.[17]

But, of course, their private lives were not taken very seriously: 'The Company is their whole life'.[18]

In addition to all these factors the *lascars* had the great appeal of providing very cheap labour. 'In 1914 Indian deckhands earned sixteen to twenty-two rupees per month (about one pound to one-fifty), Indian firemen twenty rupees,

High Pressure Turbines, SS Majestic, 1922   BBC Hulton Picture Library

against wages of five pounds ten for their British counter-parts.[19] In 1919, despite 100% inflation in India, their wages remained the same, while those of British sailors had risen to fourteen pounds per month during the war. Further economies of course resulted from the inferior and often inadequate food and smaller living space required under Indian articles, which more than compensated for the larger sizes of Indian crews. This higher manning rate, which was the only reservation the employers had about the *lascars*, was probably due less to physical weakness than to 'the eastern tradition of worksharing, and the propensity of the *serang* to pad out a crew with relatives and debtors from his village'.[20]

It was perhaps not surprising that the practice of employing Asian seamen in northern waters was not popular with British sailors, though they were apparently happy to let them do the work in the less desirable tropical regions. In 1892, when Charles Cayzer, founder of the Clan Line, was elected as Tory MP for Barrow in Furness the Liberals traded on this insularity in their election campaign against Cayzer, barracking his meetings with chants of 'coolies', in response to his practice of employing Asian seamen and thereby

depriving honest Britons of jobs. In anticipation of his defeat,
they even printed a mock 'memorial card':

In loving memory of C. W. Cayzer who got the sack from
this town, July 5th 1892 R.I.P. He took it very 'coolie', in
spite of his 'lascar'ated feelings.[21]

The xenophobia persisted in the National Sailors and
Firemen's Union, which in the early 20th century was both
anti-foreign and anti-*lascar*. It was with little help from the
international trade union movement that Indian seamen, led
by a Sylhetti villager called Aftab Ali, were eventually to
achieve unionisation and move towards equality. There is
still today a sharp difference in the wages and conditions of
service of European and Asian and African crews employed
on British merchant ships. In 1982 the Falklands conflict
provided a reminder of this when the S.S.Uganda became a
floating home for British servicemen and the living space,
previously used for Asian crews, had rapidly to be improved.
(In the same conflict, the front line troops included, in their
usual starring role 'the plucky little Gurkhas', whose rates of
pay are so markedly inferior to those of their British
colleagues.)

In the 1930's, when the young men were leaving their
villages to make their way to Calcutta, it was to a system
very little changed since the days of Warren Hastings and to
exploitation made worse by international isolation and
crushing unemployment. The first thing they had to do on
arriving in Calcutta was to find a place to stay and this was
not difficult. It was simply a matter of taking a tram or
walking across the city through the wide streets, across the
broad green of the Maidan, past the imperial absurdity of the
Victoria Memorial and the metropolitan decadence of the
Racecourse, to the seamen's area at Kidderpore, with its
dockyards, lodging houses, and teahuts, beside the slow
brown waters of the Hooghly River.

. . . We came to Kidderpore, where our people lived.
Calcutta . . . oh, it was nice, I got out of the train and saw
everywhere big buildings, and heard everywhere radio and
gramophone, it was nice.[22]

. . . beside the slow brown waters of the Hooghly . . .

Then began the difficult part – the business of finding work
on a ship, in a city where two-thirds of the seafarers were
always unemployed. Many were only saved from destitution
by putting themselves in the hands of moneylenders,
borrowing money in the village to get to the city and again in
the city surviving on credit advanced by the lodging house
keepers who were often also *ghat serangs*.

At Calcutta, some of our Sylhet people made lodging
houses. They used to make money out of our poor people. It
was in Kidderpore, by the docks.[23]

The lodging house keepers were called *bariwallahs*. They
were quite despotic, but also helpful in their way. The men
had no money of course, so the *bariwallah* used to advance
them money and give them their food and lodging on credit.
Then when the man came back from the sea, he would go
back to the *bariwallah* and give him his money, plus the
cost of his room while he was away, because of course they

didn't charge interest. He would say, 'well, if you don't pay for it I can't keep any place for you' and of course there was no other place to go.[24]

The *ghat serang* also controlled the allocation of jobs in the docks and had to have his share of a man's wages, if he was lucky enough to get casual work there while waiting for a ship.

I couldn't afford to go home. Sometimes I got work twice a week, sometimes four times, four annas a day, less than a penny. Out of that we had to pay something to the man who got us the job.[25]

They used to pay a nominal wage of eight annas per day, for polishing the ship, scraping the ship, painting, or doing many works in the ship. They used to pay very little. Payment was through a middle-man, they used to call him the *ghat-serang*, port serang, who used to pay the people . . . after doing all the work you would get six annas or eight annas, not more than that.[26]

For some young men it took years to get a ship, perhaps on their second or third trip to Calcutta. Some made their first journey on a 'country ship', going to Burma, Singapore, or Bombay:

It was a passenger ship, running between Calcutta and Rangoon. I worked there for some time . . . I saw Rangoon quite a number of times, I used to see the pagodas and all.[27]

But if a man wanted to travel more widely, getting a ship required patience, assiduous cultivation of the *serangs*, and of course co-operation with the time honoured system of bribery: 'I found a *serang* who said, "I can take you, if you give me one third of your wages," so I agreed.'[28]

In 1941, the recruitment method was changed, in theory at least, to an 'open muster system', which in the words of the 1947 ILO Report, was 'certainly open', and 'might be called a muster', but was 'most definitely not a system'. By 10 a.m.

there might be five hundred to a thousand men, squatting or standing in the courtyard of the shipping office, in the full heat of the sun. Even for the job of 1st *Tindal* (the equivalent of bosun's mate) there could be fifty applicants and for each *lascar*'s job, several hundreds. The men stood in rows, holding out their *'nollies'*, continuous discharge certificates (a merchant seaman's papers) in front of them and the ship's engineer was supposed to pick the crews impartially. Even then corruption was not unheard of – officers having been known to have had written on their hands the numbers of certain *nollies*, the holders of which had paid a bribe in advance to ensure being picked. Usually though it was sufficient to catch the eye of the officer:

> They said I had to stand in the queue, and the officer would pick out the people. When I hadn't got a job in the docks, I used to go and stand in the queue and when I had a job I used to go to work. One day the engineer passed me by and I said to him, 'Excuse me, look, what's wrong with this one? Four years I am trying to join'. He said, 'Alright', and he took me, so I joined the Merchant Navy.[29]

The first few days in the ship were usually the worst:

> They took me down, inside the ship, such a strange place. I was frightened, because I had never seen anything like that before. Then the sea started to go . . . like that . . . *oh my God!* . . . I think for six or seven days I didn't have any cup of tea or food or anything.Still I had to work. I swore to God, when I get back I am never going to leave my home and family again. The other men looked after me, they said, 'Don't worry, after a few days the sea will go smooth.' It was true, I was alright when I got used to it.[30]

The machinery was puzzling too:

> When my uncle first went in the ship, he went in the engine-room and saw all the wheels and levers and heard all the noise and he didn't know what it all was. He pulled a lever to see what would happen, and the ship stopped . . .[31]

Asian ship's crew eating on deck. SS Dunera, docked in Middlesbrough,
1910 National Maritime Museum

The work was very gruelling. In the engine-room the Sylhetti
men worked as donkey wallahs, in charge of donkey-engines;
greasers or 'telwallahs', greasing and oiling the machinery;
firemen supplying the furnace with coal and disposing of the
ashes; or coaltrimmers, trimming the coal to keep the fire
under control. Engine-room ratings worked continuous shifts
of four hours on, eight hours off, 'in view of the arduous
nature of their work'.

The Indian crew members had little contact with the
British officers, their work being organised by the *serang* to
whom the engineer would speak in *'lascari bat'* – simple
Hindustani with the verbs all in the imperative. The men
organised their own cooking together, as a *bicchu*, or mess,
taking it in turn to cook the rice and curry from the dried fish,
dried *halal* meat and *dal*, with which they were issued. In fine
weather they would eat on the deck, sitting in a circle on the
floor, and snatching some fresh air, away from the engine-
room fumes. 'However hard the life on board ship, they were
at least . . . getting regular pay, a boon to their families, for
hitherto the breadwinner and family had lived a hand to
mouth existence, at times not knowing where the next meal
was coming from.'[32] As well as the money, there was the
excitement, for these very young men, of seeing new and
unimaginably strange places:

> We went to South America, then Hong Kong, then Kobe,
> Japan. From there we went to Australia. The ship carried
> different goods, Brazil nuts from Japan . . .[33]

And so the navy men's great adventures had begun. For
some, there would be sudden death by torpedo; for others, a
few voyages and a return to the village; some would spend a
lifetime at sea, and others were to be the *Londonis*, the
pioneers of a mass migration.

The War at Sea

'We were all British, so naturally we wanted to help with the war, and get money for it.'[1]

At Tower Hill, half a mile from Aldgate, the heart of the Bangladeshi community in Britain, there is a poignant monument to the men of the British Merchant Navy who lost their lives in the two World Wars. Among the names of the 26,833 merchant seamen killed in the 1939-1945 war, there are the names of Bengali Muslims: Miah, Latif, Ali, Uddin. Strangely, however, the names of these men, whose sacrifice is recorded and honoured in bronze, represent only a small proportion of the Indian seamen who died for what they called their 'King and Country'. They were the privileged few, employed as British crew members, under British articles, for twenty times more pay and their names on the memorial. Most of the Indian seamen serving in the merchant navy were *'lascars'*, engaged in Indian ports under *'lascar articles'*, their names known only to their *serangs* and fellow crew members.

So anonymous were they that the official tables of war dead list 'Deaths among British merchant seamen, excluding *lascars*'. Indian records, however, give figures of 6,600 Indian seamen killed, and 1,022 wounded. These would, of course, have been men from all the seafaring districts of the subcontinent: Mirpur, Goa, the North West Frontier, Chittagong, and Sylhet. There is no separate figure for the number of Sylhetti men killed, but as they were the engine room crews, in the most dangerous part of the ship, they must represent a large proportion of those 6,000 dead.

There is said to have once been a record book, with the names of the East Bengali dead, which was kept in Calcutta till partition, then transferred to Chittagong, but a researcher from Sylhet, Mr. Nurul Islam, who journeyed to Chittagong in search of the precious book, found that it had vanished, consumed by fire or white ants, or lost in the liberation struggle. Those nameless thousands 'have no memorial, they are perished as though they had never been,' except in the fading memories of surviving relatives and friends:

> I lost many of my friends. One of my uncles came to my ship in Liverpool, and told my *serang*, 'Please don't give him hard work, he is a respectable man's son.' Then he sailed with his ship, but two hours out of Liverpool the ship was lost, and I never saw him again.[2]

The anonymous *lascars* appear again in the records of the shipping companies, where the names of the Indian crew members killed were not listed, presumably because they were not known, but perhaps also because they were considered of no interest. Thus, on the loss of the *Clan Mackenzie,* (in the First World War) the company's historian writes:

> through the torpedoeing of this vessel the Company un- fortunately lost the services of Chief Officer F. Temple (drowned), Third Engineer J.A. Henderson (killed), both respected members of the seafaring staff, as well as Midshipman A. McDiarmid (drowned), a very promising young sailor, and in addition five natives were killed.[3]

The numbers of those 'natives' were certainly significant, however, even if their names were not. The Clan Line's total 'fatal casualties' in World War Two were 641, of whom 508 were Indian ratings, probably most or all of them from the villages of Sylhet, where the Clan Line's *serangs* recruited their crews.

Such a large number of Indian deaths is not so surprising when one learns that at the outbreak of war, 50,000 of the Merchant Navy's 190,000 men were *lascars*, of whom 75%

SS Clan Mackenzie *National Maritime Museum*

were Indian and the rest Chinese, African, Malay, etc.
Clearly the companies had overcome their earlier doubts
about employing foreign labour in the ships (but had not, of
course, removed the differentials in their wages and
conditions).

> In general, these men, employed only as ratings, who were
> always plentiful and almost invariably docile, gave no
> trouble.[4]

The role of the Merchant Navy in the Second World War was,
of course, vital to Britain's very survival, as well as to the
Allied victory. As King George VI said, in an address to
merchant seamen in September 1939:

> Yours is a task no less essential to my people's existence
> than that allotted to the Navy, Army and Air Force. Upon
> you the nation depends for much of its foodstuffs and raw
> materials and for the transport of its troops overseas.[5]

As the war developed, the tasks of merchant shipping became ever more crucial, carrying varied cargoes without which the Allied war machine could not have run: phosphates for fertilizer from Egypt to Australia; steel from the USA to Britain; coal from India to Egypt; rice from Egypt to India; wheat from India to Greece and from Australia to Britain; and of course oil from the Middle East to Britain.

The war brought more work for merchant seamen, whose employment was normally casual and precarious and more money, even under 'lascar articles', but it also brought dreadful perils, the very real possibility of death and the certainty of extra discomfort. For the Asian seamen, who had always served in warm or temperate zones and suffered of course from the immensely high temperatures of the boiler-room, there were the new hardships of journeys on the North Atlantic, or the icy Arctic and Baltic runs, where a torpedo would mean instant death in freezing water.

Torpedoes, of course, were the most dreaded hazard. A merchant ship might possibly manage to defend herself with her deck gun against an air attack but had (until the development of echo-sounding) no warning of, nor defence against a submarine attack. If struck by a torpedo the ship would almost certainly go down. In theory, the U-boats were attacking the ship and cargo, not her civilian crew and they would not be attacked if they managed to get to the lifeboats or rafts, but even that was far from certain.

> I can see it now, the boat on the ship and too many people going in the boat and the captain talking in Hindustani, saying 'Pani pagro, pani pagro! Jump in the water! No time to put out the boat or the ropes!' But they didn't listen to him. I jumped into the water, about twenty or fifteen yards down, then came up drinking salty water . . . ugh! . . . and very cold . . . I was in the water, swimming around and holding on to a piece of wood for twelve hours before somebody came and picked us up.[6]

There were many ways to die, some of them especially for the engine room crew: trapped below, suffocating and drowning among the screams of those fighting to get out; burned to death by an explosion; swallowing the oil which was

everywhere; ripped to pieces by the barnacled hull while
sliding overboard in a desperate race against death in the
darkness; being washed off a raft in mountainous seas, or
slipping off, in the night, unnoticed holding onto the side of
the packed raft, swimming behind, hanging onto the
'ratlines', after a few hours, numb with cold, letting go;

. . . in the water . . . holding on for twelve hours   Photo Source (Fox Photos)

freezing to death quickly in the water, or slowly in the boat;
dying from hunger and exhaustion, on a drifting boat full of
dead men. As Nicholas Monsarrat wrote: 'Some men died
well . . . some men died badly . . . some men just died.'[7]

Those who saw them die did not forget:

> I have seen many people die in wartime, some with no
> head, some with no leg, some ships blown in half . . .[8]

Some, of course, were rescued by the wrong side, and spent the rest of the war in Germany, like Mr. Hasmat Ullah, now in Birmingham, whose ship, SS *Clan Cummings* was torpedoed in the Gulf of Athens in April 1941. He was one of 1217 Indian Seamen who became prisoners of war.

I was in the camp for four years . . . soup all water . . . maybe one bath full of water, one pound dal. Oh, oh, very hungry . . . only fleas, nits, cockroaches, plenty eat. One thousand five hundred people died in one day. They died because the Red Cross parcels came and they ate it all at once . . . People would fight for potato skins . . . You had to help yourself in the camp, nobody to look after you. After a few days you might manage to get a bit of food, another week manage a bit of water to wash.[9]

One must certainly remember that the men bearing all these hazards were not members of the armed forces, though in fact more at risk than those who were. As the official history put it:

Merchant seamen were civilians who could not be compelled at the beginning of the war . . . They could not be forced to stay at their posts, or having left them to return to them, when similar measures were not applied to other civilians; before the fall of France, no-one contemplated industrial conscription.[10]

In this officially civilian occupation, at least a quarter of the men died during the war, or were 'permanently injured' as a result of it – a higher proportion than that of any of the 'Fighting services' as a whole, though certain sections such as the Bomber Command did have higher casualty rates.

In the context of these deaths and injuries, the casual heroism of very young men from remote villages in Sylhet, strolling off to Calcutta to play their part in a war which would appear to have nothing to do with them, becomes quite staggering, but the survivors do not see it like that. They had three great strengths in overcoming fear: poverty, religious faith and a patriotism which only with hindsight seems misplaced.

Thousands of people from our villages that time in the war for the British. That time, if you wanted to buy a good horse, two hundred pounds, if you wanted a man to kill, you paid him eighteen rupees a month.[11]

We weren't frightened, we believed in God then, and if God saved your life, nobody could kill you, this is our belief.[12]

I was born under the British flag, and I supported Britain . . . I was in Port Said when the Queen came there, she was Princess Elizabeth then. I heard what she said. She said, 'Must be we will win this war, and when we do, there will be pensions for everyone who fought.' I am still waiting for my pension. Soon I will write to the Queen about that. Britain wanted us then, I think now people have forgotten about that.[13]

The only defence for merchant shipping against the submarines and bombers was in the system of convoys, escorted by Royal Navy vessels. The convoy might consist of over one hundred merchant ships, with an escort of perhaps two Destroyers, and five or six Corvettes. The convoy was, of course, more conspicuous than lone ships and so likely to attract enemy attention, but there was at least some protection and help on hand for survivors of an attack. The convoys assembled in the major ports of the war: Cardiff; Liverpool; Freetown; Bombay; Alexandria: sailors' towns, with all their extra hazards and excitements. There, in the bars and the bazaars, people scared each other with travellers' tales:

I was not frightened (on the convoy from Gibraltar to Liverpool), but when I was at Port Said, there were some ships coming from Liverpool to India, so we stood up there and shouted to one another. Where do you come from? What does it look like? So one ship say, 'we are in a convoy, maybe one hundred ships from Liverpool and we have come here, only two or three ships and we do not know what happened to the other ships, we had plenty trouble.' Some of those ships would have been lost, some gone another way, plenty lost, plane coming and put bomb . . . so then everybody was scared . . . we all shouted to each other and talked about it. Most of the ships had Bengali crews.[14]

It is a sad irony that the names of most of the Indian seamen who died have eluded history, but still they can be remembered for their important role in 'Winston's secret weapon' – the merchant navy convoys. In the words of Alfred Barnes, Minister of War Transport, in September 1945:

The merchant seaman never faltered. He sailed voyage after voyage . . . changing the North Atlantic for North Russia, or for Malta. To him we owe our preservation and our lives.[15]

PLA Collection, Museum in Docklands

London

'When I first came to Aldgate, it was 1925. I asked a policeman where the Indian men lived, and he said, "I don't know, you'd better go on till you smell curry".'[1]

For those on the ships, whether before or during the war, the trips ashore when the ship docked at Liverpool, Cardiff, or Tilbury, had a special flavour. Calcutta, the port from which they had come, was the Second City of the Empire and London was the first. They were the subjects of the British King, and London was their capital, as much as his.

There were already in the 1920's a few ex-seamen in East London, who had settled there after their service in the First World War and continued the tradition of the small Sylhetti community which had been there since the days of the East India Company. The homes of these men were a focus for the seamen while their ships were in Tilbury and they would call in for a meal and an exchange of news.

> I found Mr. Munshi at 16 Elder Street. He was the first of our people, he came in 1922. At that time there were only five: Ayub Ali Master; Marufah Khan; Nana; Naim Ullah and Mr. Munshi. They are all dead now.[2]

In the 1920's the number of London residents remained small, and most of the visitors returned to their ships, stopping only to do a little marketing in Club Row, selling some exotica from Aden or Alexandria, buying cloth, or maybe a sewing machine, to take home.

I told Mr. Munshi I wanted to stay, but he said, 'No, better go back to the ship,' so I went and I stayed another twenty years in the ships, till 1945.[3]

I came to different parts of London, I saw that those who had escaped, they were living here and there, they had no jobs, some are in bad conditions, some do bad things you see and I didn't feel like staying, and I went back to the ship.[4]

By the mid-1930's, however, the lure of London was becoming too strong to resist and the spreading network of contacts led to the growing fashion of 'jumping ship' in British ports, which steadily increased from 1935 until just after the war:

Seamen outside Dunbar House, West India Dock Road. 1920s
LBTH Local History Collection

Coming Glasgow, 1937, I run away from ship to London. Other people telling, 'London very good'. That time, England very good, people very respect coloured people. Coming to house near New Road – I take address when I come to London before.[5]

I jumped ship at Cardiff. I decided the night before the ship sailed. You had to do it at night. The gate was locked, but I climbed over the wall.[6]

Most people, wherever they left the ship, headed for Aldgate, where they were sure to find help and guidance, eventually:

I had one or two addresses, but they were wrongly written, they were not correct, and when I showed them to anyone, they didn't know. I was very much disappointed, didn't know what to do. At that time I cannot go back to my ship, because I have come here to stay . . . I suddenly saw a young man, about twenty-five, very dark looking . . . I thought, probably he is from Madras . . . he spoke to me in Sylhet dialect . . . I was so very glad, I held him, embraced him. I said, 'By good luck, at last I have found someone who can help me.' He said, 'You have come from the boat?' I said, 'Yes'. He said, 'Come with me, I will give you shelter, I live in Mr. Munshi's house.'[7]

As well as Mr. Munshi's lodging house, the other magnet for new arrivals was the Shah Jalal Restaurant, Ayub Ali Master's Coffee shop at 76 Commercial Street.

. . . on the corner of Fashion Street, near the big church, that was where all the Bengali people came after leaving the ship. We stayed there, or he would put us with someone else to sleep.[8]

Ayub Ali was born in the 1880's in Sylhet, where he died in April 1980. He went to sea before the First World War and jumped ship in America in 1919, following the example of one of his relatives, who 'put all his belongings in a big saucepan, and swam to shore with it.'[9] Settling in London, in the 1920's, he opened his seamen's cafe in Commercial Street and also

rented a house, 13 Sandys Row, which became famous among
Sylhetti sailors around the world, who knew it as 'Number
Thirteen'. Here he sheltered those who came from the ships
and helped them in many other ways:

> He was a very good man, he helped a lot of people, no take
> money, nothing. When people couldn't speak English, he
> helped them. There were plenty of others after him, but
> nobody like him.[10]

To start with, the runaway sailors had to go to ground for two
years, until the shipping company's warrant to catch them
had expired. The police had no reason to bother them, as they
had broken no law in coming ashore, being citizens of British
India. Their only offence was in breaking their contract, for
which the company would have to take out a summons if they
were traced. They would have no money, because the system
was that they would be paid off in Calcutta at the end of the
voyage, so Ayub Ali would give them shelter and food for as
long as was necessary and then take them to India House to
register and to the police station to get an identity card or
'police card' – as British citizens, they had no need of a
passport. It was safe to tell the police the truth about their
arrival, though most people took the precaution of giving a
different name from that under which they had signed on in
the ship, when they collected their police card, ration books,
and National card.

> Later, when they had got jobs, they would rent rooms in
> Ayub Ali's house. He still used to look after them, reading
> and writing their letters, filling up forms, holding their
> money and remitting it for them. They called him Master,
> not because he was a teacher, but because he could read
> and write and it is the custom in the villages to call
> someone with a bit of education like that.[11]

The men, of course, paid rent for their rooms, but otherwise
Ayub Ali Master did not want money for his services:

> In those days, financial transactions were not very much
> known with the village people and indeed they are still not

always used. He did it not for money, but for respect and to be recognised as the leader, so that for example he was made President of the UK Muslim League and mixed with Liaquat Ali and Jinnah when they came. In the same way, now, somebody may give patronage to the people in order to be elected as local chairman.[12]

Ayub Ali Master, and nephews

In 1943, Ayub Ali's welfare role was formalised, when he set up the 'Indian Seamen's Welfare League', with himself as General Secretary, and Shah Abdul Majid Qureshi as President. Together these two gentlemen would sit in a tiny office in Christian Street, reading and writing letters, filling out forms, assisting with identity registration, etc. for their less educated compatriots.

Another lodging house keeper, perhaps rather less benevolent and more akin to the *bariwallahs* of Calcutta, was Syed Tofussil Ali, who had a large establishment, the British Indian Sailors' Home in Victoria Dock Road, Canning Town. In the early days, until the bombs of the Blitz, Canning Town was even more a seamen's centre than was Aldgate, being nearer to the docks. Tofussil Ali had run away from home in Sylhet in 1912, after one of his friends had broken his leg at football and, on taking him to hospital, Ali had got involved in a violent quarrel with the English civil surgeon. Pursued by the angry doctor, he had escaped in a boat across the Surma River, and, afraid to go home, had fled to Calcutta and got a job in a ship. Before the First World War he settled in London and his lodging house became a big business, being used by the shipping companies to accommodate their Indian crews. Unfortunately, they also had other business with him, and he was notorious as an informant against the deserters who were sheltering with Ayub Ali, Munshi, and others. During the war, the shipping companies moved his hostel to Glasgow, to escape the bombing which had closed the London docks and in 1947 he went home. He took with him his English wife and the first car to be shipped from London to Sylhet, there enjoying a brief celebrity. He died in Shillong in 1948.

Although he was the scourge of the deserters, Tofussil Ali was, of course, useful to those who wished to return to sea under English articles, with more pay and better conditions. For them, as the shipping companies' agent, he was '*ghat serang*' as well as '*bariwallah*', arranging their papers and finding them a place in a crew.

Mr. Nawab Ali remembered another anonymous person who played the role of *serang* in London:

There was one Englishman who used to be around Dock Street (where seamen registered), he used to say he could get anyone a job on the ship, so we took them to him. I used to do it in Liverpool too and South Shields, fetch people from the Indian ship, and take them straight to the shipping office, then back to an English ship. In wartime it was easy.[13]

Those who had had enough of the sea however, had to look around for employment as quickly as possible, as London was an expensive place to live. Trusting to a change of name and quick wits to evade capture by the shipping company, they launched themselves into their new life. In the early 1930's there was little enough work to be found: 'Never mind Indian boys, English people also couldn't get jobs.' So the sailors had to become streetwise. A bright spark named Soab Ali invented the 'chocolate business', which involved investing a penny-ha'penny in a bar of chocolate, slipping into a pub, 'very hidingly, quietly you see, when the guvnor didn't see you,' and selling to the drinkers tickets numbered one to six, for a penny each.[14] 'Whoever's number comes out on top, he is the lucky one, and he gets the chocolate' while the entrepreneur got fourpence ha'penny profit.[15] 'So we got enough money.'[16] Others went down to the seaside, where they became 'Indian perfumiers', and the 'oriental fragrances' concocted in their lodging houses were in great demand from young ladies keen on cut-price luxury.

Later, with rationing, the marketing turned to a little black marketing:

> They used to have coupons for everything, money wasn't a problem, but coupons were. So we used to go to the ships, Tilbury, Cardiff and Liverpool and buy coupons from sailors, they didn't need them, and then get sweets, chocolates, clothes and sell them in the factories around the Midlands – black market.[17]

Apart from these private enterprises, the work available was either in the clothing trade (then still firmly in the hands of the Jewish community in Aldgate, 'sewing by hand, one pound or two pounds per week') or, more frequently, in some branch of catering. The boilerhouses of large hotels were another obvious place: 'In some of the boiler rooms where the temperature sometimes reaches 120°, it is understandable that a European finds it difficult to work efficiently in the suffocating atmosphere',[18] whereas for the ex-firemen and *donkey-wallahs* it was the ideal place to pursue their professions. Even now, in the basement depths of many large hotels, there is a little team of Bangladeshi boilermen, reliving the adventures of their youth with the boilers of the merchant marine.

There were jobs for kitchen porters in the big hotels and the clubs around St. James and this too was to be an enduring tradition. There are many large kitchens in the West End where the potatoes are peeled and the dishes washed by Bangladeshi ex-seamen: 'These days the Savoy kitchen is filled up with our people.'[19] Perhaps the most common first job was in some small cafe, where not too many questions would be asked:

> After three weeks I got a job in an Egyptian coffee shop in Cannon Street Road, I had to clean and wash up, and if any spare time, peel the potatoes.[20]

> So next day, I got a job for two pounds a week, washing up, somewhere in Tottenham Court Road, a Greek restaurant.[21]

It was not easy to find the way around in the big city and various ingenious systems were devised. For example, a man would arrange bricks along the pavement to mark his route to work through the confusing streets around Brick Lane . . . and get hopelessly lost if they were moved. Then there were the codes for identifying the buses to the West End: the number 8 was 'two eggs', the number 22 'two hooks'.

Once they had got used to London, some people were prepared to travel further afield in search of work: 'So we went to Coventry, to the factories. About twenty or thirty of us went, not all together, but at the same time.'[22] In the Midlands there were better paid jobs to be found, in factories producing aircraft and other war-time necessities, where the Indian men were usually employed as porters or sweepers: 'Wages weren't so high, but with overtime you could make plenty, maybe ten or eleven pounds a week'.[23]

There were other unexpected advantages too:

The job I got was in a section where there were no men, only six hundred girls. The only men were a man of sixty-four, and me. The supervisor didn't want to give me the job because I was a young man, but I said, 'No, it is against my religion to mess around with girls.' And I never did mess around, not in there, there were plenty of girls outside. The women were fitting nuts and I had to go around with a trolley and give them them the nuts and they had to sign for them. They used to give me cigarettes all the time, one here, one there, and I put them in my trolley.[24]

For these jobs, of course, it was necessary to register at the labour exchange, and that could be dangerous:

The police gave me a paper to go and get a ration book, then go to the labour office and get a card, then I started work, at a wire factory in Birmingham. But it was easy for the company to catch us, and one by one I saw my friends getting caught and I thought, 'Oh no, this cholera is coming for me,' so I left my factory without telling anyone except the man I lived with, and came to London. Then I got private work in a Greek restaurant in New Compton Street.[25]

As well as being a better place to disappear in, London was the seamen's social centre, of which the great focus were the Bengali 'coffee shops' which were beginning to spring up. The most famous of these community meeting places was the basement of an Indian cafe at 36 Percy Street (off Tottenham Court Road) which was owned by one of the most influential of the early settlers, Mr. Abdul Mannan (Chanu Miah).

Born in Nabiganj in 1907, educated a little in the village, Mr. Mannan joined the Merchant Navy first in 1932, 'to see the world and make money'. In 1942, after three years service in the war, he settled in Birmingham, working in a factory as a blacksmith. By 1944, he had saved enough (four hundred pounds) to move to London and buy the tenancy of the Basement Cafe in Percy Street, the favourite haunt of Sylhetti men in London. It was there that men would gather after work to exchange news of ships, factories, jobs, the war, politics and most of all, home, over tea or a homely meal of curry and rice, (Or, in the years of rationing, some less satisfying substitute: 'There was no rice in London for three years. We used to break up spaghetti and make it look like rice and cook it with curry',)[26]

Here those without education would have their letters read for them, and replies written sending all their news to the family, or perhaps a letter to an English ladyfriend. There were plenty of them in those days for the handsome young men from the East, to whom their advice and assistance, as well as their company, were very welcome: 'Lot of English ladies helped us'.[27]

Some young men were too religious, or too shy, to involve themselves with ladies, but of course very many did. Among the 'ladies' were many loyal and generous women, without whose help and support the early pioneers would certainly not have settled so successfully. There was a fine distinction in cafe society between those who 'associated' with women, who were known as 'betiwallahs' and those who settled respectably into marriage, the 'shadiwallahs'. It was very common among the seamen to marry their English (or Irish) girlfriends, some of whom became Muslim. Some of these marriages were shortlived, but others retained the romance of their beginnings for a lifetime:

> I never knew that people could love each other so much. We were like one life ... After she died, I couldn't do anything, I just fell apart for a while. My heart always wants her.[28]

There were other temptations besides ladies in London. Drink, for most people was easy to resist: 'I never ever drank alcohol ... When I was a waiter I used to have to fetch alcohol for customers, well, you couldn't refuse to fetch it, but afterwards I would wash my hands, really thoroughly'.[29] Gambling, the other vice particularly forbidden to Muslims, was a more dangerous trap:

> Then one man said to me, 'In Dhaka and Calcutta, there is horse racing, with the jockey sitting on top of the horse, but you have never seen a dog race! Dog is running with no jockey!' I said, 'Alright, let me go and have a look, see what

that is.' First race, he lost, I win, sixty five pounds. Then from five pounds I win five hundred pounds. So it went on, then I said, 'Let's go home'. But he said, 'Look this is the way to make money, why not stay and make some more?' Within six months I had lost all my five thousand pounds, only three or four hundred pounds left.'[30]

I did gamble once. I put a pound on a horse called *Never Say Die*, in the National, and I won forty pounds. Well, I bought a necklace for my wife for five pounds, and a present for my son and then I went to the dog track. I decided to put it all on two dogs and let whatever would happen, happen. Well, fortunately, both dogs lost, so that was the end of it and I never gambled again, it was very lucky.[31]

From the coffee shops, it was just one step to the opening of the first Sylhetti-owned Indian restaurants. The men had learned to cook by trial and error in their communal shipboard messes – none of them would ever have cooked at home or even have taken much notice of the cooking being done. On shore in London they continued to take it in turn to cook for one another in the lodging houses and in due course some enteprising soul began to sell this good home cooking in a small cafe in Whitechurch Street.

Practically adjacent to this cafe stood the London Mosque, where the local Muslims foregathered. Soon the appetising aroma of the curries reached the nostrils of some of the professional and business men and students, who travelled from widely separated parts of London to crowd into this tiny cafe, intent on sampling the appetising food. Naturally it was only a matter of time before the restaurant business expanded to other parts of the Metropolis. The Indian Muslims had discovered something at which they could excel, and which for them was proving highly profitable.[32]

Soon, it was not only fellow Indians who were patronising the restaurants, but adventurous English diners too, especially those who had served in the Raj and who liked to eat nostalgic curries, to practise their Hindustani and perhaps to bask in past glories:

They used to like sometimes if we call them *'sahib'* you know. They used to be very happy, so we wanted to have a little more tip, so why not? They used to call, 'Bearer' . . . 'Bearer'. Nowadays these fellows, if anyone call them 'bearer', they wouldn't serve him they would say, 'Go out of this restaurant.' [33]

Shafi's . . . started in the 1920s   *BBC Hulton Picture Library*

The Sylhettis were not the first in the field with Indian restaurants catering for more than a dockland clientele. Two were started in the 1920's – *Veeraswamy's,* which was owned by an Englishman and *Shafi's,* which was owned by a North Indian – both of which are still flourishing today. In 1938 however, Shah Abdul Majid Qureshi became the 'first Sylhetti man to own a restaurant', when he took over the *Dilkush* (Heart's Delight) in Windmill Street, but in 1940 in the Blitz, 'it was bombed and smashed and the story was finished there, although it was a prosperous restaurant and doing well.'[34]

The two pioneers who really launched the restaurant trade were Mr. Mosharaf Ali, and Mr. Israel Miah (Shirajul Islam). These two ex-seamen, both from the Maulvi Bazar sub-division of Sylhet, pooled their savings and borrowed from their friends to open a restaurant together. The *Anglo-Asia*, in Brompton Road, did good business, in spite of bombs dropping all around. Mosharaf Ali was 'a very extravagant type', and was soon in difficulties and forced to sell his share. Not long afterwards he opened another restaurant in Earls Court, but soon sold that one too, then 'another one here, another one there', until he had started ten or twelve restaurants.[35]. As 'his habits were extravagant, he used to have car, posh place, and all that',[36] he was constantly realising his assets by selling the current business to a fellow country-man, before starting again. Meanwhile his first partner Israel Miah, a more quietly successful type of person, was also opening new restaurants and taking others into partnership, thus bringing more people into the trade: 'I'm a bit lucky, I always did good business, I don't know why. Other people say it as well, wherever Israel Miah goes makes a fortune.'[37]

So it was that the restaurant business grew, especially among men from Maulvi Bazar, who were inspired by the example of Israel Miah and encouraged by his generous assistance and by the expansive nature of his happy-go-lucky partner, Mosharaf Ali (who eventually settled down to become a successful restaurant owner).

Israel Miah is the most successful, and he is the innovator, who took the first initiative among his Maulvi Bazar people, and they followed him. He is such a good fellow . . . he has all this money and he likes to help people of his area, so anyone who comes with a hope that he will help him to open a business, he used to give them loan. That is how the people of Maulvi Bazar were successful, because they had fellow feeling and Israel Miah is the fellow who helped most of them.[38]

Without such patronage, nobody had the money to start himself in business, so people would group together in partnerships, or lend each other their savings, until such time as they might need help themselves, to start a restaurant or for some other emergency. These finance schemes, were conducted without interest, entirely on trust, which rarely failed: 'What shall I do with a receipt? He will not deny that he has had the money from me. Why should he?'[39].

By 1946 there were 20 restaurants in London and they began to spread all over the country until in 1960 there were 300 Indian restaurants in Britain and in 1980 over 3000, of which the vast majority are owned by families from Sylhet. The names of many of the restaurants are tried and tested names of the early successes, *Anglo-Asia*, *Koh-i-Noor*, *Taj Mahal* and their distinctive red flock wallpaper style is a survival of their luxurious air in postwar austerity.

The restaurants of course have done much more than make the fortunes of the ex—seamen of Maulvi Bazar and those who came after them. They have changed the eating habits of the whole nation and even the packets of dried 'instant curry' and jars of 'curry sauce' in every grocer's shop – however little relation they may bear to Indian food – have origins in the dinners sold by Mosharaf Ali, Israel Miah and the other reckless entrepreneurs of the early days.

In order to obtain licences to open restaurants, the seamen had to formalise their position in Britain. For some this meant the acquisition of passports confirming their British Citizenship, to which they had been born:

Then I got my British passport . . . I never had Indian, Pakistani or Bangladesh passport, all along, since I had my passport, I am British.[40]

Side by side with the business ventures the beginnings of community organisation were stirring around the two themes of religion and politics. It has been suggested that the consciousness of living rather worldly, not to say occasionally sinful lives in London made the seamen particularly anxious about getting things right in the Hereafter. Certainly the

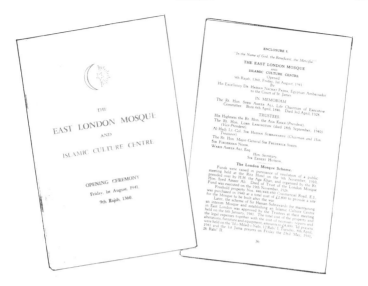

earliest forms of community organizations were the Muslim Burial Societies which sprang up around the country wherever Indian Muslims congregated. A pioneer in this movement was Haji Taslim Ali, *Imam* of the East London Mosque since 1956, who opened the first *halal* butcher's shop in the 1940's and later became the first Muslim undertaker.

East London Mosque, Commercial Road

Friday prayers at the East London Mosque, a small house in Commercial Road, were always an important occasion, even for those whose religious observance was not much more than the avoidance of pork and alcohol. The prayer gatherings were a focus for the formation, soon after the war, of the UK branch of the Muslim League. Prior to this, some of the Sylhetti settlers had been active, with other Indian expatriates, in their support of the Congress Party. But becoming disillusioned with the Congress they threw their weight behind the Muslim League's demand first for fair treatment in a future independent India and later for Pakistan. The leader of the Bengali-speaking Muslim League activists was the barrister Abbas Ali, who was very influential in the early years of the community of the ex-seamen.

In August 1947, the two hundred years of British rule in India ended at last, and the subcontinent was partitioned into India and the new state of Pakistan – its East and West wings divided by a thousand miles of northern India. The referendum held in Sylhet in July 1947 to decide the future of the district brought it out of Assam, and into East Bengal and East Pakistan. From the early days of Pakistan however, the people of East Pakistan were aware of the oppression by the dominant western wing.

In London, the ex-seamen experienced West Pakistani discrimination first in the condescending attitudes they met whenever they had business at the Pakistan High Commission, where the prosperity of 'illiterate villagers' turned restaurant proprietors was clearly resented by the clerks. The disrespect at the High Commission reminded them of the early days when, going to register at India House, they had been sent to the back door. Now they vowed to end the 'back door treatment' and began to stick up for themselves, telling the officials: 'You are only postmasters, come to send our money home.'[41]

By the early 1950's, the community of men from Sylhet living in London had grown to about 300, and they were conscious of the need to organize themselves.

They had two key meeting places: in the East End, Moktar Miah's cafe in Cable Street, and in the West End the *Green Mask* Restaurant in Brompton Road. Abdul Mannan had moved in 1946 from Percy Street to the *Green Mask* (then serving 'Continental cuisine') and made it into a successful Indian restaurant. There the men who worked in restaurants and hotels would come in their afternoon breaks for meetings. The weekend meetings however, were in Cable Street and it was there in 1952 that the Pakistan Welfare Association was formed, with Arshad Ali as Secretary and Monfor Ali as President.

In its first few months, the executive of the Welfare Association continued, in their sessions in the cafe and in restaurants (like the *Green Mask*) owned by members, to carry out the 'welfare' functions that had always been so important – the letterwriting, form-filling, etc. But increasingly also they began to lobby and organize on behalf of Sylhetti working people. Both in their welfare work and in their political struggles they had the support of a succession of singularly dedicated and capable friends who devoted a great deal of time and effort to the cause of the East London settlers and with whom they had warm (if sometimes turbulent) relationships. The first of these activists were the barristers Abdul Hamid and Abbas Ali. Then in 1953 Mr Tassaduq Ahmed volunteered to act as 'office secretary' to the PWA, a vital community development role.

The next few years were to see a significant politicization of the leaders of the community in London, through their growing consciousness of the mass movement for autonomy in East Pakistan, a movement which was born with the Language Martyrs (students shot in Dhaka on February twenty-first 1952, while protesting at the government's attempt to enforce the use of Urdu in place of Bengali) and was to lead eventually to the liberation struggle and an independent Bangladesh in 1971.

Every event and ideological development in East Pakistan sent ripples through the community of exiles in London. Political activity was at first centred mainly among the student community and in particular the Pakistan Student's Federation, which numbered predominantly students from East Pakistan.

In 1954, however, a new element was introduced. In March 1954 provincial elections held in East Pakistan had resulted in a landslide victory for the United Front led by A.K. Fazhil

H. S. Suhrawardy. 1955   *BBC Hulton Picture Library*

Huq and H.S. Suhrawardy. The new ministry was seen by the centre in West Pakistan, as too much of a threat, and in familiar fashion was displaced after a few weeks by a military coup. Major General Iskander Khan, an 'iron man' of the Pakistani bureaucracy, was sent to take over the administration of East Pakistan. One of his first acts was to declare a number of political leaders 'enemies of the state' and to expel them from the country. Prominent among these leaders was *Maulana* Bashani, the peasant political and spiritual leader from Mymensingh who was a focus for much of the early struggle for autonomy. At the time of the Mirza coup, the Maulana was in Stockholm attending a World Peace Conference, so he travelled to London for his exile.

For the next year he stayed, along with other activists, at Mr. Abdul Mannan's house, 29 St. Mary Abbott's Terrace.

There he was visited by all the exiled political leaders from East and West Pakistan – over sixty of them in the course of the year. Mannan's house thus became the centre of Pakistan opposition politics, and without ever intending it he became involved himself. The sojourn of the 'Red Maulana' in London, holding court in Mannan's house and at the *Green Mask* to mixed gatherings of exiled leaders and Sylhetti restaurant workers, was something very akin to Ayatollah Khomeini's years in France, and crucial to the eventual emergence of the liberation movement in East Pakistan.

From that time most of the restaurant owners and community leaders in London were, loosely at least, allied with the Awami League and prepared to give financial support to the activities of the students.

Meanwhile, the feelings of discrimination by the Pakistan High Commission, of which the Sylhetti community had been

Left to right. Abdul Manan, Aftab Ali, Maulana Bashana, Dr. Basu

conscious, had become a concrete issue, when the Pakistan government refused to allow passports to East Pakistanis who wished to come and work in Britain.

In the days of the post-war economic boom when labour was urgently required in the factories and mills of Britain as well as the transport and health services, there were no restrictions from the British side. The restrictions all came from the Pakistan government, which made it known that it was shameful and demeaning for Pakistani citizens to 'go to Britain for labour,' and ceased to issue passports in East Pakistan. Passports were still available in West Pakistan, perhaps because many people in Mirpur (Azad Kashmire) had lost their homes in partition and were a source of potential trouble, so the government was happy to allow them to flock to labour in the Yorkshire mills. For East Pakistanis, the only way to get a passport was to go first as a labourer to West Pakistan, or else to get a student's passport on the pretext of coming to read for the Bar, or to one of the notorious establishments like the 'Tailoring Academy' of Piccadilly Circus which supplied appropriate prospectuses. Then, when the Pakistani authorities saw through that, there was the 'medical line', with a sudden upsurge in the numbers of people for whom it was vital to be treated in London.

Clearly something more satisfactory had to be done. In 1954 the Pakistan Welfare Association organized its first big meeting at the Grand Palais Hall in Commercial Road, to receive the Foreign Minister of Pakistan Mr Hamidul Hoq on a visit to London and to press him to redress this wrong. Prior to this meeting the PWA had a membership of about one hundred, but from the packed hall the membership increased enormously and a mass signature campaign was started on the passport issue.

Among those on the platform at the Grand Palais Hall was Mr Aftab Ali, the champion of the Sylhetti seamen, who returned to Pakistan to take up the struggle there ...

The Next Generation

'**Mr Suhrawardy invited the Queen to Bengal, then he and Mr Aftab Ali explained this history to her, how for two hundred years the British ruled India and how the Indian people were poor and wanted to come to England and earn money and when they had explained it to her she said she would come back and tell Parliament to give the vouchers, and she did, so they started to come.**'[1]

Whether or not the Queen had anything to do with it, there is no doubt that the man who did most to make it possible for thousands of migrant workers to come from East Pakistan/ Bangladesh to Britain, was the late Mr Aftab Ali, 'the most well known Sylhetti man of his generation'. Aftab Ali was born in 1907 in the village of Katalkhair near Gualabazar, Sylhet. His father though not formally educated was a prosperous landowner. He ran a flourishing business, and wished that his son should be well educated and become a barrister. In his early teens however, he gave up his studies (a mistake that he bitterly regretted in later life) and ran away from his father's wrath to Calcutta, where his brother Jafar Miah was a powerful '*bariwallah*' a lodging house keeper. In 1923 he slipped away again, as a stoker on a ship bound for America. His elder brother having failed to catch him at Calcutta docks rushed to Madras to stop him there, but missed him again.

In the ship he was teased by the other men who called '*burra bap ka beta*' (rich man's son), because he was fussy enough to pick the stones out of his rice. But the insights he gained then into the terrible conditions suffered by the Indian seafarers were to cause him to spend the rest of his life in struggles for their rights.

Arriving in America, he jumped ship as he had intended, and wandered around for two or three years, taking casual employment in stores and barber shops, reading, listening to trade-unionists and exploring politics.

On his return to India in 1925, Aftab Ali began to involve himself with the Calcutta-based Indian Seamen's Union at the invitation of the leading activist Manfur Khan, who came from the village of Secunderpur, very near to Aftab Ali's home. Within a few years Aftab Ali had become the union's General Secretary.

The situation of Indian seamen was at this time quite desperate. Crippled by 70% unemployment and by the poverty which forced men to accept inhuman exploitation; shunned by European trade unions who were concerned to protect their own jobs, they were at the mercy of the powerful vested interests of the *serangs* and the ship-owners, who combined to resist any changes in pay and conditions on the ships or in the corrupt recruitment system on shore. There had been some reforming legislation after the report of the Clow Committee on Seamen's Recruitment in 1922, but it had made little impression. As Aftab Ali later wrote:

Here in the city of Calcutta under the very nose of those in authority the entire advances received by seamen on signing articles are being forcibly taken away from them by the *serangs*, aided and abetted by some of the lodging house keepers, on the plea of having provided them with employment . . . punishment for such extortion has never been applied by the authorities in spite of their attention having been repeatedly drawn . . . Every seaman during voyage is made to pay to the *serangs* another two months wages which completes the circle of extortion . . . On a modest calculation the total amount of money thus extorted annually from seamen engaged in the port of Calcutta reaches the horrible figure of two million Rupees . . . Here in the city of palaces and gardens these seamen are housed like cattle in filthy quarters and amidst unhealthy surroundings . . . Our immediate necessity is to root out bribery and extortion of the three months' wages of seamen by *serangs*, aided by certain lodging-house keepers.[2]

The first essential for Indian seamen was to unite their various unions, and in this complex task Aftab Ali was remarkably successful, becoming the first President of the All India Seamen's Federation in 1937. Despite gradual improvement, it was not until after independence that Indian Seamen's conditions at last became tolerable, and even now the conditions of Asian seamen on European ships are inferior in wages, living space, etc., to those of European crews. Still, it was a measure of Aftab Ali's achievement that James Mowat, on his Mission of Enquiry into Seafarers' conditions in India and Pakistan for the International Labour Organization (ILO) in 1947, found that the seamen were 'among the most extensively and effectively organized workers in India'.[3]

Aftab Ali's relationship with the ILO had started in 1929, when he represented Indian seamen at the International Labour Conference in Geneva. This he did again in 1933, 1936 and 1939. In 1947 in San Francisco, he was elected to the Governing Body of the ILO, and in 1951, as one of its vice-presidents, presided over a session in Geneva where he attended thrice yearly conferences from 1948 to 1957. He and his wife were the guests of the Trade Union Movement of the USSR in 1957 and in 1947 he led a Pakistani Labour delegation to the People's Republic of China.

In 1939, Aftab Ali became vice-president of the All India TUC, and from 1937 to 1944 he was a member of the Bengal Legislative Assembly. In 1947, although he had not been in favour of the partition, Aftab Ali went with the other East Bengali seamen to Pakistan, where he sat as an independent MP on the Legislative Assembly. In Pakistan he continued to concern himself with the rights of the seafaring community from which he had come. In 1947, when the port of Calcutta became lost to Pakistani seamen and he had failed in his efforts to get Khulna and Chittagong established as major ports for the foreign lines, he advised Pakistani seamen to leave their ships at British ports.

Those who took his advice, and sought work in the factories in Britain, swelled the numbers of the small community of the earlier settlers. Others however, weary of war and travelling, returned to their villages with their savings thinking to live a quiet life on their farms. But within a few years poverty again had them by the throat and they were in urgent need of income which was impossible to find in East Pakistan. With most international shipping concentrated in Calcutta (though there were a very few jobs to be had in Chittagong) the sea service was closed to them. Some started to return to work in Britain, but then came the Pakistan government's passport clampdown.

After the Pakistan Welfare Association's meeting in London in 1954 Aftab Ali returned to Sylhet, where he convened a conference of ex-seamen in the 'Jinnah Hall', near the mosque of Shah Jalal, and formed the Overseas Seamen's Welfare Association. Aftab Ali was the President: Osman Ali a *serang* who never came to England was the General Secretary; and Mr Shafiqul Hoq, a relative of Ayub Ali Master who had spent some time in London, was the Organizing Secretary. While the seamen in Sylhet were organizing petitions, Aftab Ali went to the ILO in Geneva and the government in Karachi, pleading their cause.

In 1956 the government of Mr Suhrawardy, who had always been personally sympathetic to the seamen, agreed to grant one thousand passports to 'distressed seamen', their survivors, or nominated dependents. At that time, it was

Aftab Ali, General Secretary of the Indian Seamen's Union   Mrs Aysha Ali

usual in India and Pakistan for a quarter of posts in government departments like the railways and the post office to be reserved for the relatives of former workers and this was the same principle. So the word went out that the door to Britain was open again, and the sailors or their sons or nephews, clutching their creased and dog-eared *'nollies'*, made their way from the villages to register their claims. Aftab Ali opened the first of the travel agencies in Sylhet, Crescent Travels (with another branch in Johnson Road, Dhaka) to process the papers of the first thousand migrant workers. Meanwhile in London, Ayub Ali Master was also

Aftab Ali – representing the ILO in Geneva   Mrs Aysha Ali

starting the travel agency business with his Orient Travels, at 13 Sandys Row (now at 96 Brick Lane). Later, due to further pressure by Aftab Ali, the rules were relaxed to permit men other than ex-seamen to 'proceed to the UK for employment', and the great movement had begun, of men from Sylhet coming to sell their labour in Britain.

1956, the year of the passports, brought about a sudden change, as the three hundred or so ex-seamen in East London were joined by two to three thousand more men – a new generation of adventurers. After the first arrivals there was a steady stream of migration until by 1962 the community was perhaps five thousand strong.

Meanwhile, far more people were travelling to the North and to the Midlands where there was more work, though a less established pattern of settlement. That there are now some 200,000 Bangladeshis in Britain – about 35,000 of them living in East London – is the result of the work of the early Welfare Association: Suruth Miah, Nesar Ali, Abdul Mannan, Ayub Ali Master, and their colleagues, with the support of Aftab Ali, Hamidul Hoque Chowdury and others in East Pakistan:

> Our great success was that thousands and thousands of our country people have come here and they don't know that it was we few who came before. Bangladesh depends on the foreign exchange sent by our people, and it was we who started that.[4]

For the next few years there was little difficulty in coming to Britain except in raising the fare for which people were often forced to mortgage their land to wealthier neighbours. By the 1950's the normal means of travel was by air, at first by scheduled flights, until Jorif Miah, Israel Miah's enterprising brother in Maulvi Bazar, chartered an aeroplane. In London, the old network could still just about support the newcomers, though it was getting strained:

> They used to come to the airport with just my address and take taxis to my house. Some people had addresses in Bradford or Birmingham and they used to take taxis there too! They got cheated, because they didn't know anything.

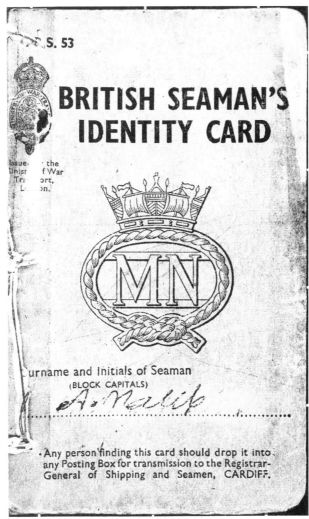

*'. . . at the outbreak of war, 50,000 of the Merchant Navy's
190,000 men were lascars . . .'*

When they came to my house, they would sign on at the labour exchange in Settles Street, then get work in the factories. At one time there were 95 people living in this house . . . They weren't all sleeping here, they used to sleep here and there, but they were all registered at this address, my wife went mad when she saw all the names on a letter! You know the room upstairs? There were 35 living up there![5]

Then came new restrictions with the Immigration Acts and the voucher system, whereby those who wanted to come to Britain had to have a job to come to. Those who were already settled became the latter-day *serangs*, finding the jobs in factories, sending vouchers, arranging passports, advancing money, for the tens of thousands of men who left their homes and came to live in crowded rooms in the industrial towns of Britain, in search of something more than bare survival for their families.

The Bangladeshi community in Britain began to take root, on the territory marked out by the first few casual pioneers who had found the way 'across seven seas and thirteen rivers' from Sylhet to Aldgate. Here at last was the memorial to those thousands of nameless sailors who died in cold water and blazing engine rooms. The Empire had finally come home.

Mr. Nawab Ali

I was born in Sylhet, that time India – Gulabganj *Thana*, Mirganjbazar, near Badeshwar. South Badeshwar is a very educated place – all educated except me, I am not educated at all! My family had plenty of land – I have land too. I have never been to school, not for one day! My father, yes he went to school.

When I was nine months old, my father and mother died, both on the same day – it was some epidemic. At the same time, four hundred and fifty people died in the village. We three brothers lived with our grandparents after that. Still we live in the same house, my uncle's father is still there, we just made a new house very near, and I put my brother there – my elder brother . . . and I still live in that same home. I just went, in 1977, and moved my brother into the new house. He has four sons, I sent just one of my girls. My village is called Sheikpur, beside Kushiara River. I ran away from home when I was ten years old. Actually, I am seventy-two now, but the way this country register, I am sixty-six.

I jumped on a small boat – just, you know, for playing and seeing. All the kids jumped on to ride to the other side of the river, and I didn't get out. Nobody saw me – I was hiding. It wasn't a very big boat, like those little launches that run up and down the Thames *Nadi*. There were nine crew. They all loved me very much, made me like their son or grandson, and everywhere we went people used to give me presents. I did all sorts of different work – ran about fetching things, making tea. The Captain gave me four rupees a month.

Well – everybody was looking for me at home – they asked all the children, about forty of them playing there, but nobody knew. So they decided that when I jumped off the ship I had fallen under the propellor and drowned. By that time

my grandparents were dead and we were living with my
uncle and aunty, all the family was there . . . our *gusti* had
about twenty houses . . . everybody was looking for me.

There was a disciple man, a *fakir*, he lived far away in the
jungle. He came to my home, and everybody asked him about
me. He said, 'He's not dead, he is coming by the door, and
nobody sees him.' This man knew everything – if he saw you,
he could tell your grandfather and great grandfather's name,
just like that. He was born like that. If anybody gave him
food, he would take, but he wouldn't ask for anything.

One day, a few months later, my brother and my cousin had a
lot of a vegetable called *Kodu*, so they took them to the
market, in Fenchuganj – three miles from our home. That
time there was plenty of water, so this boat could go in the
small rivers. We wanted to buy vegetables to take to Assam
. . . We went to the market. Only I could speak *Sylhetti Basha,*
everybody else spoke *Chittagong Basha* – it's a quite different
language you know. I went to buy about sixty of these *Kodu*
from them. When I went to them, my cousin ran away,
because he thought he wouldn't understand me – and he
called me *'Bhai-sahib'*. So my brother came.

I had changed – completely different dress, different
speech, grown taller . . . it was from January to October.

Coming behind me, my brother, my cousin, my friend from

next home. We went in the coffee shop . . . the ships crew and my friends behind me. The cook in the coffee shop . . . he had a plate in his leg instead of his knee, so he walked like this . . . Everyone called him 'Grandfather'. I told him 'we want *paratha* and *kebab*' (*Kebab* is our language – now they use it here too, because we taught them). We were seven, so I asked for seven *parathas* and seven *kebabs*.

Then when the *kebabs* came, my brother said 'I don't want to eat it.' Then I didn't say anything, but water came· in my eye and I started crying. And my brother and cousin jumped up and embraced me, and said, 'Oh, where have you been? Everybody is crying for you! Only the *Pir* knows where you are, and he said ". . . everyday he passes the door, and nobody opens the door!" '

I didn't go with my brother then – he had to go somewhere else, and he would meet me at Karimganj . . . The Captain gave me a thousand cigarettes, two thousand *biris*, two tins of small biscuits – called jam biscuits in our language, and a dozen tins of thick Nestle's milk. And all my clothing and everything.

Two villages went there to meet me . . . The riverside was full of people come to see me. Nobody understood what I said, and I had to show them that the milk was for eating. My aunty is still alive, I think she is over a hundred now. She said, 'Oh no, it's woman's milk! Nobody will eat it here.'

When I went in 1968, a lot of people came to see me, and my aunty was making tea, and she said to somebody, 'in my *kuta* there is a tin of milk, go and fetch it.' I said, 'I want to see this tin!' I said, '*Chachi-ama* (because she brought me up remember), I brought this milk from my ship, and nobody would eat it, so I took it back again to the ship, now this milk, how you eat it now? Woman milk! England woman milk!' Everybody laughed! Still she doesn't forget that!

I lived five days there – nobody understood me at all, I had forgotten Sylhetti altogether. I went home in 1968 and spoke our language again, otherwise I had forgotten it. I only stayed five days then I went again to my ship, when it came by. I had nothing to do there, nobody understood me, and I had seen so many different things. I couldn't stand to stay there – you know how it is in my country villages. Five days I stayed, but it seemed like five years!

So I went back to the ship, and stayed four and half years, and in that time, I passed two exams to be a pilot. I am qualified to test the depth of the river – whether the boat can go there or not . . . and I learned to steer the ship too – we call in my language 'seacunny'. Many times I went to Chittagong, stayed in Captain's home – his name was Ali Hamsa. I passed my river exams, but the Captain didn't give me my pass book. Yes, without going to school, I learned to measure the depth of the water. I learned it in six months, you know, with a line and lead weights. The rivers in Bengal are very dangerous, even a little mistake, and the ship can finish. From Calcutta to Assam, I knew which side of the river to go, in all the rivers. From Calcutta to Assam . . . I don't think I would know it now! We had to go through *Sunderbans* all the time, there was no other way to come to Calcutta. Tiger and deer – we saw them many times – tiger this side of the river, deer that side, tiger jumping, and deer run away. That was over forty years ago, I don't think here's much jungle left now. In Sylhet the same . . . you know where is Sylhet airport? I remember when that was a big jungle, bloody tigers living there. No more tiger in Sylhet now. They used to come out, and people shooting and killing you know. And elephants – thousands and thousands of them used to come out, looking for water, and food. Now – nothing.

At last, I had to leave that ship because I beat up the Captain in the dry dock in Calcutta. I told you how I pass my exams and he didn't give me my certificates. And there in the dry dock I found out that he had given them to his son, who had just finished in school, and come from his home in Calcutta. He had done very well in school, and his father wanted to make him a pilot – with my papers! The engineer told me, 'Ayub,' (that was my pet name), 'the Captain has given your pass to his son.' That night I said to the Captain, '*Ami dui bar pass korechi, aur ekhon, ami boi pai na. Kene, Bolun?*' (I passed and I didn't receive any papers. Tell me why?) He said, 'Yes, I have given it to my son. You will get it back after eighteen months!' When he said eighteen months, I just fell off my chair, I was so shocked! Four and half years I had been waiting for the pass.

I ran to the cabin and brought out my spring knife . . . You

know, before, there was fighting between Hindus and
Muslims, and many people were killed . . . me and my friend
Yunnus, in Chittagong we used to be very dangerous . . . he
died in the war with Pakistan – West Pakistanis killed him.
That spring knife was fifteen inches long – I bought it in
Assam for nine rupees. When he saw the knife, the Captain's
grandson ran and told them. Then the engineer came to me.
The engineer was not from Chittagong, he was from
Noakhali. He said, 'Be careful, you are a very temper boy!' He
was afraid I would knife the Captain. In those day, I was very
dangerous. The engineer was very wise. He said to me, 'Don't
kill the Captain, because he is a clever man, although he
made a mistake. There are very few clever men in the world.
So it would be a pity to kill him. Hit him if you like, but don't
kill him!'

In the night, there is nobody at the dry dock. I came to
where the Captain was sleeping, and I started to hit him with
his own shoes. I hit his face, his chest, his head. His face was a
mess. Then I tied him up with thick rope that he couldn't get
out of. If he hadn't been asleep I could never have done it,
because he was a big man. When he shouted there was nobody to hear him.

I didn't take anything with me, not even clothes, and I went
to a lodging – house keeper I knew in Kidderpore. The Captain said he wouldn't make a case, because then he would be
shamed. Later he asked me many times to go back to him, but
I always refused because I said, 'If you cheated me once, I can
never trust you again.'

Then I got a job as a dry dock *serang*. There was an
Englishman who had the contract to clean and paint the
ships in the dry dock, and he gave me the contract to bring
men to do the painting and cleaning. I had to go to the coffee
shops around Kidderpore and fetch the men. I met that
Englishman when I had to carry something to his house, and
I told him I was a good painter – I had learned it in the ship –
so he said I could paint a room in his house for him. He asked
me what paint I would want, and I said 'Gloss', so he knew
that I really did know painting, and he gave me the job for the
dry dock. I did that for five years. I didn't make much money,
and what I did get I used to spend on going out to the cinema

and things, and some I sent home . . . people were always
coming and going . . . I never went home at that time – I had
nothing to go for. Then I got the ship job through a boarding-
house master in Kidderpore, and there were five or six
serangs from Badeshwar – they all knew me.

Painting the ship in dock   PLA Collection, Museum in Docklands

First time I came to England it was 28th August 1939.
My ship came to Cardiff, and I just came to London, and then
went back to Calcutta. When I got back to Calcutta war was
declared – Saturday, twelve noon. The Government put in
the newspaper that if a family had three sons, one should stay
at home, and one go in the Army, and one in the Navy or Air
Force. Most people didn't think that was right, but anyway I
went straight to Calcutta and got another ship for England –
City Line.

I was a fireman – well a coalman really – it was very very
hard. I had to carry coal like from here to Ashfield Street – it
was a very long ship. We worked four hours on, eight hours
off, day and night. The crew were all Sylhetti but nobody else
from Badeshwar – all from other places like Ballaganj side. I
have never been to that side – although I know nearly every
corner of England.

We stopped in Bombay on the way. I found out afterwards that my middle brother had come to Calcutta to see me. And when he heard that I had gone to London, he got another ship for London. And we both arrived in Liverpool on the same day, and I ran to see him when I heard it.

After that, I didn't know that he was in hospital for five months, after getting a cold or something – I didn't know he was there and he didn't know where I was. I didn't know until he was leaving Liverpool on another ship. That time I was living in Coventry, and a man came to see me, from a ship. He got my address from another friend, Sekonder Ali. I was eating when he knocked at my door, so I opened the door with my other hand and said, 'Come in, here is rice and curry, sit down and eat.' But he just looked at me and said, 'Have you got a brother – such and such name?' Then he told me my brother had been in hospital for five months, and he had just seen him on a ship at Liverpool waiting to go home. I said, 'How did you know it was my brother?' And he said, 'You have got one face.' So I said, 'Here's the key, live here till I go to the ship. I offered the man a hundred pounds to take me out on the boat to the ship, Arcadia line, but it wasn't allowed. I couldn't even send a message, because wartime you see – France was occupied by then. If my brother had known I was there he could have come on the deck and seen me, but he didn't know. He died after he went home, and I never saw him again. My eldest brother is still alive – he is eighty-three now.

I have got out of order now . . . I jumped the ship at Cardiff. I decided the night before the ship sailed. You had to do it at night. The gate was locked, but I climbed over the wall. I went first to a friend of mine's house – his wife was half-caste. They took care of me and hid me for a few days, then he brought me to London and put me in a house on the other side of Commercial Road – that house is still there. My rent was four shillings a week. I didn't have my own room, I had a bed in the kitchen. The house was full of sailors – English, Arab, African. I had about four pounds in my pocket when I came to London. After three weeks I had got a job in an Egyptian coffee shop in Cannon Street Road. I had to clean and wash up, and if any spare time, peel the potatoes.

I had no papers. Once the police come to the coffee shop, and they asked two people at the next table to show their papers, and I said, 'Do you want to see mine?' – I didn't have any. But they said, 'Oh no – that's alright.' I think it was because I always used to look smart – suit and tie and all. I wore English clothes ever since I first ran away from home. That Captain used to take me to offices and places and even clubs. I went to a drinking club – men and ladies – English people, in Assam, so I knew about English clothes, and the Captain used to buy them for me. The next time the police came they just said to me, 'Oh yes, alright, we know you.'

After five weeks, I went to India house to get some papers. You know India House is in the Strand – I had to get a number eight bus. One man came with me, and he pointed – 'India House' is there.' But I walked past it and missed it, because of course I couldn't read the name – I can't read at all. I walked past it and then I walked back again, and I was standing right behind it, smoking a cigarette and wondering where it was. Then I see two girls looking at me from the bus stop across the road. They came over, and one of them punched me and said, 'What are you doing here?' Her father was that man who had the contract for the dry dock in Calcutta. She was born in India, and she could speak Hindustani. I used to play with that girl at her father's house. They had a big fish pond, we used to put our feet in it. So there she was at India House.

I went to India House. I had to get my proof, so that I could get a proper job. The man was from Bombay – he asked me if I come from the ship and I said, 'Yes'. He asked me too many questions, then he said he would send me my papers. When I got outside, those girls were still there. One had bought me some cigarettes and the other bought me a tie – I had a shirt but no tie. She put it on for me – I said, 'I know how to tie it.' But she did it. Then they took me to Marble Arch by walking. Then he came back, and they left me outside the Savoy Hotel, to wait for them. They were working there because they had no money. Although her family was very rich they had some problem, so she had to work. The other girl was from Bombay – they were both English but they spoke Hindustani as well as English, like our children here – speaking two languages. While I was waiting for them, I talked to the gateman.

I couldn't understand much of what he said, but I said 'Yes' and 'No', and he gave me a cup of tea. When they came out, they said, 'It's all arranged – you start work here in the morning' but they all had to go to work.

I forgot to say – I left that place where I was staying, because there was some trouble, and for three nights I slept on the street – in Settles Street, down some steps in a doorway. A Jewish shopkeeper gave me some soup. If a policeman came I had to get up and walk around. On the third day I was in an Italian coffee shop, and one of our people came in and sat down near me. He was looking at me, and then he said, 'Are you from the ship?' I said, 'Yes'. 'You come from Badeshwar, and you are one of three brothers, your father and mother are dead.' 'How do you know this?' Then he told me his brother's name – his brother was my friend – I used to play with him. I said, 'Your name must be Razzak, I knew you were here, but I didn't know where to find you.' Then he took me to the place where he was living, it was 25 Golden Street . . . there's a park there now. He shared a three-quarter bed with another man, but they were both fat, so there was no room for me and I had to sleep on the sofa – it was very small. Then the owner of the house came in, with this English wife, he heard us all talking and he came in. His wife gave me tea, and she said Razzak and the other man were stupid, because there was a spare bedroom for me. She pressed my clothes, they were very crumpled. 'Now you are a smart gentleman.' So that was where I was living.

They wouldn't take me to the Savoy Hotel, so I got up early in the morning, oh, too early, and I walked and walked, past India House, till I got there. Those girls were waiting, they said, 'It's very late, past seven o'clock, we have to get everything ready before the chef comes.' The job was to keep the kitchen clean, wash up, and all that. These days the Savoy kitchen is full up with our people, but then there were none, I was the first. The chef said I could work there if I got my proof, so after a few days I went again to India House, and this fellow told me he posted my letter. So I went back to the hotel, and they gave me a letter to take to Settle Street Labour Exchange. I got in there at ten o'clock, gave my letter to the man, and he took it and never looked at me again. So at last I jumped over the counter and caught him, and started shouting to give back my letter or give me a card. Then he said alright, 'I give you a letter, take it to the Savoy Hotel' – then he called the police.

I took the letter to the Jewish coffee shop next door – that was the one I bought later – and I asked the governor what the letter said. When he read it, he said, 'You mustn't take this to the Savoy Hotel, it says you are a spy.' The police came, and I called Razzak from the factory and he said to the police, 'No, he is not a spy, he is from my village,' actually . . . not quite same village, but nearly . . . he came from the ship.' So they let me go.

Then I went to India House again, and found this man from Bombay and started to beat him with my umbrella . . . his face was cut and his nose was bleeding. Then a law student from Badeshwar came – he used to work at the High Commission sometimes but he was really a law student, a very qualified man. He shouted at this man, and said, 'Where is the file?, if you have really written a letter there must be a file.' But of course he was lying, so there was no file, but then he had to give me a proof, because the law student said he would make a report to the High Commissioner.

I only stayed at the Savoy Hotel a couple of weeks . . . I earned one pound two shillings a week there – that was good money. Then somebody took me to Veeraswamy's, to work in the kitchen. After a few weeks, they gave me the job to put rice on the plates – a cup on each. But they still came back with rice on them and it went in the dustbin, so I spread it out and put less on, and still some used to come back. One day the governor came to visit the kitchen. He was in the Air Force – as a volunteer, not for pay. The manager was Indian, but the proprietor was not. He saw what I was doing with the rice and he asked why. I told the manager, and he told him it was because the rice that came back used to fill two dustbins, and I didn't like rice to go in the dustbin. The governor gave a tip to everyone – I didn't look at mine, I put it in my pocket under my apron. The chef looked at his, he had five pounds – they asked me what I got. I looked and I couldn't believe it, it was twelve pounds. The manager said, 'That is your business, don't tell anyone.' At the weekend I had a rise, two pounds in my packet. The manager said, 'This is not my idea, this is the boss, don't show your wages to anyone.' The chef didn't like me there, I used to be very quick and learn to do any job in the kitchen, and he said, 'Why do you do all those things? That is not your job.' So I left there – it was alright if you wanted to quarrel but I don't like to quarrel.

So we went to Coventry – to the factories. About twenty or thirty of us went, not all together, but around the same time. First we lived in lodgings, then four or five of us rented houses . . . Fussell Road. First I worked in the American factory Dunlop, but I didn't like it because you had to change buses four times to get there. So I left it and went to the aeroplane factory in Fussell Road, very near my house. The job I got was in a section where there were no men, only six hundred girls. The only men were a man of sixty-four, and me. The supervisor didn't want to give me the job, because I was a young man, but I said, 'No, it is against my religion to mess around with girls.' And I never did mess around, not in there – there were plenty of girls outside. The women were fitting nuts in there, and I had to go around with a trolley and give them the nuts, and they had to sign for them. They used to give me cigarettes all the time, one here, one there, and put them in my trolley.

I used to do some other business there, when I wasn't working, you know. They used to have coupons for everything – money wasn't a problem, but coupons were. So we used to go to the ships – Tilbury, Liverpool, Cardiff – and buy coupons from sailors – they didn't need them – and then get sweets, chocolates, clothes, and sell them around the factories . . . black market . . . After the war I was a pedlar in the markets, all around England. I was a long time in Plymouth, opened a restaurant there, but that is a later story.

When we went to the ships we used to bring men away too, if they wanted help to come. No – not for money, just to help them. We brought them to a factory, or many times I just took a man to India House . . . got his papers, then straight to Dock Street Shipping Office, to sign under English articles. That was no problem – they wanted a lot of men.

I used to hold a lot of people's money for them in Coventry because they were afraid of fighting. I worked very near where we lived, so I could easily go to the Post Office at lunchtime, and send the money to India. We all send money home – I used to send to my brother. Wages weren't so high, but with overtime you could make plenty, maybe ten pounds or eleven pounds a week. Sometimes I would be sending two or three hundred pounds. Once the Post Office called the police, because they didn't understand where I get all this money, but I explain them. People were frightened to carry their money because at that time was a lot of fighting in Coventry – white people against Indians . . . they wanted us to go.

No – it's not true that everything was good in those days, not in Coventry, there was too much trouble – some Indians were killed. I'm surprised you never heard it before. We didn't start it, we were quiet people, only wanted to work, but we were very dangerous though. One Indian killed three Irishmen with a knife – three! He got a life sentence, but he came out again after the war, and he killed another in Birmingham, but then they said his head was wrong. They put him in prison again, but when the Queen came to the throne, they let him out as long as he went home. He was from Sylhet, his name Zobbar. He is still there – I wanted to see him when I went, but his village is a very remote place.

The man in charge of the City of Coventry gave the Indians eight weeks notice to leave, because there was so much trouble, but Winston Churchill said we should stay, because England need us to work. In those days they wanted us to work. And after, when more people came, they came because the Government called them to come and work, so many jobs we did.

Then I got notice – I have to join the Army or the Air Force, but I refuse it, and so they called me before a War Court, like an Army Court. My adviser was Krishnamenon . . . India's Minister of Defence later. I knew him well, we used to meet at Hyde Park Corner – *Lascars'* meetings for Indian freedom. We were all in the Congress then, even in India I was in Congress, taking up railway lines in Assam. Krishnamenon couldn't come in the Court, Lord Goddard banned him, but he told me what to say – my parents died too young, but Government never helped me . . . only my family helped me, so why I should fight for Britain? I had an interpreter to help me, and I told them these things, but they didn't accept it, and they said I had six months to join up or I would go to prison till the end of the war, and not even have cigarettes. Plenty of English people refused too. If you had enough money you could manage it, or a doctor's sign – I know three doctors here in East London who signed so much that the Government wouldn't believe their sign anymore.

I did want Britain to win the war – I was born under the British flag, and I support Britain. I didn't support Subhas Bose. I know all about him – he escaped from Bengal in women's dress, and went to Rangoon, and then Japan, and the Japanese made him Prime Minister of India, but we didn't support him. Only I didn't want to join the Army because I did six weeks Army training in Calcutta, and it was terrible – they never let you out. And I didn't like the ship because it was like a prison. They say in the Navy you see the world, but not true, you only see down inside the ship, and the water, and you can't get out.

But when my six months was running out I went to London without telling anyone . . . went to Dock Street . . . met a *donkey-man* who said he was looking for crew, and I just went in and signed . . . went back to Coventry, and said goodbye – then back to join my ship. I stayed in the Navy till May 7th 1945, that was when the war ended – after they dropped the atom bomb on Japan.

We went to France first. I had an accident – I learned to be gunner, passed my tests . . . and I was on top of a tower and fell – injured my back. Another time, another ship was hit, and there were men in the water and I was throwing a piece of wood to them and the Captain was angry with me. He said, 'They may live or they may die, but if you stand up here you will be hit – go down below.' It was the same in the bombing in Coventry – I didn't like to go to the shelter, and the police used to tell me to go, so I said, 'What about you, why you don't go?' And he said, 'I am a policeman.' I said, 'You are also a man – if I can be hit you can be hit – I won't go.'

The most terrible time was in the Bay of Naples – Barrio Island. We had taken that, although the rest of Italy was occupied, and there was a big party there for all the troops – lots of singers and dancers. Suddenly the bombers came and nobody could escape. In the morning, Christ – it was terrible! The water was full of nothing but bodies – I think there must have been thousands killed. They came with lorries, and just piled the bodies in.

I was in Port Said when the Queen came there – she was Princess Elizabeth then. I heard what she said, she said, 'Must be we will win this war, and when we do there will be pensions for everybody who fought.' I am still waiting for my pension. Soon I will write to the Queen about it. Britain wanted us then, I think now people have forgotten about that. The Princess said too that all the women must work to win the war. That time all the men were away, and the women of England were the men – driving lorries, working in the Blitz and all that. The other day on television a woman was saying that women could do everything without men and the men could starve, and people said, 'How can it be?' But I said, 'It is true – I saw the women in the war, they can do everything.' I was very surprised when I came to England and saw that, because in India the women couldn't even go out. In our country it is still very backward and women need to be educated. But look in India now they even have a woman Prime Minister, she controls six hundred million people.

I hope I am not going to live to see the next war – I remember the atom bomb they dropped. But if they did not drop it Japan would have fought for another five years.

Well, after the war, I came back to my business. I didn't tell you about that. I bought that coffee shop in Settles street, in 1943, when I was still in Coventry, and I put a partner in to run it. His name was Ali, his wife was half-caste – West Indian.

The coffee shop was 11 Settles Street, I decorated it and all, but I didn't change the name, it was the *Settles St Cafe*. A lot of people used to come there because it was near the Labour Exchange – English, Indians, Arabs, Africans – all kinds of different people. We sold tea and coffee, rice and curry, fish and chips – all the usual things. I came back there after the war, but not as the owner, only as a worker. That Ali was telling everyone he was the owner and I was only the worker. After a while I got tired of it, so I went off to Cardiff.

In Cardiff I went to the house of someone I knew, and we

went out together to a coffee shop. It was a Punjabi place, and the owner made trouble with us. So I said to my friend, 'Isn't there a Bengali restaurant here?' He said no. I said, 'Well, I won't drink a cup of tea or coffee in Cardiff till I open one.' He said there was a Maltese place that was for sale, so we went there. The governor offered us tea, but he said, 'No, he won't drink tea or coffee till he opens a coffee shop here.' and they laughed. He said he wanted four hundred pounds for it. I had five hundred pounds cash in my pocket, money I had saved from the Navy, but I didn't say anything . . . There was a business girl there – Irish. She was a real business girl, no messing about – she used to take the Indian and Somali sailors upstairs – five minutes and then they were out. She helped me to arrange it with the Maltese, so I got it for three hundred and fifty pounds. She was trying to kiss me and all that, but I said, 'No – not now, maybe later – now we do this business.'

We went to the solicitor's office and signed all the papers, then I got a builder to come, and he gave me an estimate to paint and repair the place for one hundred pounds . . .you wouldn't even do one room for that now . . . I made a new signboard and everything. I gave it the name *Calcutta Restaurant.* When I first heard about the place, they said there was a problem with rations . . . only five pounds bacon, half pound tea, one pound sugar, and so on. I said, rations are not a problem when you know where to look, and of course I didn't want bacon. Anyway I knew how to manage for rations. There was a house above the restaurant – I had that decorated too and furnished the rooms. Then I went to London to fetch my things.

When I told them about the place, they said, 'Why don't you take this place, and we will go to Cardiff?' Her family was there. So I agreed, and I even gave them some money. I didn't bother to go to a solicitor to put my name for the Settles Street place – it was not in my name because sailors were not allowed to have licence – I don't know why.

After a few weeks they were back. I asked what happened to the restaurant. He was a gambler man and he lost it – couldn't manage it. They said they had only come to visit me, but I heard from other people that he was saying, 'I am going to take the cafe from Nawab Ali.' I asked him why he was

saying that, but he said he wasn't. One day his wife was in the shop with me, and she said, 'How much did you take today?' I said, 'A hundred pounds.' She didn't believe me, so I took out the money from the till and counted it in front of her – a hundred and ten pounds, and some shillings – ten pounds was my cash float, so that left a hundred pounds. She told me he did want to take the cafe.

Then one day an African came and said, 'You'd better be out of here in two weeks.' So I asked Nisar Ali, 'Why did you say you don't want to take the cafe, then you send this African.' Then I did go to the solicitor and put my name on the licence, and they went away, they owed me plenty of money. He owned three restaurants when he died, he was very rich, but he never gave me back my money. He was a big gambler, he lost thousands.

Before he died he called me and showed me a ring he had – he said it was worth three thousands pounds – he bought it after he won on the horses. He said I would have it after he died to pay back the debt. But when he died his family didn't even tell me – I heard it a few weeks later from someone else . . . and I never got the ring!

One of his daughters was a very good dancer. He had a gambling club in Caledonian Road, and a dancing club in the basement and she used to dance there, but somebody murdered her and put her in the bath . . . the other daughter is still alive. I had a gambling club too, in Umberstone Street, the Commonwealth Club, you must have heard of it. The police closed it down, I'll tell you about that later.

I used to be a big gambler – dogs, horses, everything, I used to go to the races all the time. I used to bet in thousands. Now if anyone comes to try to make me bet I say, 'Go away – you are my enemy!' When I had a lot of money coming in I could afford to take the risk, but now I have only my pension and odd bits and pieces, and small gambling is no good.

I have had so many restaurants. The first was in Calcutta in 1937 – a seaman's coffee shop. Calcutta was really something in those days. Before I die I would like to go to Calcutta again – it was such a wonderful place. I remember every Sunday I used to go to the *Churirkhanna* – the Zoo they call it in English. There were two *mahouts* from Sylhet town and they

made me like their younger brother. I used to go there and see the animals, and sit and play cards with them – oh not for money, just for fun – and eat with them. You love Calcutta too, so you must really love India – a lot of people go to Calcutta and they don't understand it, and they think it is a bad place.

Shillong . . .

Another place I love is Shillong . . . cold like England . . . and that twisty road to go there. Is that road still the same? I think it is very sad that Sylhetti people live all their lives and never see Shillong. Of course it is not easy to go there now, used to be it was all one country – Sylhet and Shillong. Lord Mountbatten loved India you know, but he broke it – he believed the Hindus and not the Muslims. Of course there

was a lot of fighting between Hindus and Muslims in those days – in Calcutta, Noakhali, Chittagong. I was in a crowd once that nearly broke the Victoria Memorial – we chased a lot of Hindus in there and twenty-four people were killed. Of course the Hindus started it and we had to defend ourselves.

Now the Indian Government neglects Calcutta, because they expect that any day Calcutta may become part of United Bengal. That is what the people really want . . . of course I supported Pakistan. To start with we were in Congress, but even before I left Calcutta I supported the Muslim League. Jinnah wanted to have six seats on the Council and give the Hindus five, but Nehru made it the other way round, and gave five to the Muslims and six to the Hindus. They said we were a minority, but we were all one . . . they were majority, but all divided up . . . When Jinnah came to London, we invited him to a cafe in Backchurch Lane and gave him a party, and told him we wanted Pakistan. That cafe is still there – it is Italian now. That time it was Punjabi, there were quite a few Punjabis in Backchurch Lane – they had scent and clothing factories.

I supported the Bangladesh struggle too. Not immediately of course – because we fought to make Pakistan, so we didn't want to lose it. But when we saw the newspapers – the photographs of what they had done to Bengali women – then we supported it. Eight of my family were in the *mukti*, what they call in English 'guerrillas' we call *Mukti Bahini* – freedom fighters . . . eight of them. There was heavy fighting around Dakhadurkhin.

We had meetings about Bangladesh in London, and we collected hundreds of pounds to send for arms. There was a big meeting to discuss how we should persuade the British Government to support Bangladesh. After that we had meetings with Peter Shore, Malik and I – he is our friend. Malik used to go every day to the House of Commons – I paid his taxi fares. I did a lot for the community – never made anything out of it. Look how I spent six thousand pounds for the Citizens Advice Bureau – I tell that later.

India is exploiting Bangladesh now – stopping us from getting our gas and oil. I am afraid there will be war between India, Bangladesh and Pakistan before long. You know Pakistan has got a bomb . . . It is only for India.

You want to know how I opened the gambling club? Well really it was because of the Welfare Association. The Welfare Association first started in 1942 as a Seaman's Welfare Association, with an office in Christian Street. Ayub Ali Master was the cashier. They called him 'Master' because he used to be a schoolmaster at home. He was not the first to come, there were plenty of others before him, but they are dead now, most of them. There are some left – Aftab Ali in Watney Market . . . and another one in Shadwell Gardens . . . and Moyna Miah of course, in Delafield House – he has eighteen children. The adviser of the Welfare was Nisar Ali – not that restaurant one, another – Qureshi Nisar Ali – a barrister at law, very educated. He used to work at the High Commission – that same barrister at law who helped me at India House, from Badeshwar. The Welfare was really started by the High Commission, to help them register people when they came to London. When people left the ship they used to come there, and we would take them to Dock Street to sign on British Articles.

Anyway – the Welfare decided they wanted to have a place for a social club, where people could sit together. There was the Punjabi place in Backchurch Lane, and there was a Maltese place too, but people were always getting into fights. So the Welfare decided they should open their own place, not for gambling, just for a place to meet. So they gave me the job to look around and find a place. I was the joint cashier, I and Noor Miah – 'Sergeant' Noor Miah we used to call him, because one day I said, 'Oh, you are so tall and straight, like a Sergeant!' . . . I don't know if he is still alive . . . he had a restaurant in Croydon.

We found a place in Backchurch Lane, but it was too expensive – then we found another in Cannon Street Road. The landlord wanted six pounds per week, for the ground floor and the yard. I said that was too much, so he said, 'Alright, five pounds.' I paid four weeks rent in advance, then another sixty pounds to get the place fixed up, so that was eighty pounds altogether. Then I went to a meeting of the Welfare, above the Taj Majal restaurant in New Road. They were all there – Chanu Miah, Noor Miah, Motlib, and about twenty others. They started to tease me and say I would never open the club so I got angry – I got my knife out. Somebody telephoned my

wife and said, 'Babbi – come and get him, he is getting mad.' I
said to them, 'Give me my money eighty –pounds that I spent,
and I will open my own place.' But they only laughed at me
and went on with this monkey business, so I left.

Next day – it was Saturday morning – I was going out in my
van to get the chickens for the poultry shop, and I saw a sign
in the window of a place in Umberstone Street. I couldn't read
it of course, so I went straight back and fetched my wife. She
had her hair in curlers, and she said, 'What is the matter with
you?' but I just said, 'Come on, quick!' We went to that place,
and I asked her what the paper said. She read it, 'To Let', and
the name of the agent – so I went there straight away. He said
he wanted twelve pounds a week for it – it was a lot of money –
but for the whole house, room for a sitting place downstairs
and a restaurant upstairs. I had cash in my pocket, and I gave
him a deposit, then I went to fetch my chickens.

The next week, I told some other people to come with me to
look at it – they were trying to open a place too. I told them to
come at ten o'clock, but I made the appointment with the
agent for nine forty-five. I went there and signed the lease.
They came to my house at ten o'clock, and my wife said, 'Oh,
he just had to go out – he will come soon.' When I came I said,
'I've got the key to this place.' And he said, 'So what – I've had
the key lots of times.' But I said, 'Yes – but I've got the lease
too!' We fetched two tables from the shop, and brought twenty
chairs from the second-hand furniture shop in Christian
Street, and we opened it as a restaurant on the Monday. Then
I had to get a club license.

I decided to call it the *Commonwealth Club*, because people
from all different countries came there – Pakistanis,
Africans, Arabs, West Indians . . . very few English. They
used to play poker, rummy – all kinds of cards games. There
was food, but no alcohol. Ladies could only go downstairs – no
business there.

At that time, I also had my two businesses in Hessel Street –
the poultry place at number 12, and the *halal* butchers at
number 42. That was the first *halal* butcher in Britain . . . I
had two others – in Lisle Street and Paddington. I started the
poultry shop first – we got the chickens live and killed them
there. We couldn't do that with the big animals, so I used to go

to the English place and do it. The Jewish one was at Tilbury Shelter, in Commercial Road – it's still there, but I didn't do it there. For the cows, I used to stand up on a ladder and shoot them with something that made them fall over, but didn't kill them and then one man used to hold them up while I cut their throats. The sheep – I just held them down on the ground and cut their throats. I killed hundreds of cows and sheep, thousands of chickens. A Jewish butcher used to come to the shop and bone the meat, and we chopped it up. We were four – my wife and I and Taslim Ali and his wife.

I had done many things in my life, bad things and good things – the money I made in bad ways, I spent it in good ways. I used to make the money with one hand, spend it with the other, all my life like that.

I gave up black marketing after a few years . . . '47 or '48. Once we went to Southampton Docks, there was a lorry load of nylon stockings and women's things, you know, under-wear. You couldn't get those things then. We settled it with the driver, told him to go and drink tea, and then in an hour he could say that the van was stolen. Our driver took the lorry to Plymouth, and we sold the stuff in the markets. We were four partners – me, a Maltese, a Jewish fellow, and a Turk. We were *dacoits* in those days. I always had a gun, I got rid of the last one in 1974. Only a few weeks ago, I threw away the bullets I had, you ask my wife. She found them in the storeroom, and said, 'What are these?' I threw them away. I don't have a gun any more. I expect my family have guns in Bangladesh, they were in the *Mukti* you know, so probably they kept the guns.

I only used my gun once, that was in 1948, when I had a restaurant in Plymouth. Some Royal Navy men came and tried to break up the restaurant. They had been in Bombay when the Navy was fighting with the Indian freedom fighters – that time three or four British ships were blown up. When they came to Plymouth, and they saw the name, *Bengal Restaurant*, they wanted to make trouble, so they came in, about twenty of them, and started to break the place up. One of them – he was an officer too – brought out a gun. I ran into my little office – just a little booth I had, and brought out my two guns – German pistols. . . . Never mind where I got them,

I had them, and I had two toy guns too. I ran out with them and I said, 'If you don't get out I will shoot you. See! I can shoot – I am a sailor too – I had the practice.' . . . I was a gunner, remember. And I fired at the table legs – left, then right – to show them. I made them put their hands up, then leave one by one, by the back door. There was a park behind. Then I told the Greek boy who worked in my kitchen to go away with the guns. The police came – oh too many of them, all around the restaurant. They came in and said, 'Have you got a gun?' 'Yes . . .' I said, 'here you are.' and I gave them the toy ones. They looked like real, but they said, 'No – these are only toys, where are the real ones? Somebody has fired a gun.' 'Yes,' I said, 'somebody fired it – it was the Naval Officer – you better search him.' Well, the police not allowed to search Navy, so they called Navy Police, and they searched and found five guns. They kept me in the police station for twenty-four hours, while they searched my place . . . thirteen rooms above restaurant, and they searched them all – but they didn't find the guns. How could they, when they were five miles away! That was not the only time I was arrested.

Once I spent six weeks in prison, for not paying my wife's maintenance – my English wife. At first, I had to pay her thirty pounds a week, and I paid her for years. But then, when I lost my gambling club, I couldn't pay her anymore. I had to go to court, and my barrister told the Judge I was a poor man, and if he give me time I can borrow the money. But he wouldn't and I had to go to Pentonville. I shared a cell with a Turk and a West Indian – both of them knew me, they were too happy to see me. Everybody knew me there. They used to queue up outside my door for tobacco – I always had tobacco, people used to give it to me if they were going home. Even the wardens knew me – one said to me, 'Ali, how is it there's always a queue outside your door?'

I was always spending money for the people. When I had my club I used to give so many money to the Berner Settlement, Dr Barnardo's Home and all that – I still got receipt. The biggest thing was the Advice Bureau . . . Malik came to me and he said, 'So many people coming, they don't understand English or nothing, we got to help them.' That time, I was taking the lease for the place in Umberstone Street, so I took the lease for 48 Hanbury Street as well – ground floor and basement. My idea was to have the Advice Bureau on the ground floor, and another gambling club downstairs. But Peter Shore said it wouldn't do, so we used to use the basement for the drama. We had so many meetings with Peter Shore in the Central Lobby. And there were other people too ... Councillor John Orwell – he is dead now. I spent six thousand pounds for that place – for the rent, decorations, paying Oluludi's salary when the grant didn't come. Ololudi was the secretary of our Afro-Asian Society at Toynbee Hall so we put him in charge of the Advice Bureau.

We opened a school here – I and Malik – in Toynbee Hall. We put Anne Evans in there to help our people. First we had the English classes, then the drama. I found Mr Bose – he was living in Bow at that time and earning thirteen pounds a week in a factory. I asked him to come and teach drama, and I would pay him. I took him to Leman Street Police Station, and they took him as an interpreter.

Oh yes – in those days people used to be running after me –'*Nawab Sahib* . . .' When they bought the Welfare Association house, the agent said they wouldn't get a mortgage unless my name was there, because I had so many properties – so I had to run about, here and there ... building societies and banks. I think the price was six thousand pounds. They made me a trustee – Motlib and I, Gaus Khan, and Noor Miah. It was called the Pakistan Welfare Association then, but all the people were Sylhetti. I will tell you why there were too many Sylhettis. It was because we all helped each other. I brought twenty men myself, when the vouchers came in, and I must have brought two hundred from the ship in the war, so if each of them helped twenty more ... you see how it happened ... of course in those days we never imagined there would be so many people – we just wanted to help our brothers. There was one Englishman who used to be around Dock Street, he used to say he could get anyone a job on the ship, so we took them to him. I used to do it in Liverpool too, South Shields ... fetch people from the Indian ship, and take them straight to the Shipping Office, then back to an English ship. In wartime it was easy.

In the 1960's we had to organise to get the vouchers. The Pakistan Government said the Welfare couldn't do it because it was political, so we formed the Pakistan Caterers' Association. There were seventy restaurants then, I used to have all their telephone numbers in my book, now there are about a thousand, all over the country. The Caterers' Association joined together with twenty-eight organisations – Indian, Pakistani, everything – to ask for labour vouchers. We wanted to bring people to work in the restaurants, and the Government wanted people to come and work too – they wanted our people to come. Aftab Ali came from Pakistan, and we told him to go to the Parliament House and ask for the vouchers, but he said he couldn't do that because it would be shame. So instead Mr Suhrawardy invited the Queen to Bengal – then he and Aftab Ali explained this history to her, how for two hundred years the British ruled India, and how the Indian people are poor and wanted to come to England to earn money. And when they had explained it to her she said she would come back and tell Parliament to give the vouchers, and she did – so then they started to come.

They used to come to the airport with just my address, and take taxis to my house. Some people had addresses in Birmingham or Bradford, and they used to take taxis there too. They got cheated, because they didn't know anything. When they came to my house, they would sign on at the Labour Exchange in Settles Street, then get work in the factories. At one time there were ninety-five people living in my house . . . they weren't all sleeping here, they used to sleep here and there, but they were all registered at this address. My wife went mad when she saw all the names on a letter! You know the room upstairs? There were thirty-five living up there.

One night there was a knock on the door at two o'clock. We went down, and there were two taxis there, with twelve men from the airport. I didn't actually know any of them, but I knew three of them by name, by family. The taxi men said they wanted ten pounds for the two taxis. At that time the fare was about thirty shillings, or two pounds. I said, 'Why do you want to cheat them – they are poor men, they have come to earn some money, they have got nothing in their pockets!' The drivers came inside, they were arguing about it, and one told my wife to 'f.... off', and pushed her, so she fell down. I had a big knife and a chopper lying on the table. I took the knife in one hand, and the chopper in the other, and I kept those men standing againgst the wall while my wife called the police. When they came I put down the knife and the chopper, but I kept them on the table – I didn't hide them. Well, we had a case about it, and the Judge asked me, 'Why did you take a knife, and a chopper?' and I said, 'They hit my wife! What else do you expect me to do ?' The Judge said it was not right to cheat those men, because they were poor men, and they only came to work, and he said he should only pay four pounds for their fare, but he told me not to use the knife again like that. That driver is still living in Mile End.

That was my English wife I was talking about. She is wrong in the head now. I still see her sometimes, she lives in Peckham. We were really married, but she left fifteen years ago. We had three sons and one daughter. The eldest son lives here in this house, with his wife and four children. They have just come from Bangladesh. Before there were two other women, but I wasn't married to them. The first girl went away with my eldest son – he is a Naval Officer in Newcastle. The next one was Australian – I lived with her in Plymouth. Before the baby was born her father died, and her grand-mother sent for her to come back to Australia, so I have a son over there too. She wrote and said she would send me a ticket if I wanted to go. With my Bengali wife, I have three daughters, and the last baby is a boy. So I have ten official children, and there was another in Alexandria, and one in Italy you know – from the ship.

I didn't go home until 1966. It was mainly because I wasn't very friendly with my elder brother. After my middle brother died we didn't really write to each other. Sometimes I would get a letter from him, and ask somebody to read it. It was always because he wanted money so I used to send him some, and throw the letter away. But after I sent my son he got friendly again, and so I went home in 1966 and five or six times since then, and I started to send him more money. My English wife never went there – there were the three businesses to look after, so how could she go. I married this wife in 1972 – that was years after my English wife left me.

There have been a lot of changes in Sylhet, it used to be just a little place like Dakadurkhin, now there are so many buildings. I remember when the bridge was built. The British built it to use in the war – now it is broken, and they need a new one. Before the bridge was built you had to cross the river by boat. I remember going Sylhet to Calcutta by boat in those days. There was no road from Sylhet to Karimganj before the war, they built that for the army. Before that, those places were very remote, no buses or anything. Now people in Badeshwar are more used to new things, because strangers can come by the road, and the people have been to Dakadurkhin and Sylhet and seen many things, so they are not so backward. The people in Badeshwar are the most educated in Sylhet. I am not educated at all. I have never been for the *Haj*, I could go any time, if it feels right. I don't think much of people who talk a lot about religion. Going for *Haj* and growing a long beard doesn't make you a good person – the important thing is in here – the heart. All religions can be good – it doesn't matter if you call yourself Muslim, or Christian, or Jew, it is what you do that matters. It is no good praying five times a day very nicely and then cheating people.

Mr. Nawab Ali and his family   *Tom Learmonth*

I have never learned to write, only my own name, and I can't read at all. That is why I have been cheated so many times. My wife can read and write our language a little, but she was cheated too – she and my son gave eight thousand pounds to that person for the restaurant in Stoke Newington while I was away, and we have lost it. That is why I am to learn machining at my age. I can learn that, but I can't learn to read at all, I tried it a few times. I think it is better to know a lot, or nothing at all. When people are only a little bit educated, it makes trouble. I want these little girls to be very educated, this little girl, Lutfa, is six – she will go for doctor. My other sons I told you – one is Naval Officer, one went to University College, one is still at grammar school, this side. He comes over from Peckham. Only the one who lived in Bangladesh is not very educated. I have told my wife, 'If I die, go on with these children's education.'

Just now, I want to move to a restaurant in Stoke Newington. I have a partnership in it with my wife's relative but I want to take it over. That is why we are working day and night at these linings. I have never done this work before – I'm only a learner.

I would like to move from this house now – you see how it is full of cockroaches and rats. I have had the Council men to spray it three times, but the cockroaches always come back. I was offered a council flat once but I didn't take it. Well, you know in this place you can be private – nobody to mind your business.

Although I am so busy with the machining, I don't mind how long I spend telling you this history. I will tell you why – it is because when I am dead this will still be left, and I think it is important to tell the history of people like us.

Our family was not rich but our grandfather was, you know, middle class – good family. We have a lot of land now – seventy or eighty acres – a great deal of land. I sent the money to my brother, and he bought it. It all came from my money – my grandfather didn't have very much land.

You might think it would be better to live there, not in this broken house in Sidney Street, but you don't understand what living in Bangladesh is really like. You might think it is nice to visit, but you wouldn't like to live there. It is true that if you have money you can be comfortable in the house. But when you go out of the house there is nothing but trouble – people twist things round and round, tell lies, make trouble all the time. They seem like very bad people – if they are bad people ... it is because being poor makes people bad. People in this country are not poor – they can afford to be good.

I want my children to be able to live in this country – I am worried about all these new laws that might stop them. In Bangladesh there are no jobs, no factories or anything.

This country has changed so much – it is like living in another world from the old days. I think the reason for the change is that the young people, they don't understand why we are here – they have forgotten that we were born under the British flag, and we have come to our mother country – and they just want to get us out.

Tom Learmonth

Haji Shirajul Islam (Israel Miah)

I was born in 1912, that time it was British India, Sylhet. The place is called Keelgau, near the Maulvi Bazar. We did have a lot of land but unfortunately my parents died when we were young, and the land went bit by bit. It is hard to explain how it was lost, those things happen. I went to school, just ordinary school, and I didn't like to go very much, I just liked to play. My father wasn't very educated, but he could read and write. I learned to read and write Bengali, and a little bit English.

At that time many people were going to the ship, they used to go to the ship, then come back after a year or ten months, fifteen months. They used to go to Calcutta and get the ship. That was what I had to do too . . . when everything was gone. I had four younger brothers, I had to save them. They were still at school, my mother and father were dead. There were no uncles to help me. My mother had brothers, but they were separate.

I was about twenty-two or twenty-three when I went to Calcutta with one of my uncles, he was a *serang* – a boss. I stayed there for six or seven years working on Indian ships, then I found two gentlemen who were working on English ship, and they were talking about good money and I thought to myself, 'This is little money I am getting in there.' Two times I came back and went to Calcutta again, the money was not very good.

How I came to England was like this. My ship went to Africa. That time cloth was quite cheap in India, quite dear in Africa, but I didn't do that business. I had only my suit, and underneath it half pants . . . summertime, quite hot. Somebody came to me and said, 'Sell it?', I said, 'No, this is my

only suit.' But he offered quite a bit of money, and underneath I had my khaki half pants and shirt, so I sold it to this
African man. Then afterwards some detective of police came
and caught me, with another gentleman who had done the
same. Another two innocent people were with us, and they
arrested them as well. It was not allowed you know – to sell
things like that. We were nearly all day in the cells, then
someone came from the ship to take us out. They fined me
more than my wages. I was in this ship for another five
months, and when I got to Calcutta, the fine was still over my
wages, so I couldn't give it to them, and I said, 'No!' Then one
of my uncles wanted to pay it, but I said, 'No, if you pay it I
won't pay you back. If I haven't got the money, how can I pay
you?' We had quite an argument. At that time we found these
people talking about the English ship, and they were getting
quite a bit of money.

At that time too I had in my mind that my uncle the *serang*
was the boss on the ship, and he was always shouting this and
that . . . I got a bit temper, and said, 'This is not your ship, if I
am suffering it is nothing to do with you,' and we had quite an
argument. Then I made up my mind not to stay in this ship.
Then three or four days after going to Calcutta I found a ship,
to come to England. I was a very good worker, a fireman. Very
hard work, but I don't mind working hard . . . The English
engineers liked me so much, because I could speak a little bit
English, I could understand even if I couldn't speak.

The ship I found was the *Clan Baxter*. It was very hard
work – just like slaves we worked. When we came to Tilbury
five or six people ran away from the ship. I didn't go with
them, and I thought, 'Oh my God, now they have all gone, and
they have put a watchman on the ship, so nobody can go any
more.' I was thinking, 'How can I go now?' Then I took some
clothes in a bucket to wash with another Indian boy. When
we got to the gangway there was no watchman, so we just
came out. In the ship they used to say the watchman and the
serang going to do this and that if they catch you. Some
afraiding things, you know. The watchmen were English,
from the dock. But we were lucky, no watchman, and we just
walked out, free. Cold . . . 1937, in December . . . ordinary
clothes we got, ship clothes, can't put the suit, just like khaki
jeans.

Deck crew on a P&O steamship.   *P&O Group*

I had no money, and the other boy had just a little. He paid my fare, one-and-six (seven and a half pence) from Tilbury to Aldgate on the bus. We had been to Aldgate before, coming from the ship and walking around. That time we were not afraid of anything, we could ask, 'Where is Aldgate?' and this and that. We could speak a little bit English, and that time people helping – oh God, how they helping us, English people . . . Then one of my friends, he say he know someone, and he

take me there, but when we got there this fellow was drunk –
blind drunk, and sick, making mess, and two girls were there
. . . I never smell drink before, and I feel sick, and so we had to
get out of there. And then we didn't know what to do. So then
he know another friend – that friend was alright. He was in
the West End, he helped us a lot. In the middle of the night,
my friend said he was going back to the ship. He said, 'Come
on, let's go'. I said 'No, I'm not going. I'm not going back to the
ship. If they catch me, my knife is open – I will have to go to
hospital or to prison, one or the other, I'm not going back to
the ship any more.' He still wanted to go. I said, 'Look, I have
one of my . . . not relations, but 'uncle-friends', in Aldgate.
Give me the tuppence to go to Aldgate'. The man we were
staying with was married to an English girl, and he said we
couldn't stay because his wife was coming from the hospital
with a new baby, so I said, 'Give me the tuppence'. Then this
fellow told me that my near enough relation was in West End,
but I didn't know the address.

Then I wanted to work, but couldn't get a job. It was so cold
– got no coat. But I did have a thick pullover. Can't get a job in
West End, then at last I went to Aldgate. My friend took me,
and I was working in a tailor's shop . . . a shop boy in a tailors.
Just I had to take the clothes from one shop to another, put
buttons, things like that. It was a Jewish shop, no other
Bengalis there. I worked there for a few months. I was
staying in a different house. By then I had found quite a few of
our people, maybe twenty or thirty in Aldgate, not a crowd
like now. We were all friends.

Again I left this job for some reason, and I got another job in
Clapton, in a tailor's shop. Then I came to the West End, to a
waiter's job, in the *India Burma Restaurant*, Leicester
Square, Leicester Place. Mr Chowdury was the proprietor.
When I went there, two of us went, and I did one thing – the
menu, you know menu? One of my uncle friends said, 'You
can't get restaurant job unless you can read and write the
menu.' I said, 'Can you bring me one?' And I read it again and
again, and when I go there, there were two of us for the job . . .
which one better will get it? He was a bit older than me, that
time I was a bit young. When I came to read the menu, I
already read it again and again, and I could do it very well,
then he give me the job, so alright.

But when I went to the job. Oh – morning to midnight you
got to work. It was a small restaurant but decent customers,
mostly English sometimes a very few Indians. Then one day,
I was tired, and they were three or four brothers – one is
doctor, one is engineer, another one I don't know, and one is
Mr. Chowdury, the manager. His father was there too, and
Chowdury's wife – six or seven of them, sitting at the table,
late at night. It was my time to come out. Then one said, 'Give
me this thing' and another said 'give me that', and another
wants something else . . . it was in a way just like you know
slavery job, and you got to do it. Then I had some glasses on
the tray. And I was temper, and I dropped the tray, like that,
and smashed the glasses and walked out. Well, but how can
you do the work like that? One calling this way, another
calling that way, another the other way – what to do? So then
this job is finished.

Then I get a job in *Khayam Restaurant*, Holland Street off
Tottenham Court Road. These were all small restaurants –
the main ones were *Veeraswamy's*, *Shafi*, and *Koh-I-Noor*.
I don't know which was the first. Well, I came to work there,
and it was like this. People say they want *chapatis*, and there
were two staircases, up and down to the kitchen. 'One *chapati
lau*, one *chapati lau* . . . ' each time bring one *chapati,* how
many times have to go up and down? You got to do it, otherwise where you go? . . . What to eat? . . . Where to stay? Then I
said, 'Alright, I don't mind for job, hard work.' Then, one day
. . . I was never late, always I was at work before everybody
else, I always thinking, if I go late somebody will be say
something . . . then one day somehow I slept, and came fifteen
minutes late. When I came, the governor came – there were
three governors – students, and one of them came and said,
'Mr. Miah, you are late.' I said, 'Yes, I am sorry sir, I
overslept.' 'No, my restaurant is twelve hours work, nobody
can come late. Twelve hours job.' Actually it was not twelve
hours . . . fifteen hours, eighteen hours we worked . . . It was
quarter past nine when I came, so I said to myself, 'Right, now
it is quarter past nine.' You know, I had no money, but still
my mind was quite strong, and I said to him, 'Is it twelve
hours your job?'. 'Yes'. 'Alright', I said.

That day, we were two waiters, one waiter is off. When the
twelve hours came, at quarter past nine I said, 'Well, I'm

going now'. He said, 'No, you can't go.' I said, 'I'm going,' I went upstairs, changed my clothes . . . he was shouting. 'There are customers here'. The chef came running and said, 'Mr. Miah, go back'. I said, 'No, I'm not going.' '. . . but he'll give you the sack'. 'Let him give me the sack, I don't care – fifteen minutes late and I said sorry, and still he said his restaurant is twelve hours.' Then I was in my trousers and braces, and always I kept a small knife – penknife – in my pocket. I came down and he said, 'Serve these customers!' and I said, 'No, sir, I won't, it is already your twelve hours, so I can't'. I said, 'Can you give me overtime?' He said, 'No'. Then he came and tried to hold me and force me to do the job. Then I am getting mad . . . I am swearing, 'Bastard, I am not your slave.' He ran upstairs, I ran after him. He locked the door, I said, 'Bastard, come out'. Then I went out, and went home . . . if he hadn't locked the door, I would have got him with my knife . . . that time I didn't know what I will do, because temper is temper you know . . .

Next day, I came about eleven o'clock. Three of them were sitting at the table. I had come for my card, and the oldest one asked 'Why?' I said, 'Well, we had trouble last night.' He knew, but still he was a gentleman. Then that fellow said, 'Why take the knife out?' Two or three times he asked me. That time I have no temper. Then I said, 'I was going to hit you.' 'You were going to hit me with the knife?' I said, 'Yes sir. When you come to hold me, to do the job by force, that time I don't know where I am.' He looked at me . . . they didn't know what to say, because I was a very good worker. Then the oldest one said, 'Alright, get your clothes on, do the job, forget it.' Next day, when he sees me, before I get a chance, it was 'Good morning, Mr. Miah, good morning.' Now it was alright.

Then, you know, my mind went off . . . if you got thirty-two stamps, then you could get labour . . . labour exchange give the money. When I had the stamps, then I give the notice . . . When I left the ship, I didn't have to worry about the ordinary police only some kind of CID. They used to come and look around the houses sometimes, but they never found me . . . To get a card I just had to go to the labour exchange, and they didn't ask me anything. I said to myself 'Look this job is no good, I work from morning to midnight for fifteen shillings a week.' Of course living was all cheaper too. Rent is two-and six . . . meat is a shilling a pound . . . twenty Players with a box of matches a shilling . . . all cheaper. The labour exchange wouldn't give me money because I didn't get the sack. So for four weeks I didn't get the money – that time my friends looked after me. I was staying at 8 Leicester Place, top of the Prince Charles Theatre. My friends were all our country people. Quite a few people came within six months of me, from the ship. That was a big time to come – 1937 and 1938.

After four weeks I got the labour money, I couldn't make them understand when I went to the labour exchange, they wouldn't give me anything. There was a fellow called Mr. Nandi, a very educated fellow, and one day I seen him and I told him, and he fill out the form and write something, and they give me the labour.

Then who going to work for fifteen a week? Better to lie in bed and enjoy yourself with seventeen a week. Many people told me, 'Why don't you work?' I said, 'No'. Then after about a year, they stopped the labour money. Then I got a job in South Kensington, Earls Court Road, a Sikh fellow – an old man. We called him *Nona*, grandfather, he was a good man – I was happy to work with him. Then the war was about to start, and people talking, 'Money coming, money coming.' I said, 'Look, why don't we start this war.' Then they tried to start, and they stopped for a few months. Everywhere, when a war starts, people's wages go up, I don't know why.

Then it stopped again, and I swore. I said, 'Why don't we start it, then we can all make some money,' I knew all about what the war was about, but I had made up my mind I wanted some money, and I am very determined. Then it started again, and I went to the ship. Then my friends and relations cried. They said, 'If you are killed, you won't have even a minute to think about your life, and get ready to die. You know, this torpedo, when it hits the ship . . .' That time it was really war . . . But I went on the ship, and I was alright, I was on that one for four or five months then I came back. It was very hard work. We went to Australia.

Next voyage I went again, this same ship, everybody else come out, but I stayed there. It was hard work, but hard work won't kill you. They paid ten pounds or twelve pounds a month . . . not bad . . . quite a lot after the Bengali ship. Twice we came back to London, then the whole crew wanted to come out because of some trouble with the engineer, but I said, 'No, I'm going to stay. All of you can go, but I am going to stay.' Them say, 'No, you coming out,' I said, 'Look, now you are telling you are going to leave the ship, but this is wartime. The Captain can't control when is wartime coming, can't leave him just like that. After war everybody may agree to stay, but if I don't agree they can't make me – they can put me in the gaol, but if I say I'm not going to stay then I won't.' Then we all agreed to go, and the captain tried to put a case on us, but our . . . what do you call them, insurance people . . . they fight for us, and we were fined ten shillings each. That was in Cardiff.

When I left the ship, I am coming again London, coming to work. That time quite a bit of job in London. Indian restaurants – I didn't go to English restaurants because I was always thinking about ham and bacon and those sort of things . . . because we are Muslims . . . I love the money, but . . . then afterwards we were looking for a little money . . . my brother had come in 1940 . . . he used to work in Oxford. Then we made a little money and we decided to open a restaurant. Then one friend, he is still here, his name is Moshraf Ali, he was quite clever and educated, better than us in one way. He was from very near Sylhet town.

He was looking for the place, and he got a place in Brompton Road, just past the Harrod. He got the licence in his name, and we gave the money, he had no money. We were partners, and it cost seven hundred pounds, complete . . . we had four hundred pounds of our own, and three hundred pounds we had borrowed . . . nowadays anybody can give you two or three hundred . . . five hundred . . . a thousand . . . but that time it was quite a lot of money, ten pounds from one person, twenty pounds from another, and we opened the restaurant. So I told my friends, 'Look, I'm going to the ship again.' They said, 'Why?' I said, 'Well we're not busy, how can we manage? How can we pay the rent?' Rent was nearly two hundred pounds a year. Then my brother said, 'No – business is alright, don't go.' Then the bombing really started, and nobody went about in London at all. We wanted to sell it, but nobody buy it. I said, 'Look, you are your mother's only son, you better give me your share. We are five brothers, if one die, my mother still got four.' So he said, 'Alright, give me your money.' Well, there was two thousand pounds written on the paper, but I gave him a hundred less, and he was quite happy. I didn't give him the money then, but I said I would give it to him when the business improved . . . business was very quiet at that time. Then my brother didn't like it, he said, 'Look, how can we pay that money back?' I said, 'Maybe in seven weeks, I'll pay back seven or eight hundred pounds'.

I don't know how God helped us, but the next week there was quite good business. When the bombs were dropping at night, a lot of working people used to come there and eat . . . a little bit rough as well, but I am rough myself, I don't care. That restaurant was called *Anglo Asia*. Then we were making quite good money, and in seven weeks I gave him back his seven hundred pounds. In the meantime, my brother didn't like my partner, he said, 'He can go.' I said, 'No, he's not going, you can go.' Because he didn't do anything wrong, and he found the place, and he got the licence, and without the licence what would we have done with our money? So I said no. Then my brother said, 'I'm not coming there.' and I said, 'Alright!' So we bought another cafe for him, in Gerards Place . . . they've just pulled it down, I went there the other day. During the war it was full of Americans all the time – there was quite a bit of fighting there. Then . . . Mr. Mosharaf Ali went, he did business in Charlotte Place.

Then we bought a house in Nevern Road, a big house, ninety-nine year lease, eleven-thousand pounds. What to do? My brother was at home that time – he wouldn't come. I had a bit of money doing the waiter job, very good tips that time. I always worked as a waiter in my own restaurants . . . what did it matter, they gave me tips, and money was what I wanted.   One day two customers came – I was working in the kitchen. That time there was one waiter . . . they walked out . . . the waiter came and said to me, 'The customers walked out, they didn't pay the bill.' I took my apron off and went outside and brought them back to the restaurant. . . . thirteen shillings and fourpence . . . I won't forget that amount. They got a revolver, like that. Then one of my uncles, not a blood relation, he came up. I said, 'No, you go down.' Then they said, 'Do you know what this is?' I said, 'Yes, I know what it is, but you have got to pay my money.' We were talking for six or

seven minutes. They were tall people . . . I am a small man. I
said, 'You got to pay the bill, otherwise you can't go. Then you
can kill me or shoot me down . . .' I had locked the door. Then
they paid the bill. Afterwards . . . now . . . I am thinking to
myself, how silly I am, for thirteen and fourpence they could
have shot me and finish my life. But that time I just thought,
why are they coming to my place and eating without paying
. . . by force? Maybe they wouldn't have shot me, they just
want to make me afraid.

Then this house in Nevern Road, always losing money –
not many guests. It was a lodging house, with twenty-one
rooms – a very big house. So I decided to sell it. I put it with
the agent, but nobody buy it. I said to him, 'Sell it for whatever they offer.' Somebody offered five thousand pounds I
said, 'Sell it.' When I say something, I mean it. After that I
had eight hundred pounds clear, and I went to my good
friends the agents Christies, and I bought a small restaurant
in Russell Square, with room for only twenty-two people to
sit. That was such good business, really good. It was called
New Karachi. Then afterwards when they made the big block
in Marchmont Street I took a corner shop, seven hundred
pounds rent. Then we closed this small *New Karachi*, because
the customers always queued, and we made the bigger one. It
was nice – a very nice job we did there. At that time, with the
decorations, it was one of the nicest restaurants. It was all
canopies and things . . . quite different. Then we did very good
business . . . afterwards the landlord company wanted to take
it and they took it for twenty-five thousand pounds, about
twelve or thirteen years ago – that was a lot of money then. I
bought another then, at 3 Glendower Place, that's still my
restaurant – *Moti Mahal*, and another in Chelsea.

I had quite a few restaurants . . . not now . . . I sell
everything when my wife died . . . just kept a little bit of
partnership – very little. They are running it – I stay in
Bangladesh. I tell them, if they don't like it, they can give my
money back and take it, but they want to keep it like that
because the lease is in my name. I'm a bit lucky, I always did
good business. I don't know why, other people say it as well –
wherever Israel Miah goes makes a fortune. I don't think I'm
very clever, just a bit lucky, and I work very hard, I try to give
very good food, and clean. Of course the food is not like in

Sylhet – there we use all fresh things, fresh spices, that makes a lot of difference, and the meat and fish and everything, all fresh. I know cooking, but I've never been a restaurant cook. You've been to Sylhet, you know that no boys cook there, but when they came to this country they learned it, first as kitchen porter, then cooking. Of course if I cook in my home it's a bit different to the restaurant. Take my son, he likes to eat curry. When he goes to the restaurant he eats Madras – hot one . . . me I always eat in the house. When I offer him food, he eats it, but he says not tasty like restaurant food, because he's the other way round now.

I went home in 1945 and stayed ten months. I had a little farm, and I looked after that, and a small shop. I enjoyed it. When I can do some work my mind is busy and I enjoy . . . I had to come back again because I had taken only a little money and it was all gone . . . That time there was only the one restaurant, the *Anglo-Asian*, and when I was away the business went really down.

At partition time I was in East Pakistan. There was another trouble. At that time I was not yet married to my wife, but she was working in my restaurant. My one nephew was born here. Mother and father always quarrelling and father go home and left this boy. I promise to my brother that if I went home to India, or Pakistan – or whatever it was then – I would take this boy. But he was very young, and I was thinking, 'How can I look after him?' Then she said she could go too. I said 'Oh, no – you don't know this India how look like and where you have to live.' I tell her worse than how it really is to make her afraid, because if I just bluffing and take her there then afterwards what she going to say? So I make it sound worse. I said, 'It is jungle' . . . well it is . . . and I say, 'All snake and that and this, no electric light, no proper toilet . . .' this sort of thing. But she not afraid – she said, 'Well, so many million people live there, they don't die, so why should I die?' . . . She came from Durham – she was in the army during the war.

She went with me there, and she stayed quite a long time. We were married and we had one boy there. I took her to Shillong when she was pregnant, it was hot weather . . . One of my friends had a big house there, he was a very good friend, when we went there he gave me half his house, that helped a lot. She got on well in Sylhet – she could speak our language, and she liked our people very much. She went there three or four times, and stayed quite a long time. She was a very friendly woman, everybody knows. I had so many restaurants, she used to go and collect the money and letters and everything. Once I told her, 'Look, if you go to the restaurant, if they offer you a cup of tea, you can have it, but don't ask them to give you tea. If something is burning in the restaurant, don't tell them, don't talk to them this sort of talk, just come and tell me, and I'll go. When you got two, three bosses, is no good.' The boys liked her so much – income tax letter, this paper, that paper – they waiting for Thursday when she go there. We had only one son – he had a business in France, now he is back here.

I retired when she died, I changed everything then. I never dreamed I would go and live back in Bangladesh, I never dreamed this, but when she died I had nothing to stay for. I don't care where I am really, I never go anywhere, just I look after my little bit of farm, my mind is quiet, I like to keep out of gossiping and politics and all that. For quite a few years they put me in the Welfare Association, Caterers Association, other Associations . . . few things you know, I was the president all the time.

I have a nice house in Dhaka, and my farm is in Maulvi Bazar. Yes quite a lot of restaurant people come from Maulvi Bazar – it is not really through my doing, except that when they see me . . . how I am making money, buying land, buying this and that . . . then others think, well better I go too – just like that they follow me.

I have another family in Dhaka, with my Bengali wife, I built them a house in Gulshan. My English wife and my Bengali wife were really like sisters – they loved each other so much. I was surprised how they look after each other. When my wife died I was packing for a trip to Bangladesh. She lay down on the sofa and said she didn't feel well, and I held her hand, and she died – she had a heart attack. I never knew that people could love each other so much, we were like one life. When I came in, I used to tell her everything that happened, and she used to tell me everything. After she died,

I couldn't live here anymore, I couldn't do anything, I just fell apart for a while, my heart always wants her.

In 1971 I went back to my religious practice. I never stopped being a Muslim, but my business used to distract me from practising. Then I started to pray five times again. If anybody rang I used to tell my wife to say I was in the bathroom, but she told me to stop it, she said people would think there was something wrong with me because I was always in the bathroom. The point was I didn't want to make a fuss about being all religious, claiming to be saintly person. I have been to *Haj*, (pilgrimage to Mecca) for myself and my parents, but that doesn't make me a saintly person. It is just the duty of Muslim to go if they can afford it. When people tried to call me '*Haji Sahib*' I said, 'Don't call me that, my name is *Israel*.' My passport name now is Shirajul Islam, that is my real official name from when I was born, but I was always called Israel Miah, that was the name I used when I went to the ship. I don't like to make a lot of fuss about religion. I have built an orphanage near Maulvi Bazar, to do something for the people.

২টেঠ সামুল

I never ever drank alcohol, and I wouldn't even have it in my restaurants. People used to say I was crazy not to get an alcohol licence, but I made more money than them anyway. When I was a waiter I used to have to fetch alcohol for customers – well you couldn't refuse to fetch it. But afterwards I would wash my hands really thoroughly, like we do before prayer.

I did gamble once. I put a pound on a horse called *Never Say Die*, in the National, and I won forty-eight pounds. Well – I bought a necklace for my wife for five pounds, and a present for my son, then I went to the dog track. I decided to put it all on two dogs, and let whatever would happen. Well, fortunately both dogs lost, so that was the end of it and I never gambled again. It was very lucky.

Things have changed here, in the old days, people were just the same as our people, we were all one. I remember once I came out of South Kensington Station and I asked a lady the way to Chelsea. She told me, and she said, 'Have you got the bus fare, or shall I give it to you?' Can you imagine anyone doing that now? All they want to do now is bashing and stabbing and beating. But there is some fault with our people too. The young boys who have come here behave badly, they go around the streets and do bad things, they don't understand the way to live . . .

When you come to Maulvi Bazar, come to my house. I hope you will come.

Mr. Abdul Malik

You wanted to know about my life story. My life story is very very long. I will try to take short cuts, as much as I can. Maybe sometimes I can't speak English and I have to say Bengali.

I born Sandwip, 1902. That time Sandwip in Noakhali district but now it is in Chittagong. When Sandwip was broken by water, then we came to another village. Still I have my village there, still have some lands and everything there, my part went to my sister. I got a letter to my sister: 'Anything of mine there is all yours, I will never come to take it.'

My father is disciple of one of the priests – come from Joinpur. His name Maulana Karamat Ali Syed. He was a priest, friend of God. One day when he came, he said to my father, 'Amin Miah' (my father's name was Amin Miah), 'Amin Miah,' he said, 'you are helping me a lot – but now something is worrying you, I can tell.' My father said, 'I don't know why it is – I have plenty of money, plenty of land, but I haven't got no children, only one daughter, that is what is worrying me, nothing else.' He said, 'Alright – I will pray to God and maybe He will help you, but promise me one thing, that if you have a son, you will have two sons, and the first one for your *haram*. That means you mustn't use him – he is ours, second one, he is yours – he can do your farm jobs and everything, but the first one, you mustn't use, after he is seven years old – he is ours.' ... Making it very short – after we went he never returned, he died in Dhaka, his *Mazar* (Tomb) is still in Dhaka.

After I was born, my father forgot all this. I grew . . . I went to school . . . and religious school as well. I was a very experienced boy – also I was a bit of a *Shaitan* (Devil). I used to play too much, I made a little house to play in with the other children. I used to play with the cows and the buffaloes, and I liked to help the workers in the rice fields. My father, seeing these things, was happy, and he forgot his promise to the *Pir*, and let me carry on working. Sixteen or seventeen years passed, then one day Maulana Karamat's grandson, Maulana Abdul Assad, who taken his place after he died, came to Sandwip for the Ramzan Id ramaz. Then Maulana Abdul told my father, 'Mr Amin, before I came here this time, I checked in all the books, because I don't think I will return here again, like my grandfather. You have got one son – his name is Abdul Malik. You got another son – Muntaj Ali (four or five years after I was born, my brother was born). I think you promised my grandfather that you would give the older son to us. You never did it.'

As soon as my father heard that he cried out – he shouted at me, *'Shaitan!'* Then he told my sister and my mother what happened, but he never told me. When I came near, he said to my mother and my sister, 'I can't talk in front of him . . .' Three days later, he was dead. He died in my arms, and before he died he said, 'the first son is not mine, he belongs to

Karamat Ali.' The rest of the story my mother told me, then I am thinking, what does it mean, 'that first son of mine, that belongs to Maulana Karamat Ali?' My sister and mother talking, but I can't hear anything.

After that I left home, and went to Narayanganj, without telling anyone. I found the *Pir* . . . how I found him is a long story. When I got him, I told him, 'My name is this, my father's name is that. Now I have found you I won't let you go – I am going with you,' He said to me, 'One thing you need . . . big Arabic education . . . and I don't think I have very long, to give it to you. Best thing to do . . . I know in Sylhet district, one of my *Nana's* disciples – his name is Kari Anjub Ali. This is the letter – carry it with you, but not now – give it another three years then try to meet him.' I said is he going to die? And Maulana Abdul Assad said, 'No . . . not going to die another five years, I tell you that, another six or seven years.' I said, 'I am going to your home, to see your wife, who is my mother also – I have to go.' He said, 'Yes, you can come with me one night, and tomorrow after breakfast you got to leave.' Because that day he going to die, and he don't want me there in his dying time. He know he going to die that day. He said, 'I am not going to keep you after breakfast – soon as the breakfast finished, you got to come down.' I say, 'Alright.' Went there, stayed one night, then I called her mother, I salaam, she holds my body and my head, I slept there and in the morning I left and came to my home. Four days after, I heard, Maulana Abdul Assad died, so and so day. Which day? That day I had the breakfast there, exactly the same day. He was not an old man, very young . . . they know when they will die, our country's *Pirs*, I can't explain why.

After that, I couldn't stay at home, I went away . . . came back . . . can't stay. When I stay home, like a fire come to me, I don't like to eat, or talk to anyone. Then one day I left, go to Calcutta. Started working on the ship. Not a big ship for coming London, local journeys, Dhaka . . . Calcutta . . . Dhaka. When you get to Calcutta, you go to the seamen's hall, then you find a job. I knew some other seamen, from my district and other places, my brother-in-law himself was a seaman, *Bilait* seaman, he was a quartermaster. I was about twenty then – I understood too much, but not much educated – could only read and write my name and address.

Then I heard my mother was ill, and I went home. When I was about three miles away I went to my relative's place near the road, to drink water. They told me, 'Your mother is dead. She is dead five days ago.' My mother dead . . . I just receive a letter from my brother, she is ill . . . Then I did not go home, why should I go there? My mother dead.

When my brother went to the market, somebody told him, your brother coming. No, he said, my brother no coming. Yes. . . he came to our village yesterday. So somehow he came to Sandwip to find me, my younger brother, Montuz Ali. I said to him, 'Look brother, first my father die in my hands and now. . .' I know, because my *Pir* told me, that he who doesn't see his mother die is the worst man in the world – we call him '*Kombok*'. If you are lucky man you will see your mother die in your hands, if you are unlucky you never see your mother die . . . When old people talk, it is like a Bible.

I know that when my mother died, must be she said, 'His father done wrong to him, and now he is not near me.' And with that in her heart my mother died. I can't forget that. Must she be thinking, 'I never done any wrong to my son – done the wrong his father, not me.' That was what I kept thinking, as I wandered here and there for two years. I learned a lot of things – how to make a dead person come to life, and I did it once . . . that is a very long story . . . .

Two or three years gone by, and I remembered that letter, and started looking for that priest. Went to Fenchuganj, Sylhet, found the village, found him, gave him the letter, he read it. Then I saw that he was not a *Pir-sahib*, but a madman. I didn't like the way he spoke, but I had to like it, because my *Pir* gave me the letter to come to him. 'You go to do *namaz*, I don't – I go when I like,' Like a madman! He said to me, 'Oh, you are all mine now, your *Pir-sahib* give you to me, you are mine, you got to listen to me.' He said to me like that. I said, 'Yes, sir.' What he did to me, and what happened, I don't want to disclose.

I saw him do many things. Somebody came and said, 'My son is very ill, please come,' He said, 'Alright, bring him near me.' He touched the dust . . . that type of man he was, lots of thing I saw, *Pir* activity. This knowledge comes in a long line . . . back . . . back . . . back. Same way, a schoolmaster must have a master, and he must have another master, wayback . . .

Before he died, he said to me, 'Look I give you everything, all my people, all yours Malik.' So after he died, it was me they wanted in his place, absolutely one hundred percent of the people. One day in one village I was sitting down to the Maripathi (Sufi) songs, and about two in the morning, I said to them, 'Can you try to carry on, I will have a little rest.' I lie down, like asleep, then I see running down behind my bed, a small gold ball, gold colour, running behind my head, I don't know how I could see it. It went on about two hours, and then I got up. When I got up, I felt something funny . . . 'Who am I? Where am I? What am I doing here? What's that? What's this?' Feeling everything strange. About seven or eight people always with me. I asked them, 'What's your name?' I forgot all their name. It is absolutely true, on my Koran. About two hours gone by, everybody surprised what happened. Then I asked for a glass of milk, I drink it, then I say, 'You people stay here, I am going to Pataikandi' – Pataikandi a *mazar* of one saint. I went there, I stayed there. At night tigers came and big, big snakes . . . I saw tigers at Shah Jalal's nephew Shah Puran's place. I was there at two o'clock in the morning, but I was not frightened – I had power . . . I had such power when I was young . . . the kitchen might be far away but I would know what they were doing there.

After, some of them came to fetch me. I said, 'No, you people following me, you are wasting your time, I got nothing to give you, I lost everything.' They said, 'You are bluffing, trying to hide the power from us.' I said, 'Oh no, it is true, better go home and find another person to teach you, I can't do it any more.' They wouldn't believe me, said, 'It's not you who gives to us, but God, and you are still our *Pir-sahib*.' I said, 'I can't, I can't, I got nothing, I can't put up with it. I'm *Pir-sahib*, I'm this, I'm that, It's no good to follow me any more, I can't give you anything, I got nothing left.' . . . That time, I did look like a *Pir-sahib* – long hair, robes . . . and my singing voice was lovely.

I went to Rangoon, Burma, on a ship as a passenger, I learned many things there. Then I learned how to cure snake bite without medicine, that was at Kamrup kamakhya, the place in Assam. I went up there, nobody could stop me. Then I came back to Sylhet, and I was doing *Kobiraj* medicine. Then someone called me, and said my brother is ill, and so I went to that house, and when I had finished I had to take a bath. I wouldn't eat there, because my teacher told me, 'Where you do this thing, mustn't eat or take any money, if you do, next time no good.' So I took my meal outside, and when I was coming back to their home, I got a fever, dangerous fever. All day and night I lay there with fever, and next day I couldn't breathe, pain in the side. Yesterday I had God-power, I swear, now I got no power. I called the women, 'Go away from here, because I got to swear . . . '

Next morning – I was better. I like to hear the children read with the *Miah-sahib*, I love to listen to them. In this village the *Miah-sahib* was Fazul Ali. I go there, sit down, about twenty or thirty girls and boys reading together, very nice, like a song. Then he called the children, 'Come on so and so, let me hear you read'. Then all of a sudden he said, 'Come on Atusan, give me your studies!' I thought to myself, 'Atusan!

One thing Kari Anjub Ali told me before he died, he said, 'Look Malik, you have learned a lot of things, but you played the devil too much, and you had better stop, or you will lose your knowledge, . . . if you marry you will keep it. If you marry, must be a name with five letters, and first letter must be A.' This was for a very complicated reason – to do with the letters of my name – like a puzzle.

. . . AH . . . TO . . . SA . . . Na . . . My name AH . . . BO . . . Do . . . LO MALIK.' Eleven letters and five, or something like that. I said to myself, 'This must be the one.' I asked the *Miah-sahib*, 'Whose daughter's that?' He said, 'Why, the man you treated yesterday, his daughter,' Then I remembered – this one gave me *paan* and tobacco. Went home, sitting down with her grandfather, I found out that his uncles also of the Shah Jalal line – their name Mansur Ali Ashfar.

Then I know this is the place I got to marry in. Then I told the grandfather, 'Make me your grandson-in-law.' My father-in-law accepted it, but I said, 'There is one important thing, nobody should tell her that she is married – that I am her husband, keep quiet.' She called me *Bhai-sahib* – two years she called me *Bhai-sahib* . . . two years she was with me – she didn't know that she is my wife. Then after two years she knows, but I didn't know what going to happen. My *Pir* told me if I want to do all these things, I can't have children – got to be careful. I want to stop doing these things. One day it happened – a woman got a devil. I go there during the day – I call the devil. The devil say, 'I can go, night time, twelve to two o'clock I can go out. After two o'clock I am coming in again, or that *Pir* sahib who put me out, I will kill his son or daughter, before seven years old, somehow or other. If you give me permission to do these things, I can leave this woman now.' I accepted it.

Her mother knows, her aunty – all the village . . . more than half the people still alive. About two years after, I found that she was to have a child in two or three months. I said, 'Now I have got to leave this country.' I didn't stay very long after I heard all these things. Another son was born, and his name is Kolunder, but he is not that one, can't be that one, impossible. He is still alive. If he had been that one, I wouldn't have left my country – I would still be there.

The war started, and I went to Calcutta and joined the army. I was too clever then, although I am nothing now. Went to Rangpur district for training, then started as assistant *ganger* – working class army called *gangers* and things like that. Slowly, slowly I became a *jemudar*, means sergeant . . . After I lost my God-activity I did everything wrong – I didn't know what I was doing. I was not a poor man, that I should have to join the army to come to London – in my country I could have made plenty of money. But I joined the army. The army came to Burma by ship – the officers went by plane. The Burmese people talking, but we can't understand them . . . small, small people.

Then the bombing started '. . . *vroom vroom vroom!*' everywhere. I am standing with an officer – people dying all around me, one yard, two yards away. Then I got hit – I don't know how. They took me in a jeep through the jungle, then to some airport . . . They brought me to Calcutta. Three days and three nights I am unconscious. The British doctor say, 'You better bury him.' but a Bombay doctor said, 'No he's not dead.' British doctor say 'Twenty-four hours like that he must be dead, every book say it . . . how can you say he still alive?' Bombay doctor say, 'I don't know about your book, but I am doctor too, and I know sometimes can be like that. Snake bite patient three of four days may be like that. If he was dead his hair would come out when you touch it . . . ' This doctor very smart . . . When I start breathing again, at DumDum I heard it all. They kept me there till I was better – fit – then they take me to Calcutta in a jeep . . . big party . . . song and dance. Anyway, after I got better they said to me, 'We don't want you in the army any more.' I said, 'What have I done wrong?' I was *jemudar* – lot of money, sixty rupees a month. Forty rupees I sent home, twenty I kept in my pocket, the twenty I spent like a king.

Then they said they would give me a contract, to build soldiers quarters, in Sylhet district. So I went home, fetched her uncle, and some other relatives. The bank loaned me five thousand rupees, without security. The officers said, 'You got a miracle life – three days without breathing. We can't use you in the army because you got a miracle life, so we got to use you some other way – do the contract, building barracks.' First house I made a profit one hundred rupees – paid everybody. Second one I did four houses together. Profit margin only one anna in the rupee. That was no good for me, only good if someone had contract for lots and lots of rupees, then they could make enough. I lost two-hundred rupees on that job. So I said, 'I must have four annas in the rupee'. They said, 'We can't give you that,' So I said, 'Then give me something else to do – send me to London.' But they said, 'No that is against the law – we can't send you to London.'

Then one day we meet together, one officer said to me 'Come to my place, I want to talk to you.' I go to his place, he says, 'Look, take my advice . . . don't tell anybody I told you . . . Go to Calcutta, get a job as a seaman, get to London and then go to your relative (my wife's uncle was there . . . still alive now). As soon as you get to Liverpool, you run away from the ship. Try to find Brook Line or Star Line. When you have been in London one month, go to India House, they will give you a paper to take to Bethnal Green Police Station. Don't tell anyone I told you for at least ten years.'

I wanted to come to London for money, because she had got used to having money, and also I don't want to stay home because of my son– remember I swore that nobody going to see my face there any more. I had to come to London because of what happened to my son. If you break a promise you make on the Bible, what is the use of living? . . . If you don't keep your swear on Koran, what the use to go to the mosque and

Mecca – it won't do any good. That's the way I feel, and that's why I want to keep my Koran swear – and if I want to keep it I have to come away from the country.

The first time I joined in the sea, I was called a *bunkerman* – in the coal bunker – it meant bringing the coal out from the store and putting it on the fire. There were different classes: *coalawallah, ag-wallah, tel-wallah, donkey-wallah. Tel-wallah* means engine greaserman, *coalawallah* has to bring the coal in and give it to the fireman, to get the steam up, *ag-wallah* is fireman. On that ship, I came in as fireman, and got promoted to greaserman. When I became greaser it was not hard work – very easy, only to check the engine and see that it wasn't too hot. It was dangerous though, the engine-room goes up and down, you had to be careful. It was hot – oh yes, it was hot.

When I came to London I went to India House, then Bethnal Green Police station. I told everybody the truth, never one word lie. Police gave me papers, they love me very much because I am honest . . . I tell truth. I joined the ships again in this country. Three ships died under me, gone down . . . bombed, torpedoed, mined . . . here in the docks. Everybody live – only one officer lost in one ship, the rest are alive. I decided not to go to sea any more, and same night we heard the war was over. I finished work, came home, laughing, singing, jumping, all in the street. I think we were two or three Bengali men together.

I lived in Old Montague Street, No.8, Prospect Place – it was Atusan's uncle's house, her mother's brother, cousin brother. Moktar Miah kept a house in East London – he was one of the first people . . . he died last year. He had a boarding house in Cable Street. I think he came in 1932. Ayub Ali Master was another early one. They came because they were poor and they wanted to make some money – that time we were British, now it is very difficult. It was not only Sylhetti men who came – some from Noakhali and Chittagong. But there were not many people here – it was very hard to find one if you wanted to meet one. There were only about ten or fifteen when I first came, and all living very far from each other. In 1957 and '58, they started coming to work and Aftab Ali came, to see the Queen and get permission for the vouchers. Then too many started coming – but not until 1957 . . . by that time it was very difficult. Anybody could get a voucher at that time – I never thought about it – I could have brought in my family. But I never expected to stay so long – I thought I would go back. I started making money as I told you, and my intention, whatsoever, was never to stay in London all my life. That was why I never bothered to bring them.

I worked in three restaurants, and then Lansdowne Club, then Piccadilly Hotel – I was cook. Sixty names for ways of cooking potatoes, fish – three names, chicken – five names, steak – three names, all French names. How I knew all this? Well, I had to learn. One French chef was there – he told me in his language, I wrote it down in Bengali, and when I had time I would study it. Nine *commis* under me. My wages were fourteen pounds a week. After that I became ill with a gastric ulcer. The doctor told me not to work in the kitchen any more, so I left and started tailoring work. At that time seamen were coming here from Bangladesh . . . India. No – that time it had become Pakistan . . . I had a Pakistan passport.

While I was working in the tailoring, the gastric ulcer put me in hospital plenty of times. I was in hospital a month, and the ulcer was cured, please God. Then I did my chest in, in 1963, in the fog. I walked from Aldersgate to Cubitt Town – no bus or train. I walked from four in the afternoon till two in the morning.

When the Indian seamen came to London, they gave them clothing coupons . . . I used to go to Liverpool, Tilbury, and buy the coupons from them. I bought them for ten shillings, and sold them for five pounds. Well, ten shillings was a lot of money for them – they could buy three or four suits in Pakistan with that. Then I became a peddlar businessman. They used to sell clothes without coupons, they had to get the cloth from the wholesalers, they needed coupons . . . In two years like that, I made five thousand pounds, very easy – I was ready to go home. I didn't want to stay any more. Five thousand pounds was a great deal of money.

That was in '48 or '49. That time I wasn't married to Lily – I was by myself. I had no need to stay – I got what I came for and I wanted to go back and make business over there – why should I stay here and take another man's job? I had enough money.

Then one man said to me, 'In Dacca and Calcutta, there is horse-racing, with the jockey sitting on the top of the horse, but you have never seen a dog-race! Dog is running with no jockey.' I said, 'Alright, let me go and have a look, see what that is.' First race he lost, I win – sixty-five pounds. Then from five pounds I win five hundred pounds. So it went on . . . then I said, 'Let's go home', but he said, 'Look – this is the way to make money, why not make some more?'

Within six months I had lost all my five thousand pounds, only three or four hundred left. I was caught by Atusan's uncle's wife, a Jewish lady – very good woman. She caught me somehow, she said, 'Why don't you go home – sign on as crewman in a ship?' But I didn't get round to it, and in the meantime I lost the money. My uncle came and said, 'Show me your savings book.' He took it and then he called me. Ayub Ali Master was there. Ayub Ali Master said, 'Well, where is this money?' I said, 'I will tell you in the morning.' My idea was that in the night I would pack up and run away. I was too shamed to tell him what had happened. Then my uncle's woman told them. For five minutes, nobody said anything, then my uncle said, 'Well, never mind, what's happened has happened. Next year, I'm going home. I'll give you a hundred pounds cash, and I'll buy you a ticket to come with me . . . '

So then when I lost that money, I had to start working hard again, and I wrote to Atusan that I must have a woman otherwise when I come home from work place won't be clean, and I am a very clean person as she knew already. So she wrote back, 'Do what you like.' So then I found Lily. We had four children. In 1968 she said, 'Let's go to Pakistan.' I said, 'No – only a few months to go to my pension, then we will go.' Two months before my pension she jumped from the window and now she is crippled like this.

In 1959 I told my brother-in-law when he was going home, 'Tell your sister I am not going back no more, I got children here already . . . this and that. If she wants, I can write that it is finished and she can get another marriage.' I was thinking about her as if she was my younger sister. She said, 'No – I don't want another marriage, and whoever says I should, I am going to kill them or I kill myself.' Then I was thinking too much, after I had the letter from her brother. I am thinking, I done wrong, and I am guilty. After all these years and all her young life gone, still she looked after the children alone, and never got a bad name. Nobody can say she messed about with any man. What can she be thinking? Her brother say, 'Your husband is going to divorce you if you agree.' then she is thinking'. . . when I was nine years old he married me,

through all my childhood he taught me, he put me in the bath, combed my hair, and all these things, and why he say today he don't want me?' That is the meaning of the song I wrote then, how inside she is feeling that way. I wrote it that she is Radha and Krisna is away in Matura, and why does he want to leave her, when he is far away. I felt all these things, that they must be coming into her mind. That is the meaning of the song, and that is how it affected me, so much.

At that time it would have been very hard to call her. After the fire in the house where I was living, I had to pay back one thousand eight hundred pounds I had borrowed. How the fire started – one man was smoking too much in bed. He had a lamp . . . he fell asleep . . . the lamp fell over. His bed caught fire first, then the window curtain. I carried him out, but he died in the hospital after a week. I don't know how I carried out all those people. My foot was on fire, and I didn't know – the fire brigade put it out. The police took me to the police station, gave me a glass of milk . . . this and that. Two or three nights they watched me, I had gone like mad. Then I am thinking, thinking, and I write that song.

In 1972 the immigration act came, and my young friend Tipu came to London, having resigned from being an MP. And he wanted to help me something because I helped him before and he remembered. He wanted to buy me a shop or some-thing, because in one year he made fifty thousand pounds, from his cement company. That was how he became rich, now he has started other factories in Bangladesh. I said, 'I don't want you to give me a shop, I would only lose the money. But if you do want to help me, well, you know I have got a wife in Bangladesh. I married her when she was nine years old. I left her thirty-one years ago, she never see me, I never see her. I left a daughter three months old.'

I took citizenship in 1973. In 1975 I wanted to bring my wife, and I said to Tipu, 'If you want to help me, help me that way. Whatever needs to be done from here, I will do it with the help of Peter Shore. But something needs to be done there, because in Sylhet, Gualabazar, they are absolutely backward people, they doesn't know nothing. I can't go there, and leave Lily like this. Somebody better go there to talk to my wife,' And Tipu did it. He went from Dhaka to Sylhet, to Gualabazar, and two or three hundred people sat down to discuss it, and the Chairman came and made the paper – then Tipu took it to the British High Commission, and they accepted it. Then they sent a form, and they said, 'We are going to give Mrs Malik British Citizenship before she comes to London.' Then they sent a form for her to fill up over there, and called her to the High Commission, then gave her British Citizenship and passport and everything. Then she came. On the First of May, 1975, we first met together after thirty-one years.

She got her passport on the Monday, and she came on Sunday. We each have our own pension books . . . Atusan, me and Lily, and we all live here with our cat Timmy. That is my life story.

Now I will tell you how I started social work. When the Pakistan Welfare Association was started, by T. Ahmed and others, I knew we needed something like that, and I helped them to enrol members. The cost was ten shillings a month, then they put it up to one pound ten shillings, then come to two pounds, I said, 'No, I can't pay.' That time I was earning ten pounds a week. I said, 'I can't pay two pounds, but I can pay twenty pounds.' The people were laughing at me in the meeting. I said, 'You got to take my advice – build up the Welfare to help the people. What we have to do, we got to go in our own time, to the people's houses. The people are in trouble, they don't know nothing, they got no education. They need some education – they need somewhere to go when they are in trouble. During the day I am working. Evening time I will go door to door – find out if anybody got any trouble, tell them, if you got trouble, go so and so place, Welfare Office, and get help.' That time they didn't have the Welfare House, that time it was Mr Miah's place. They bought the Welfare House in 1961 or '62 . . . 39 Fournier Street. 'So give me twenty houses in my area, and I will look after those houses. So I will go door to door, and visit the people, ask the landlord, "How many people living in this house?" In that way, I could get twenty members, give twenty pounds to the Welfare.' I said to them, 'The Welfare should do some work, Welfare is to help people.' Came big argument – I said, 'This is not my cup of tea,' and I resigned.

After resigning from there I thought, 'Now, what to do?' When I go to the Labour Exchange, I see the people got trouble. Some people sign only three days and before that maybe one week sign, then again like that. Labour Exchange officer knows he got not much money, he need money and he give him a letter, to take to Assistance Board. 'Me no Assistance Board, me money here – sign today! Me money here . . .' I hear from the other queue. Then I left my queue – I go there, to try and stop that argument, they swear at each other. When I hear all these things, believe me, I can't bear it.

They need education so much, and they don't know it. So I ask this man, 'What happened?' . . . 'He don't want to give me my money, bloody white bastard, it is only because I am black. Terrible!' I say, 'Look, you can't claim three days money, that's not the law.' But he won't believe me either. Then I force him – bring him to my home, give him a cup of tea – make him understand . . . to take a letter from the Labour Exchange.

Next day, I took him to the Assistance Board. I said, 'Look, I also go myself, I got five pounds from here, and another five pounds I will get from there as well, tomorrow.' I explained it all to him. But I keep thinking, there must be some sort of education given to them, so that they can understand all this. Otherwise they are wasting their lives coming here. When we first came here, the white people loved us like anything – whenever they saw us, they helped us . . . where has all this gone? The reason is our fault.

Then we tried to open the school. I tried for two years, and no good – then I started in Toynbee Hall. You know Abdul Gafur, I call him *Pagla* Gafur because he talks so much, he was a trade union member at that time, and I asked him – you try at Toynbee Hall. At that time I knew Mr Walter Birmingham at Toynbee Hall very well, and he said, 'Alright, if you come as one society, we can give you the keys to do it, free.' The society was called Afro-Asian Society . . . but the Africans never did anything. In that name opened the school. Then Gafur came to me, and said, 'Well Mr Malik, we opened the school last week, in the name of the Afro-Asian Society.' I said, 'No, that's no good, I don't want the name of the Afro-Asian Society, all the benefit is to come from this country's Government and if you put that name they are not going to help us, they will say, Let the Afro-Asian Government help you.' I called a general meeting in the school. I gave the nominations . . . Mr Birmingham – Chair, Mr Sabur – Treasurer, Mr Ololude – Secretary. I heard that there was a Workers' Education Centre, more than eighty years ago – that was the name I wanted to give. When Mr Birmingham and the Trade Union Secretary heard it, they said it was a lovely name.

Then seventy students enrolled. I was making the tea, because I couldn't teach. I said I would do it in two shifts, because you can't do tea for seventy people all at once. Every day the same group were first, and the second group started to complain, and said they should take it in turn. It's correct, it should be like that, but when I told the others there came an argument, then a fight. I tried to stop it – I said, 'Look this is not my cup of tea!'

Then somebody called Abdul Hussain, some people called him Abdul Barrister, he opened another school, in Toynbee Hall, where was C.R.C. office . . . bloody Bengali people coming against each other! I said, 'That's not the way to do it, one against another – I don't like it.' So I resigned from there. Not only that reason, another one also. The teachers came from Queen Mary College, today one, tomorrow another . . . each one with a different way of teaching. I said we should pay for a permanent teacher. Then somebody advised me to go to the Bethnal Green Institute. Before this I had started the Drama, with the production of Sirajdula, Abdul Hussain had introduced me to John O'Reilly, Mr Hilton and all.

Mr. Malik (centre) with Peter Shore to the right   *Mr. Abdul Malik*

Then I said, 'I don't know how it can be done, but I want some sort of Welfare Centre,' So John Orwell gave me the advice to put the name of Citizen's Advice Bureau, so then I opened it. I still got a film of the opening . . . Whole Brick Lane blocked – about four of five dozen police officers on duty – the house all decorated, with lights and all . . . The film cost thirty pounds. Mr Khan keeps it, once a year we invite him and he shows us that picture. The opening was by Mr Peter Shore.

When I started to do drama, Danny Connolly invited Peter Shore, Ian Mikardo and everybody. They came to the show, and they were introduced to me, and that was when I first met Peter Shore, in 1966 – face to face. We became close – he gave me his home telephone number – I said, 'Can't write, can't read.' I been to his place many times . . . still if I want I can go, but I don't like to disturb him because he's a Minister now. He has been to my place – not once, many times.

I always voted Labour from the beginning, because I'm a working man. I joined the Labour Party in 1968. 1967 20th December opened the Advice Bureau . . . 1968 I joined the Labour Party – I was an E.C. member. Then last year when I was in hospital they advised me to give up all this, and I resigned then and put Ashik Ali on the Committee instead. They said that they miss the Committee's father.

In 1968 I met Mr John Brown, Principal of the Bethnal Green Institute, then we opened the classes in Tower Hamlets Girls' School. Amar Bose was the first teacher. On the first day there were eleven pupils, second day three . . . four . . . like that. Carried on one month, Three, Four, Five, no more than that. Then Mr Brown said, 'Can't do that way, I think you better stop, must have at least twelve students.' But Amar Bose said, 'If it takes six months or one year to build up this school, I am willing to do it without pay.' Then Mr Brown said, 'That's lovely, then you can carry on.' So Amar Bose carried on with the culture, and Barrister Shahjehan carried on with the English class – I knew him for a long time before, from the time when we began the drama. Then Mr. Brown wanted a music class, so I brought in Jyoti Hassan as a music teacher. Then he wanted a dancing class, so I said 'Yes, lovely, I like that' and I brought in Manesa Bose. Then she had to leave, and Amar Bose brought Manju. Then we moved the classes to Myrdle Street. My daughter

Rabia was in the dancing class, and she collected two hundred pounds to send to the East Pakistan Cyclone Fund.

I also got John Brown's telephone number at home, and disturb him at home many times. Many things he helped, I can't forget that. The other day at that exhibiion at the Whitechapel Gallery, he said, 'So many activities are going on today, and the father of them all is Mr Malik.' He said it in front of Ian Mikardo and everybody there.

So that is my life – up to today now. I had a lot of trouble in my life. I am an uneducated man, how much can I bear? . . . I can bear a lot . . . in Bengali is called *itihash* . . . English word is History . . . you mustn't forget history, you must remember your history – if you don't, you are not human. That is why I would like to put my history in a book. And the cultural side – the dramas – nobody done as much as me. Some people may say they done it, but nobody try in East London like I done . . . maybe they try in Birmingham, or West London, but it didn't last, one or two days after it's finished . . . mine still standing.

Without education, I can't do nothing. So therefore, my name is nowhere, and I don't care about that. God knows – God sees it. I don't want to say 'I did this and I did that' – why should I?

Haji Kona Miah

'A hot night on the Red Sea' (from 'P&O Pencillings') P&O Group

My father was in the ships long ago, fifty or fifty-five years –
when I was young – he came to Liverpool twice. But he didn't
do much, he stopped after two or three years. He told me how
it was working in the ship – how you make friends with
people, how to treat people, and that helped me when I came.
He was a fireman. He went because in my country there is no
money, everything very cheap, if anybody want to make
money, he can't get job. So some got the seamen's jobs, going
from Sylhet to Calcutta and signing with the ship. My father
was one of the first to go. The money that he made . . . oh well,
at that time it was much money in my country. He bought a
farm, and did this and that other things.

I was born the first of January, 1921. I went to school in the
bazar to the west. That was the school for five or six villages,
now every village get a school. I didn't learn much, I only
went for three years. I learned reading and writing – Bengali
but not English, I never heard English. I have just learned

English from hearing people and that is why not very good. I never learned to read, only my name and a little bit printing – no handwriting. I first saw English people when I was about fourteen, in Sylhet and Calcutta.

I came to Calcutta with some older men – local fellows – with one *serang*, fireman - *serang*, just like foreman. My father asked him to take me to Calcutta and get me a job. The *serang's* name was Joirul Hoque, he came from the next village. The fare to Calcutta was seven rupees eight annas. That was the first time I had seen a train. The train came to a place called Chandpur, we had to change and after get a boat. Boat take about six hours and after get train and come to Sealdah. There we got out of the train and got a bus to come to Kidderpore where all our people lived. Calcutta . . . oh, it was nice. I got out of the train and saw everywhere big buildings, and heard everywhere radio and gramophone . . . it was nice.

The Hindu people there wouldn't go to sea so it was all Muslim people from East Pakistan. Hindus don't go to sea because they don't eat meat.The Muslims were all from East Bengal and a few from Calcutta. The Sylhet people were in the ship because these people follow each other,and some went there and others saw them and thought they could get jobs too . . . It all started before we were born. Some people came home from Calcutta, and them got nice new clothes – not suits but just nice shirt and dhoti – and they had nice health, and when they go home everybody say, 'Oh so and so man came from Calcutta' . . . that time everybody said they came from Calcutta, even if they'd been abroad. So everybody used to come and look at them, all the village. Sometimes a man might have been away six months or a year and everybody would come to see him, and everybody would enjoy coming in the house and sitting down, and looking his face, asking him all kinds of questions. And the young people used to think, 'Oh – if I go there people will come and look at me too, and ask me things.' So that was why they went – for money too of course – that was the most important thing.

When we got to Kidderpore, they took me to a house, this house belonged to my village man . . . we paid cheap rent. Every morning we used to go to shopping, to buy meat, fish, rice, then we used to cook. Then at ten o'clock go to the

. . . and everybody would come to see · · ·

Shipping Office at Takta Ghat in the town – that was where we used to start from. When we got there we used to just look around and see which ship was taking crew. There was a list up – so and so ship take crew . . . it was written in Bengali, so I could read it . . . so then we would go to the master. Every day some people came from the ship to be paid off, and some people joined. Some ships were in Calcutta, some in Bombay, some Karachi, some other ports. Before I got a ship I went to Calcutta twice, stayed two or three months and then went home . . . no ship. In that time I sometimes worked in the dock – some ship chipping, some ship clean up – pay by the day. We used to work one or two days, then again off. It was hard work. Then afterwards we used to come home, sleep, then go to the coffee shop, talk with the seamen. They used to talk all the time about the ship, travelling.

The third time I came to Calcutta, I waited about two weeks, then my serang got his ship, and I got it too. He went to the shipping master and said 'I want to take this new boy.' That time because it was wartime, we were not all from the

same village – two from the *serang's* village, and myself, and
the rest were all mixed up – but all from East Bengal, Sylhet,
Noakhali. That was Harrison line, SS *Advise* carrying half
passengers. We travelled first from Calcutta to Karachi by
train – all the crew. They took the crew in Calcutta because
Calcutta men better. Oh! Five days and five nights we
travelled in that train, and it was hard, sitting down. We had
two or three cars reserved for the crew. At some stations we
used to come down and buy fruit, *roti, bhaji* . . . no rice . . . very
bad!

When we came to Karachi we stayed in a boarding house
and next morning came to ship – and evening time ship go to
sea. That time wartime, January 1944. Easy to get ship then,
plenty people frightened and stayed at home. I wasn't
frightened because I had one brother already dead on the sea,
so we needed money – when you worry for money, you don't
worry for death. My brother was killed in 1943 . . . he came
from Calcutta to Durban, and before he got there his ship was
torpedoed. He had made plenty of trips before then, all
through the war. Some people lived, and they went back and
told us in the village. We had an official letter afterwards . . .
they sent an inquiry, who was his guardian? That time he
was married, he was much older than me. I had five brothers
and four sisters . . . My oldest brother went to the ship too.

When I first went on the ship . . . oh . . . it was terrible . . .
because when it was bad weather everything went up and
down like this . . . it was alright after. We slept in bunks, four
to a room – two down, two up. It was up on the deck, so we had
fresh air. At that time it was blackout in the night time –
nobody put a light on the deck – we had to be very careful.

I was a fireman, I had to get the steam up, put coal in to get
two-hundred and fifty pounds steam in the boiler, the ship
would do fourteen or fifteen knots. It was very hard work,
very hard, very hot. We used to have ten or fifteen minutes
rest in the watch.

The passengers were English – some going to Africa, some
to Liverpool. We went down the African coast – went to
Durban, took some passengers. From there we went to a place
called Bairo I think, in East Africa, left cargo there . . . then
went up East Africa – Mombasa . . . Katanga . . . Dar-es-
Salaam. Then from Mombasa we had a convoy to get to Aden

*Oh! Five days and nights we travelled on that
train . . .*

– some troop ships, some man of war. That time no U-boats
coming. When we came to Aden, we stopped there one or two
days, then through the Suez Canal. Then again we waited
one or two days, for ships for a convoy – then to Alexandria . . .
then a very big convoy – fifty-six ships. When we were out in
the sea, everywhere you looked you could see nothing but
ships . . . one change position – everyone change position, one
make noise – everyone make noise . . . But before we came to
Gibraltar . . . one day I was on the four to eight watch, about
six o'clock at night, and the Captain said, 'Everyone be
careful, because there are some submarines underneath, inside the convoy.' I don't know which, but I think some troop
ship hit – '*tawawww!*' like that, and we shook. The *serang*
sent some men to call me, and they came and said, '*Serang*
wants you'. When I went the *Bandari* was there – the cook for
the fireman crew. He put water in the bathroom, he say
'Quick, come and wash!' but them not tell me why, because I
am new. So when I finished washing they came to my cabin,
and they gave me some curry and rice and they said, 'Well,
when you finished eat you got to go on deck'. So then everybody going on the deck. Nobody knows what's happening, and
the captain said to everybody, 'Don't sleep – everybody stand

by.' There were four or six lifeboats on the ship, and everybody was told by name which boat they would go on – this
boat go you, another boat go he – we had practised it before.
The *serang* told me my boat on the boat deck, two boats
upstairs. He tell me, 'If anything happens, don't go to that
boat, go to this one, it would be safer'. So we waiting . . .
everybody waiting . . . and then my sleep time coming, and I
said, 'I cannot stay, I feel so sleepy'. And everybody said,
'Don't sleep, nobody sleeping!' And I said, 'No, I can't stay any
longer, I will trust in my God, if God gives me life, well I will
have life, if not, well I will die', and I went to bed. Three
o'clock, somebody knocking . . . four o'clock I went to the
watch . . . eight o'clock finish – we had four hours on, eight
hours off. Then in the morning we came to Gibraltar. It took
twenty-six days to come from Gibraltar to Liverpool – very
easy passage, seven ships went in a separate convoy, not
roundabout – they were there in fourteen days.

I was not frightened then, but when I was at Port Said,
there were some ships coming from Liverpool to India, so we
stood up there and shouted to one another, 'Where you come
from, what does it look like?' So one ship say, 'We are in a
convoy, maybe a hundred ships, from Liverpool, and we have
come here only two or three ships, and we do not know what
happened to the other ships, we had plenty trouble.' Some of
those ships would have been lost, some gone another way,
plenty lost, plane coming and put bomb . . . So then everybody
was scared . . . we all shouted to each other and talked about
it. Most of the ships had Bengali crews.

Then we came to Liverpool – discharged cargo, then came
to Manchester through the canal. Ship empty – two or three
weeks here – shore people working got ship ready . . . but we
went out on shore . . . oh everything was nice. I didn't talk to
English people – there were some Bengali people there, we
used to visit them. One said, 'Do you want to stay here?
Plenty job here . . .'. But I didn't stay that time, I went back to
the ship . . . to South Africa . . . round South Africa and back
again to England . . . Liverpool . . . then back to Africa again
. . . then after that Calcutta – I had been away for thirteen
months.

We went to Calcutta, paid off and went home. Shopping
first in Calcutta then go home, stayed two weeks, told my

father I go back again. My father say, 'No, you stay.' I took about six hundred or seven hundred rupees home – that was a lot of money then. Now if I go to the market with five hundred rupees I will have nothing left when I come home at night, but then it was plenty, you could live for months and months.

When I went home the people came to look at me, like they used to with the others, and asked me so many things: 'When you go to ship, how is the sea? How is the fighting? How is this and that?' But I said, 'Well we never see any fighting, we just walking round, hearing plenty, but we never see nothing – we never see plane dropping bomb . . . only that every week they try the machine guns on the ship . . . machine guns, '*boooom bapapopopop*'.

So back again Calcutta one week after – go to shipping master's office, join another ship, crewed in Bombay. So again by train to Bombay – stopped there one day then next day ship, go to sea – that was SS *Defender*. Ship came by Africa to Liverpool – when came Liverpool, I left. That was my idea when I left Calcutta – I knew that I would do that, but I didn't tell my father. When we came into the docks some English ships were lying beside ours and we found some of our countrymen there and they gave us ticket. Then we came Lime Street Station, before we run away, to see how it was. They showed us how to take the ticket, and next day we took the train to London – Kings Cross, or maybe Euston. Then by bus to Aldgate, 76 Commercial Street – the coffee shop on the corner of Fashion Street near the big church. That was where all the Bengali people came after leaving the ship. We stayed there, or he would send us with somebody else to sleep. I stayed in Buxton Street first night, 25 Code Street – gone now.

Next day coming again to the coffee shop, three o'clock, and my friend was living in the city, so some people going to the city. Ayub Ali Master asked them, 'Do you know the so and so man?' . . .'Yes'. . . 'Well, you take this man and show him the way.' So he took me to Tottenham Court Road, by under-ground – cost threepence – then to the Bengali cafe in the basement in Percy Street. That was the place where the bomb dropped before but by this time Hitler was finished, though Japan was still fighting. Well I sat down there, and my friend came. He said, 'I've been waiting for you, I've got three jobs

waiting.' He knew I was coming because I had spoken to him
by telephone from Liverpool – he was from my next door
village. Then I stayed the night there, and next day he said,
'Well, do you want a job, or do you want to wait another two or
three days first?' I said, 'No, if I can get a job now I want it.' So
next day I got a job for two pounds a week washing up
somewhere in Tottenham Court Road – a Greek restaurant.

At that time the wages on the ship were four pounds a month.
I worked for two or three weeks for two pounds, then after got
another job for five pounds . . . after six pounds . . . in Percy
Street. I stayed in 195 Drummond Street, at Rashid Ali's
coffee shop. While I was living there one of my friends came
from a Greek ship and he asked me, 'Do you want to go to a
Greek ship?' I said to him, 'Is there any *rice*?' He said, 'Yes,
plenty rice . . .'There was no rice in the town then, we had
Indian curry, but we had to eat it with bread . . . there was no
rice in the country after the war – no rice at all. You couldn't
buy rice from anywhere . . . So we had to go to the Greek ships.
That was why I went, getting twenty-eight or thirty pounds a
month, and some rice – and when we went to any foreign
place we could buy some more rice, and so it was alright.

I did two trips with that ship, then signed off in Newport, then
that time we heard that some seamen were signing in South
Shields, so we went to South Shields, we were five or six
weeks there waiting for a ship. South Shields was nice – a
lovely place – small place, but good for seamen all foreign
people there, more Arabs and Somalis than Bengalis. Then I
joined the ship, Court Line, ship called *Stancourt* – ship to go
to West India, Tobago, Trinidad, back again to Cairo. We
went ashore in Trinidad, looked around – very nice. Paid off
in Cairo, got another ship – then one after another after
another, from January 1947 till 1958. Then I take holiday for
a while and went home and got married – then back to
England and in the ship again. Then after three years and
three months in that ship I went home again. Then one year
later Dudu was born, but two months before he was born I
came back. My wife complained maybe but I didn't take any
notice.

So I was back again, but at this time shipping was very slow, and I had to leave the sea and come to Manchester, to shore work. I worked there from 'sixty-three to 'sixty-nine. I had plenty of friends in Manchester. Two or three times I went home and came back again, by plane. Then in 'sixty-nine, when this one was born, I tried to get a job in the ship and they wouldn't give me, so I went to a solicitor and tell him, 'I been so many years Merchant Navy, and now I am doing shore work'. Solicitor tell me, 'Bring your book and everything'. and he wrote to them and within a week I had been called for a medical exam . . . I went back to the ship, stayed one and a half years.

That time the Bangladesh struggle was starting, so I stayed in Manchester working in a factory for eight or nine months then went back to Bangladesh, made passports for the family and brought them here . . . because there you could not guarantee your life, and now you can't come to this country from Bangladesh without a lot of bother. So I have brought my boys here from my small village, and they are doing well in school and college, and they have grown well . . . And because they have come while they are young and gone around in this country they have learned well and got on. I am glad that I brought them, they are all happy – when they want a job they will find a job. In Bangladesh, if there is a job a hundred men will be after it, but here I need not worry about them – that's good, isn't it? They are all clever and if they want more education they can stay at school and college.

I brought them first on the fourteenth of February 1974, to Hyde . . . came to London first and stayed two or three nights, then to my brother-in-law's house in Hyde. We stayed there one year, then we came to London – first Turin Street, Monkbritton House – we stayed in a friend's flat there for three months. Then I bought a flat in that broken house in Sheba Street – I paid fifteen-hundred pounds for that place. Then I tried to get a council flat, because I had five babies, and we only had one bedroom . . . no bathroom, no hot water . . . rats everywhere . . . but we couldn't get. If we had stayed even longer there we would have got a flat in the end, but by the time we got it maybe we would be dead. Then after we came here to this housing co-op and it is not bad.

From 1947 to 1958 I was in the ships all the time, and I went round the world. England is the best place in the world – people are nice, everything is nice. I have been all over the world, I have been to Holland, Germany, Sweden, Norway, Poland, Italy, South Africa, North Africa, East Africa, Australia, New Zealand, Sydney, Melbourne, Newcastle, Fiji Islands, Malaysia, Japan, China, Panama Canal, Vancouver, Argentina, Kiel Canal, Suez Canal, Montreal, America, Mexico, San Francisco . . . What do you want more?

I enjoyed it all, every place I went ashore – South Africa, North Africa, West Africa, East Africa – everywhere. There were some very bad places, some good places – but the best place is England. If I had wanted to I could have stayed in America plenty of times – a lot of people stayed there – but I like England, England is the best, England people very nice.

Now, I have told you everything that is in my heart, what more can I tell you?

Docks, Calcutta

Mr. Sona Miah

I was born in Baushi-Moyshabari. My father's name was Maulvi Mosharaf Ali, he was the *Imam* of the Mosque. I had two brothers – no sisters.

I went to school for five years – there were only boys in the school. We had no books – we used to write on slates . . . I can write Bengali, a little. The teacher was a Hindu . . . there were seven Hindu families in the village.

I didn't need to go away to sea, my father had enough land to keep us in food, but nothing else. I was fed up in the village with nothing to do, just running around. I ran away without telling anyone, with three or four others who had been before. The train fare from Sylhet to Calcutta was seven rupees. I stayed in Kidderpore, in a *totta bari* – a boarding house. The landlord was a Sylhet man. Everybody helped me, then after I got a ship I paid them back.

I got a ship after three months. First time going to Colombo, Australia, England, Calcutta. First Benglen Line, then Clan Line. I was a coal trimmer. I got eighteen rupees a month, had to give ten rupees *ghoosh* (bribe) to the *serang* first month. Next ship I got the Clan Line, going to Africa, Aden, England, back to Calcutta. Three or four ships, *Arcade, Mclean, Mcvitie* . . . big ships.

Coming Glasgow 1937, I run away from Arcade ship, to London. Other people telling, London very good. That time England was very good, people very respect colour people. I came to house near New Road, I take address when I come London before. Big house – eight people, no jobs. Only chocolate business – six tickets one penny each, chocolate cost penny-ha'penny. First man starting it – Soab Ali. Afterwards find out Jewish people give job, one or two pounds a week, sewing by hand.

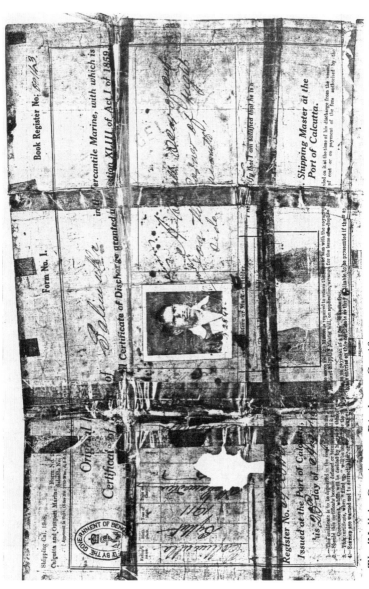

The 'Nolly' – Continuous Discharge Certificate

1939 –I got English articles – go ship. Fireman, afterwards donkeyman. Africa . . . Montreal. . . good money, twenty pounds a month. I sent it to my brother – if I died money no good to me. Too many people die – ship sunk . . . me very lucky. Wartime . . . five different ships. New Road house finish – broke by bomb. I stay in London sometimes one week, sometimes three days. Tilbury Shelter . . . plenty girls . . . before war good girls . . . after war bad girls. I not like face powder, make girl wash it off. This why I not marry English girl.

1943 ship go Calcutta, I run home, my brother and everybody tell me to come. They want me to stay but I refuse – after war I come again England. Worked on twenty-two ships . . . 1954 to 1967 . . . Avis Line. Here are my *nollies*, on them all written 'very good'.

I like the sea life – America, New York City, Baltimore, Washington, Australia, Shanghai, Hong Kong . . . Communist countries, nobody talking, only in seamen's clubs. In Russia I seen girls working in the docks. Australia, big farms . . . fruit . . . everything. America very good. Shanghai, before the war too many girls, after war, no fun any more. Alexandria . . . Basra . . . business girls all dirty, all seamen going to them! I work very hard in war – never got nothing – some people got money from company. I go home now – I stay if family get entry – come again for holiday.

I married 1943, went home again three times when my ship went to Calcutta – got six children . . . but the immigration don't believe they are mine.

Bangladesh people very hungry, that's why I come back to London. I send money to buy a farm. Enough land now for food, but no extra for cloth. England very bad now – no much job, too much trouble. After war good . . . about 'sixty-seven going bad – English boys bad . . . My wife don't like me going ship, can't help it! Nobody else from my village came . . . can't get voucher . . . When I go home I tell I live very well in England – good food, water, electric – easy work, easy cooking. This country good for food and everything. Bangladesh, hungry . . . hungry . . . too hard work. If my son could come, I happy, he happy.

Mr. Qureshi as a young man   *Tom Learmonth*

Shah Abdul Majid Qureshi

Since you have visited Sylhet, you know most of Sylhet District, where I come from is called *Patli-Qureshibari*. I am a direct descendant of Shahkamal – one of the saints who went to Bangladesh or Sylhet with Shahjalal. I am sure since you have been to Sylhet you must have visited the *daroga* (tomb) of Shahjalal. Well – he was one of his disciples – Shahjalal's – and he was one of the important leaders because he was a very learned man, and with the permission of Shahjalal he came to Shahapara to settle there. And the rest of Shahkamal's descendants live at Shahapara . . . A few generations back, one of my forefathers went to Patli, where he got married, got a family and acquired land and all that . . . so I come from the place called *Patli-Qureshibari*. Shahkamal is the descendant of Abubakr – the first *Caliph* Abubakr Sidikqureshi al-Quraish – so we keep this title after our name – Qureshi, and some call them *Kamali* . . . *Kamali* and *Qureshi* . . . both. The place I come from comes under Jaganathpur *thana*, where you have been and visited one of the villages of Jaganathpur, Dowrai.

Let me tell you about my area, Jaganathpur. Jaganathpur is a very renowned place of Sylhet, because there was an independant King, named Rajah Vijay Singh – a hindu *Rajah*, and that is why in all the locality, before the time of Shahjalal and my forefather, Shahkamal, it was mostly populated by Hindus.

At one time, Jaganathpur was mostly under water – most of the villages now you can see standing – the places were all under water once. In the low lying area of Sylhet, when it is flooded, the people used to have good fun with big boat races – with very long special boats, nicely built – like your boat race. There are songs, and musical instruments – accordion.

Sylhet district is divided into two regions – upland, hilly area, and the lowland area. The lower part of Sylhet is called 'Batti'. During rainy season, the whole of the low-lying area is flooded with water, and during monsoon people use boats to get about. During the summer, spring, and winter the lowlands are dry, but the communication is still very bad – people have to walk on foot, miles and miles. Upland areas . . . fortunate to have all sorts of communication – bus, rickshaw, rail.

The people of the *Batti* area never thought of going to any foreign country to earn money, or even to take an opportunity to join the sea-service and see the world, because they possess more land for cultivation, and they are always engaged in farming, and they grow more food – in excess of their needs. By selling the excess food they earn a lot of money, so it hardly occurs to them to seek job outside the country. The *Batti* is the west of Sylhet. Where I come from – Jaganathpur – is more close to the upland area than the *Batti*. In the far west – the lowland area – they have vast lands, they cultivate it and they make plenty. In Ballaganj and Visnath,

At the Tomb of Shah Jalal

according to the ratio of the people, they have less land, whereas further west they have got far more.

Nowadays, in Ballaganj and Visnath, some people have a lot of money from London – they are building new houses. People are increasing every day . . . they have to find new houses every year, so the land becomes less for cultivation. The people who have gone to London, or have the link with London, they are the earning people, they have no problem. But the problem arises for the poor people, who never had the opportunity to come to London. The early-comers to London, America, Africa, Burma, Malaysia, Singapore . . . were from those upland areas – Visnath, Ballaganj, Birni Bazar, all these places. They were the people who took the opportunity of the sea-service.

Today, the Sylhet people have got different businesses in America, Germany, France, Switzerland – restaurants, clothing business . . . and others of course. Most are in London and Birmingham. It was the upland people who became adventurous, to go out and seek a job in the sea, as soon as the ports of Calcutta, Bombay and Chittagong were established, and the East India Company started to send ships there.

Out of all these seafarers there were a good number who took it up as a hobby and pleasure, to see the world. They were the educated men like Aftab Ali, the son of Syed of Sylhet . . . Illyas Rajah, from a *zemindar* family . . . there were many notable men who came to this country . . . my friend Hamid, who became a barrister. I had the same idea and high hope, but I myself coming from a very poor family had to be always coming to the aid of the family, contributing for their support, so I couldn't do much. Some time ago, in my early days, I took up a course for the law and I had high hopes of becoming a lawyer, but due to economic reasons, I couldn't carry on.

We were three brothers . . . I am the eldest . . . the second brother was a graduate in India. He had Honours in Philosophy and he came to London for further study . . . M.A. in Education. But unfortunately he couldn't go through with it – he had bronchitis. Afterwards when he was a little better he had a job in the High Commission, then he went home. Then he was a headmaster sometime in Visnath, then in

Habigiganj and Jaganathpur as well. And then again his bronchitis trouble started. He was sent to Dacca for medical treatment – there he stayed for ten or twelve days and then he died. He had three daughters and one son.

My youngest brother, he didn't have much education, because he was a bit of a daredevil type of boy, one day he had a row with the teacher at the school . . . then he gave up his education . . . although my father tried to give him a good education . . . and he used to look after the home while I was away in London. My father was old – when I was born he was about forty.

In my early life I lost my mother. She was about to have a child, and at that time, in our area, there was one Government surgery, in Jaganathpur, where we used to get very little medicine, and they were not good. Mostly at that time the doctors used to use that medicine for themselves, or they used to put water with just a little medicine. We were not very well off, so we couldn't do anything. My mother couldn't give birth to the child, and she remained in pain for two days, or three. The local quacks came, but they couldn't do anything. At last now, I understand it is something that women have after childbirth – there is a special medical term – and unless the person can get proper medical treatment for it, be sent to the town doctor, the person will die. So my mother died, I was about ten, it was a very sad thing for the whole family. My mother used to look after us very nicely, and my father became very helpless without having a woman in the family.

I was born on September 25th 1915. Before my father died my second brother died, . . . my youngest brother . . . somehow I managed to bring him to London, because we had some opportunity to bring them. Then I was in the catering business, I had a restaurant in London, in Peckham, namely *Anglo-Pakistan Restaurant*. At that time I was the general secretary of the Pakistan Caterers Association. We applied to bring people to help us in our business – because we couldn't get suitable cooks here – and we were permitted after long struggle to bring some of these chaps from Bangladesh. I managed to bring my brother and a cousin and a few other fellows.

My father and my uncle lived in our family home. My uncle had two sons and my father had three sons and one daughter. Of all the brothers and sisters, I am alive, and my two cousins.

We had enough land, but somehow my father spent a lot of money on us, to get us educated, so he had to sell the land and we became very poor. Among the nearest villages, apart from Syedpur and Habipur, my brother was the first graduate, and then my second cousin, he was also at the University, and then I had some education myself. We were the only family in those villages at that time who were educated. My father . . . had elementary education, and he had some learning in Arabic and our letters, but yet he was very modern in mind and he always thought that he should give his children proper education. My sister had some education, but not much, . . . my family brothers all had good educations. Mother could read, but very little you know, not much. At that time the ladies didn't bother so much to learn Bengali and English. Now it is the fashion that everybody must learn English and have proper education, otherwise, you know, the family name is not there.

I studied at different high schools, and after matriculation, then I came to London. Not straightaway, can't come straightaway, but it was my idea to come to America or London. At that time, there were a few people from our village and nearby who went to America. How? Because Sylhet district you will find a lot of seafaring people you see and the reason, I will tell you.

The men of Sylhet district are seafarers, because it is in their blood. Most of the people of Sylhet, they claim they are descendants of the Arabs. Arab people used to like travelling. Even before the Muslim rule of India they came as travellers to Chittagong, to Sylhet. They came as businessmen to Sind in India and many of them, they settled and that is why the Sylhet people, the Muslims especially, they like to travel. It is in their blood to travel the world. So that's why the people of Sylhet, and Noakhali, and Chittagong, . . . are seafaring people you see, because they like to go to different parts of the world and it was the only way out. For a poor people, it was beyond their thinking to go for a holiday or anything like that but it was usual for people to go to the ship. It wasn't thought wrong for a person from an educated family to go, it was the fashion at that time, the fashion. I can say that a good number of persons from Sylhet – not only Sylhet, other parts of Bengal – they became a seafarer to see the world you see, because it was easy. They travelled all over the world, in the ships you see. Some when they came to America they tried to escape from the boat, and some manage and some cannot.

Those who managed to escape and somehow settle in America, they always used to send big money orders. Some of them came back, and that gave me the idea that we were poor, down and out, and with our education we couldn't do much . . . if I could manage to go to America, somehow or other I could earn enough money – that was my ambition. I had the amibition to earn money due to the economic situation – that forced me to earn money, because I didn't like to see my people, my brothers and sisters in this position.

I went with the permission of my father, I told my father – I am just going to try my luck, to see if I can get the opportunity of going in the sea-service. Probably I will find the opportunity of going to England or America, or somewhere. My father – at that time he was down and out, had no money – he didn't mind, but my brothers stayed at home and they studied.

So somehow I managed to come to Calcutta. I came alone, by train . . . I think it was 1934. At Calcutta, some of our Sylhet people made lodging houses. They used to make money out of our poor people. It was in Kidderpore, by the docks. There were quite a few *latchis* . . . they used to call *latchis* 'lodging houses'. They used to have a list of different area lodgings and landlords and they used to run it through our people. They had a system – that those who stay in their lodging, they must pay monthly so much but they won't take money from you till you get a ship and have a job. Once you got a job and your voyage was finished – say for a year or six months, then come back again to the port – they count their money from the day you took shelter in their lodging up to your return from the ship you see. Even though you were away in the ship, they could count it. The advantage – and it was a very cunning system – they used to give weekly some money to everyone who used to live in their house, for your food and everything. Food was quite cheap at that time – they used to give one or two rupees for a week, and with that one or two rupees you had to manage food and everything

There were some ships at the port of Calcutta – after finishing their voyage and returning to the port they used to employ some local persons who could do the jobs. So they used to pay a nominal wage of eight annas per day, for polishing

PLA Collection, Museum in Docklands

Painting the ship in dock (photograph taken by a PLA docker for his album)

the ship, scraping the ship, painting, or doing many works in the ship. They used to pay very little. Payment had been made from the company much more, but there was a middleman – they used to call him the *ghat-serang,* – who used to pay the people from Kidderpore dock, or from these lodging houses. So through them we used to get jobs when we were waiting for a ship, so in that time we could earn a little. After doing all the work you would get six annas or eight annas, not more than that, that was extra money on top of what the landlord gave you.

I knew quite a number of *serangs*, and some . . . when they were in difficulty, I used to help them. At that time there was a system in Calcutta, they used to get their job in the sea as a *serang* and they used to bring their crews, they call it crew, those who work under *serang*. It was *serang* who used to collect them. So I approached a number of *serangs*, some who had been waiting a year you see, waiting to get a job. A job was very difficult, even for a *serang*, so they came to me to write letters to their engineers, under whom they had worked. So I used to write nice letters to the engineers – 'I have been employed for such and such and such period, and I am sure that you remember me, and I am sure that you had good service from me, and I am waiting here at Calcutta for nearly two years, unable to get a job, so if you kindly when you come back, after finishing this voyage you come back to Calcutta port I think you will select me as *serang*.' They used to be very happy, they used to give me tea and all that. Sometimes they used to give me pocket money as well, so I was living quite comfortably, but that was not my aim, you see. My aim was to get a job in the sea and either to go to America or to England. England was not much attraction to me – America, at that time America was the attraction, because those who went to America, they used to send big money orders.

So after some time struggling I got a job with a *serang*, and that was I think 1935. But that ship, they came to London and all that but somehow I couldn't escape from the boat. I always looked for my opportunity, but that *serang*, also he took up a vow from my uncle who was there in Calcutta, that – look, this young chap, I wouldn't mind to take him with me, but these literate people, when they go to a port of London or America, they always run away from the ship, but if you agree that your nephew wouldn't run . . . So I kept to that promise. They used to keep a special watch on me, they used to guard me always.

There were about forty crew, all from Sylhet. There were two sides in the ship, one is called deck department – deck is where the people work on the top, such as cleaning the ship – they have a *serang* and *tyndals* and all that, they do the up jobs, they are under the officer called the Chief Officer, and the Second Officer, Third Officer. Their job is to see how the ship goes, which way it goes, and all that, under the leadership of the Captain. We used to be in the engine-room services, to put the coal in the boiler and all that. We put coal in the boiler, and then it gets heat and then the ship runs. It is a most difficult job, very hard, very hot too. Many people died in the heat. In my sea life I knew hundreds of people who died.

We were paid eighteen rupees per month. The food we used to get was our rice, and while we were on the sea we used to get dried fish and dried meat . . . it was *halal*

That ship went to America and all that, but nowhere I could get a chance to escape, they wouldn't allow me even to walk in the port. Nowadays anyone can go to the shore, without restriction, but at that time everywhere it was restricted, there used to be watchmen in the boat and in the shore near the boat. So, by ill luck, on my first voyage I couldn't escape. I had to return to Calcutta and had to stay for another year or so without any job. I went home for a short while, then I came back again and then I managed to find a job with saloon department, in the service of those engineers and officers, looking after their food and serving them. So it was a better job, comfortable and all that. They were quite nice to me, because I was very good in my duties. Some people, due to lack of language, sometimes did not understand what the officers said and they might make a mistake. But I always did things right, so they were very pleased, and apart from my wages I used to get tips from them.

Lastly I got a ship again that was coming direct to London. I decided in my own mind that since I couldn't get to America, and last time I didn't stay at London, well, I'll try my luck and stop at London. So I came after eighteen or nineteen days to London – only passed through Port Said and then direct London.

It was about ten or eleven at night, I dressed up, wore all my clothes, and I put my religious book, Koran in my pocket . . . because I used to pray regularly – from my childhood I was religious because I belonged to a religious family you see.

I ran away, but I didn't have much money. I booked my ticket from Tilbury to London, but somehow there was a change. I didn't know which train to take and I took a wrong train, and it stopped somewhere else. 'Is it going to London?' Somebody said, 'No son! You are in the wrong train.' Then I said 'Well, what can I do now? I haven't got enough money, I bought a ticket and I finished my money.' He was very kind, this English gentleman, he gave me some money – I cannot remember how much – it was enough to book my bus ticket. I took a coach and came to Whitechapel – Aldgate – it was about twelve or twelve-thirty. When I got out of the bus I didn't know where to go. I had one or two addresses, but they were wrongly written, they were not correct, and when I showed them to anybody they didn't know. I was very much disappointed – didn't know what to do. At that time I cannot go back to my ship, because I have come here to stay, and I can't disclose anything to anybody.

I tried to find an Indian in the street – anybody – any of my countrymen, but there was none. At last I found a policeman, and he said, 'Sonny, what do you want?' I showed him the address, but he said, 'No, I don't know that.' After some time walking up and down the policeman suggested that, if you can't find a place to go, come to the police-station and we will give you shelter for the night and in the morning you can go away. But I was frightened in case they sent me back to the ship.

I was in the street. It was nearly one-thirty . . . I suddenly saw a young man, about twenty-five, very dark looking. I thought probably he is from Madras because of his colour – his skin was so dark. I thought he is from Madras, so instead of speaking to him in Bengali I spoke to him in Urdu. I said, 'Gentleman, ap kidder saya Apkar mulluck kia hay?' ('Gentleman – where are you from? What is this place?') He spoke to me in Sylhet dialect – no – in a very broken Urdu, he said 'Ham Sylhetadjmi hay. Ham Sylhetka adjmi hay.' ('I am a man of Sylhet I am from Sylhet').

I was so very glad. I held him, embraced him, I said, 'By good luck, at last I have found someone who can help me.' He was a very quick talker, you know. He said, 'You have come from the boat? Come with me. I will give you shelter, I live in Munshi's house.' Munshi was a gentleman who used to have a lodging house, somewhere around the East End, in Code Street. So he said, 'They are nice people, my landlord is a very nice man, and we are there about twelve or thirteen fellows and there is no literate person among us. Do you know English?' I said, 'I know enough for anything.' He said, 'Well, come with me, we will treat you nicely.' He took me there, and really I found them very nice. Munshi-sahib was a good man . . . it was one-thirty, everyone was going to bed but somehow the landlord was awake, and he asked his wife to cook some rice for me. Curry was already there, they fed me, and I felt comfortable. There were some people from Visnath area, and there was one fellow from my *thana* as well, not a close relation to me, but we were distant relatives.

So I felt very comfortable, all of them treated me very nicely, but I asked them, 'What do you do for your livings here?' They said, 'There is no work, but one thing we can do here in this country nowadays. During the week nothing, but in the weekend, Friday, Saturday, Sunday, three days we go to different pubs, with chocolate, and with a raffle. We make six cards, numbered one, two, three, four, five, six. First with a penny we sell the cards – all the people will come around when they they start drinking, they buy the tickets for a penny. Whoever's number comes out on the top, he is the lucky one, and he gets the chocolate. The chocolate we buy for tuppence, tuppence-ha'penny, or threepence at that time. So we get enough money.' Not at all an Islamic thing to do. You can't say that any Indian boy could get work at that time, never mind Indian, even the English boys – that was 1936 – a very bad time.

So I said, 'Do you all do this?' And they said, 'Yes, that's the only way,' And some of them did the peddling, they used to go from door to door with the silk clothes and different clothing and some go door to door, or in the streets with toffee. In the street they used to ring a small bell and they used to attract the school children, and they used to utter a few words – 'Indian taffee, ask your mummy to give you a penny.'

So they used to make their living, or else they would sell clothes to different houses, knocking on the door, and this was the other profession to go to pubs.

For three or four weeks, they wouldn't let me go to work, they said, 'No, you can't do that. It is a very nasty job.' All the publicans wouldn't allow you, and even some of them, if they do allow you, you have to go very hidingly, quietly, you see. When the governor or proprietor didn't see you, go quietly and try to attract the boys who were drinking. And when the governor sees you or the manager or someone, they would throw you out, drive you out, swear at you and call you different names. So after a few weeks, I said, 'Well, I don't like to sit aloof here and live on you, so I must also try my luck.' So firstly I found it very difficult, but then I made a different way. First I went to the publican, and I said, 'Would you allow me to sell my tickets here?' Some used to say alright, some used to say, 'Oh, your brother has just been in.'

So I stayed there some time, and kept on doing this like other boys, and with that money whatever I earned I managed to keep myself.

At that time, in 1936, and even before there used to be a gentleman in East London – Canning Town, I think it was Victoria Road – he used to have a big lodging house. . . they used to call him Ali. He was a seafarer himself, and he settled much earlier than we all, who came later. Ali was one of the old fellows who came to this country, and he had a little education, not much – he had some high school education you see, up to class six or seven or eight. He struggled in Sylhet, and then as a seafarer he managed to come to this country and settled. So he made a lodging house in Canning Town and he managed to get a contract from the shipping offices in London – City Line, Brocklebank Line, all the different lines. Because sometimes what happened . . . they used to exchange crews in London, so under contract Ali used to get the crews in his lodging for a month or two, often days, and he used to get money from the company for their food. Whatever money was allotted, out of that he used to spend only ten percent and ninety percent he used to keep in his pocket . . . that was how he became rich. And some of the old seafarers, the few who were under English articles, they used to live in Ali's house. So Ali was quite comfortable . . .

He had become quite close with the shipping companies – as a broker. And those who ran away from the ships . . . to get clue where they are, then company can sue them and take them back . . . Ali used to give the news to the company 'I found out where your crew are hiding.' So the company's police used to take a warrant against the name of the person who deserted the boat and Ali used to go with the shipping agent to get him. If you could catch one person, you used to get money from the shipping company, a good bit of money. And he used to get this contract from the company, all the crews, when the necessity arose to stop them at London, they used to send them to Ali's place – and he used to get money from them. That is how be became a monied man.

At that time, not only Ali, there were other people, quite a few, mostly in East London – one Islam . . . another is Mr Munshi who just died . . . Khan, one Maarufah Khan . . . and a few others, who used to keep lodging houses only for those deserters who used to come to stay in their houses. Ali was their common enemy, because Ali used to take people from their houses, and betray them to the shipping companies.

People of Sylhet are very daredevil types – you may say a wandering race, they like to see the world, like to go all over – very inquisitive type. You will find all over the world, in every nook and corner, not only England, but even Russia, America, Canada, Australia . . . everywhere you will find Sylhettis. And it is the seafaring men, they enter a port, they settle, they bring others after them. Here in this country the student community from my country – they boast that such and such a man is having high position, but at the bottom you will find that those Sylhetti people, they organized something here, they made a few restaurants at that time. And those students who came here, they always knew that . . . 'we will not be without shelter, because there are some at least, men of the same country . . .' so fellow feeling was there. They used to live in these restaurant people's houses, or they used to work there on the quiet, and at the same time they would be attending their classes.

The first restaurant was started by Mister Yassim and Mister Rahim, two gentlemen from United Province, or maybe from Punjab, anyway men of Western India. They opened a restaurant known as *Shafi's*, it is in Gerrard Street, W.1. The second restaurant, I think, was Abdullah's, the curry powder maker. Abdullah – we used to call him 'Uncle' – he opened a restaurant, somewhere around Old Compton Street, in the West End, but he couldn't run it very long. It was long ago, about 1920 or 1925 . . . he was an expert cook, he was from Bombay. He had a grocery business in East London near Liverpool Street, Helmet Court – his son owns that place now. Sometimes when Buckingham Palace required to have Indian food to entertain their guests, they used to call him – not directly . . . they didn't know him . . . but it was through the Advisor to the Secretary of State for India, who was an Indian gentleman, they all knew Abdullah, and through their recommendation he used to go to the Court. So he was quite popular, and he opened a restaurant but did not last long. Third restaurant was *Veeraswamy*, I think. There was another restaurant, still existing, owned by a gentleman, a graduate of London University. He had a brother, a barrister at law, another brother also quite highly educated. He – Mr. Vin – came here for studying, but after studying he found that to make money catering will be a good attraction. There were those who used to be here . . . retired from Indian service, or they had visited India . . . they enquired about curries. So he got the idea from them that if there was an Indian restaurant . . . and at that time there was *Shafi's* already . . . so he opened the next restaurant. He gave up his law business . . . he found that catering gave more profit in London than to be a practising barrister. So they were the people who had restaurants in London, in Oxford, in Cambridge, in Manchester, and all that.

The Sylhettis were not the first, they came in last – there was *Veeraswamy,* and then there was another – the *Bengal Restaurant* in Percy Street – run by a gentleman from Orissa. I worked for him, after finishing with the chocolate selling business I told you about, in 1937. I lived in number 5, Old Compton Street – there was a countryman of mine who had the leasehold of a three floor house, and he used to let rooms. I used to share the room with other fellows, and the rent was very cheap. I used to get about two pounds ten shillings as a waiter, and then I became the head waiter, so I used to get three pounds a week, plus tips.

Then in 1938, I saved enough to open my own restaurant – in Windmill Street. I can claim that I was the first Sylhetti man to own a restaurant. It was previously owned by a Hindu gentleman, from Calcutta, an artist – I don't know whether he is still alive or not – a very nice fellow. His name was Mr.

Ghosh, and the name of the restaurant was *Dilkush* – '*Heart's Delight*'. You may have seen in Calcutta, there is a restaurant called '*Dilkush Cabin*', and he named it after that. It was a successful business, I had a gentleman who helped me with the business, he is from Sylhet, he is a Hindu gentleman. He came here to study something in the engineering line – he came as a seaman, but he wouldn't admit it – he is the son of a Rai Sahib. His family was a very well educated family – his brothers were engineers, doctors, one was a Captain in the army. His name was Nandev. That Nandev is no more, he died long ago. He used to come and help me – guide me. And he used to bring me customers, because he was quite known . . . he was a very clever fellow, and he was well known among the Indian students and cultured people at that time.

At that time most of the customers were Indians, Hindus, very few students were Muslims. We used to get English customers too – those English people who had been in the Indian Civil Service and all that. They used to come, they used to speak in Bengali, Urdu and English, we used to speak to them in English. And they used to like sometimes if we called them '*Sahib*', you know . . . they used to be very happy . . . so we wanted to have a little more tip, so why not? They used to call 'Bearer!' . . . Bearer! Nowadays these fellows, the waiters, if anybody called them 'Bearer', they wouldn't serve him – they would say, 'Go out of this restaurant!'

So I was earning good money, and with the help of Mr. Nandev my restaurant was doing well. I had obtained an identity card from the Indian High Commission. The High Commissioner certifies that he is an Indian, that he comes from such and such a village, and the High Commission wouldn't do it just like that, they would send to the police authorities in India, and they would enquire, and then they issue it. After a certain time, you can't be challenged for leaving the ship, because their warrant was only for a limited period, after that can't. Then I was quite alright – free – and many like me. Then eventually I got my British passport, now I am British. I never had Indian, Pakistani or Bangladeshi passport. All along, since I had my passport, I am British.

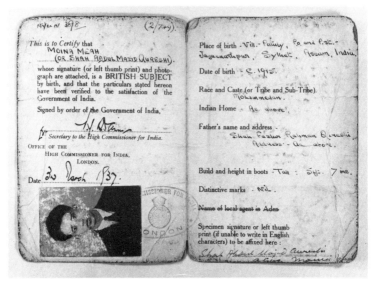

Tom Learmonth

So it was 1938 when I first got my restaurant, it didn't cost me much – two hundred or three hundred pounds for the lease and the business, and I did quite well. I used to serve the Maharajah of Siraikullah's party – they came to tour all over the world, they used to have a circus show. Something like Udai Singh who used to show Indian dances and all that. They used to come in a big party, regularly, for two months sometimes . . . the Maharajah's own son, and the people who came with him. They made a lot of money – they used to book big theatres and they used to get big audiences. They used to come and have food in my restaurant, and I was quite famous.

Then the student community from Bengal, they started coming, because they knew that they wouldn't have any worry for shelter, and they could find work as waiters, and at the same time they used to take admission in the Law Institutes, or in any institution. Students from all Bengal – East and West, Hindu and Muslim. So all the credit goes to that fellow who started the restaurants.

As well as the Sylhetti people in London, there used to be other places, such as Cardiff, Southport, Glasgow, Liverpool – they used to live there in a group in different houses, just for the sea jobs. And here in London, they used to get sea jobs under English articles. They lived with the Somalis too, who are also seafaring people . . . they are also Muslims. Chinese used to live around there too, but we did not mix with them. At that time, when I came, the Chinese were looked down upon by the English people, because they didn't speak English . . . and then they used to be also engaged in opium business, and all that. And Chinese used to do restaurants. From a very early time the Chinese people were in the catering business, and the English were attracted to them. They started before the Indians – the Indians followed the example of the Chinese . . . got the idea that wherever there is a Chinese restaurant doing well, if you open an Indian one there, it will work.

In 1939 war was declared, and we were all forced to take up some form of National Service – I took up the job of A.R.P. I was a First-Aider. We used to do very important work in London – every time there was a Blitz we used to go out with the ambulance and pick up the dead bodies, pick up the wounded and take them to hospital, give them first aid. It was not once a day, but sometime five or ten times a day, or in the night. There was no time to it, you had to do twenty-four hours on and twenty-four hours off. We started in William Street, NW1. It was bombed – the place was damaged but we were saved, somehow or other. But many a time I myself and many of my friends were wounded by splinters, when we were getting out while a place was about to collapse. Some died, many escaped narrowly . . . but I was not afraid. Many people were frightened, but I have a strong faith in God – if I die in the cause of humanity doing some good service there is some satisfaction, but if I die without doing anything, well then it does not give the same satisfaction in your mind.

We felt, we Muslim people, that it was our war too, because the Japanese were at the gate of India. And we were frightened because we – not only Muslim India but the whole Muslim world which includes Arabia – we knew that the safety of England meant the safety of the Arab world, so we supported the war effort. But at the same time we did put our demand for Independence. At that time I was a supporter of Congress – Indian National Congress – and we held many meetings.

Before that there were two platforms, one was Krishnamenon's India League, and the other was Hindustani Social Club, run by a gentleman named Surat Ali – he used to be a bit socialist type. He was also a seaman but he never admitted that he was ... He was not even *Surat Ali* – he was not a Muslim – but he came to this country, after giving himself a Muslim name ... he somehow managed to get a job in the ship. Not that you had to be Muslim, but the *serangs* and all that were Muslim, so if you were a candidate to be in the sea service it was best to be a Muslim.

So we worked together in the Hindustani Social Club. It was not much political, mostly we had social gatherings – we used to invite the High Commissioner and other big people, to come and see how we were living. We used to have Indian songs and all that . . . we were people from all India and Bengal. Then I saw the slums in East London, because I lived in the East End. At that time the people were ill-clad, children especially not so bonny ... not so healthy. Most of the houses were like slums – falling down, old ... you can see that it was a bad life. And when you go to look for work, there is no place to find work, and as I told you before, never mind Indian boys, English people couldn't get jobs.

We used to get seventeen shillings dole – somehow we managed – English people also managed. But there was not poverty like in India – at least there was some security, help from the Labour Exchange. At least for six months you were entitled to get some dole, and in emergency cases rations could be given also if you were in dire need. And the Health Service – you used to get free service from the doctor, but at that time you had to pay for prescriptions. No, you couldn't compare it with India – a subject country – poor ... down and out ... not be compared with England. Though England was poor too. But the standard compared with today and 1936 ... 1938 ... it is heaven and hell, heaven and hell. I used to work in a few Indian restaurants, say *Veeraswamy's* or even *Bengal Restaurant* – those who used to come were doctors and such, or retired Indian Civil Servants, those types. No ordinary people would ever dare go inside a restaurant, even

an Indian restaurant, never thought of sitting inside a
carpeted place, and eating . . . Now, everybody has got a car,
even a labourer gets hundred pounds a week, must have a car
. . . Who did all this? Who changed the future of these people?
The Labour Party, those were the people – Lloyd George,
George Lansbury and all that, Attlee, Morrison – they turned
the future of these people.

During the Blitz, the wartime there was a cafe – Indian
cafe – where we used to go and chat to one another . . . like a
club. At that time there was a flying bomb, and another,
Hitler's bomb, which could all of a sudden massacre whole
crowds. I went to the bath, and after my bathing, naturally, I
was about to go to this cafe to meet my friends and dine there.
I think it was about ten or eleven o'clock. I quickly finished
my bath and was ready. Suddenly I heard the sky . . .
'WHOOOOOOOOOOOOOOO! . . .' and everything was shaking. I fell to the ground . . . when I got up and got out,
everybody running. Running where? They don't know.
Everywhere I want to go, the road is blocked, in Oxford
Street, thousands of people. 'Somehow', I said to myself, 'I
want to go to that place, the Indian cafe' . . . at last I came near
to the cafe and I saw that the whole area was smashed.
Eighteen Indians died that day, and most of my friends, they
died – those in whose company I was all the time. And I went
to their burial place, in a cemetery near Woking where
Muslims used to be buried, they were all buried on the same
day.

That day Morrison came to see the cafe. He was the Home
Secretary, and I met him and talked to him. At that time,
nobody was certain who will live tomorrow, or even today.
During my day off I sometimes used to go the deep shelter, in
Warren Street or Piccadilly, but after some time I got fed up
with going, taking blanket and pillows – and you couldn't
sleep properly. So I made up my mind, if I die, I die at home.

I used to live in Green Street, near Piccadilly – No. 3 Green
Street – it was a private landlady's house, and I took one
room, unfurnished. One night the whole city was bombed –
East India Dock and all the dock area, the City of London . . .
they used to call this night the Day of Resurrection . . .
wherever you looked, you could see only fire and fire. My
whole building was shaking, not far from my house, houses
were burning. Some Greek fellow used to live downstairs, he

came and banged at my door, he said 'Hey Indian mister, get up, come on, quick, go to the shelter!' But I made up my mind, I thought, 'No!' and I pulled up the blankets and covered my head.

Of course during the wartime many of my countrymen took up jobs in Birmingham. Birmingham was massacred, Coventry was massacred, and many of them died – most of my friends were killed. Those who were in the sea-service, under English articles, some of them are still alive, but most of them died on convoys to America and Australia and all that.

At that time those who came to this country, whether from Sylhet or any other part of Bengal, they didn't bother much about religious faith, only occasionally, at *Eid* (end of *Ramzan* the fasting month) they used to have congregational prayer, but people never kept the fast. Now ninety-percent of the Muslims who are here, they fast in the fasting month. But in those days people didn't observe religious things properly when they came to this country, I myself forgot it. . . . World War Two people came in big numbers, and some of them were very religious and they thought they should apply for a licence to have *halal* meat, fellows like Taslim Ali and others did a lot to get this done. Now there are a lot of religious organizations, as well as the political organizations. Taslim Ali . . . he is a fully trained fellow – he understands Islam and he is a practical Muslim . . . Taslim . . . has always been the first one to organize for the betterment of Muslims. I was the Secretary of the World Muslim Organization, the *Jamai'at al Islami* and I had to do all this because it was my duty.

In the early days we never thought of having *halal* meat here or anything like that – we used to buy the meat from the English shop – just avoid the pork . . . pork usually no Muslim will take, though they might take drink, which is equally forbidden to them.

In the early times the only religious thing was that after *Ramzan*, they used to go for the *Eid* prayers to the East London Mosque, 448 Commercial Road, there used to be a good feast there, and not only Muslims, Hindus and everybody used to come to enjoy the feast. And our leader – *Imam* – used to give a good lecture, in English. Sometimes during the war I used to go to the mosque but there were never more than ten or twelve there, but now if you go to a mosque you see thousands of people there. The reason is that recently the more religious type of people have been coming, and they have set up religious organizations, and are always in the mosque and teaching Islam, and give the true interpretation of Islam.

I must say some words about my friend Taslim Ali . . . *Haji* Taslim Ali is a fellow who from the very beginning, since he came here – although he is married to an English lady – has been a very religious man, and a very good man. For the welfare of the Muslims, always he was the first one. If anyone is sick in the hospital, always he inquires, no matter whether he is from Bengal or Punjab or anywhere – he may be Hindu or Muslim, doesn't matter – always he will go to see him and comfort him.

Before, in this country, we never had the opportunity to be in the hospital when the person dies, to be at his bedside. But it is a custom according to our religion, that when a Muslim person dies someone utters something reminding him of his faith. Sometimes, when a person dies, he may be in the agony of death, and he may forget everything, but at that time to remind him is better. So he organized these things . . . went to the hospital authorities . . . and nowadays if anybody wants to go to the hospital to see his dying person they allow him to go and sit at the bedside and say this prayer.

Haji Taslim Ali was the first one who organized the Muslim mortuary – he rented a room near the mosque. He used to pick up the dead bodies from the hospital, wash the body, and give the funeral service according to the Muslim rites. His wife is also fully trained, a very good Muslim – she gives instructions to the other ladies, who want to perform *Haj* in Mecca. Here in London also, if any woman dies a man cannot wash her, by Islamic rites. But she is trained to do that, and she does it. He was the first one to open this Muslim mortuary, now I think there are quite a number of them.

We used to organize political parties and political meetings and all that. In early days my associates were Ayub Ali, *Haji* Taslim Ali, Mushraf Ali, Barrister Abdul Hamid, who is no more. We used to organize anything – whatever it was necessary.

I have already told you how in my early days in London, I used to be a Congressman, because the Congress party was the only platform for the Indian community. Mr. Krishnamenon was the Indian Ambassador here for some time, and he lived in this country for a long time before, and he was active on behalf of the India League, and we used to support him. In fact myself and Ayub Ali were two of his favourite fellows. We used to preside over his meetings, because he knew that we had a good following among the working class community, and with our support he could pass any resolution without difficulty. I remember I presided over many meetings of the India League, as well as Ayub Ali. Mr. Menon used to be very friendly. In the olden days, we used to be all supporters of Indian freedom. We never thought of Pakistan at that time, though Mohammed Ali Jinnah was working then, but he was not so popular at that time, and the Muslim League didn't gain much ground in the 'thirties.

I remember one incident, during the war. The Secretary of State for India had some Indian Officers. Sir Hassan Suhrawardy was in that position during the war . . . was a pious Muslim, from a learned family, highly respected in India. He visited Mecca, Arabia, and Egypt, and he was a guest of King Farouk. When the War started in the middle east, and the Axis tried to grab all the Muslim states . . . they tried to get out of the Axis.

After the month of Ramzan . . . we were celebrating our *Eid* prayers at the East London Mosque, under the leadership of Sir Hassan Suhrawardy. As usual we pray afterwards for God to give us this thing and that thing, with folded hands, as you do. Then he, leading the prayers, said in a loud voice, 'Oh Allah, give victory to the Allies!' At that time there were some Congress Muslims in the mosque – one was the Shah . . . they protested after the prayers, that, 'Why did you pray for the British? We have come for a religious function, and not to pray for the British.' They made him cry, poor fellow, he was in such a bad position, everybody was after him. Some of us being of a reasonable mind said, 'It might not be right to pray for the victory of anyone, but victory of Allies mean victory of the Muslims. The states of Arabia may be overrun at any time' . . . the grievance was that the British had been keeping us down for two hundred years. Then Sir Hassan was also explaining 'It's not that I am only praying for the British, I am praying for all those who are against the aggressors who want to attack the Muslim countries.' But they wouldn't listen to him, and then he cried, I would never forget that.

As I told you, I am from a priest family, my family are the descendants of the missionaries who came with Shahjalal of Sylhet so I have that trait in me. From childhood I have prayed regularly, read Koran and so on, so it helped me more to know Islam properly. When I first came to London I took my Koran with me and I continued to read Koran, observe fasting and regular praying. For five times prayer it is not obligatory to go to mosque, only on Friday for congregational prayer, *Juma* prayer. So we used to go to mosque only on Friday, that was the old East London Mosque in Commercial Road, now it has been demolished and they have erected this new place in Fieldgate Street.

Taslim Ali and Ayub Ali came later, in 1938 perhaps. But we ... myself, Mushraf Ali and a few others ... we came in 1936, 1935. Ayub Ali became a sort of leader, he had some medium education – not highly educated – like me or a little below me ... and in 1943 I think, we formed the Indian Seamen's Welfare League – Ayub Ali was the Secretary, I was the President. That was the first of our Sylhet people's platforms, and before that I told you I was in the India League ... I was in the Congress ... I was in the Muslim Social Club.

Then Abbas Ali came, I think 1944 or '45, and he approached me because he found that we were very popular here, and mostly the Indian working class people came under our organization – we were leading them. So he used to come after me, at that time I was owning a restaurant in Charlotte Place, near Charlotte Street, in the West End, W.I. I gave the place the name of 'Indian Centre'. Why? Because all the Indian political workers and their associates, the English gentlemen, M.P's and all that – they used to come to my restaurant and hold meetings there. I was very popular with them because at that time I used to support the Congress wholeheartedly . . . So when Abbas Ali approached me he said, 'Brother, I am approaching you because you are in a good position, but you are forgetting one thing. India will be free, sooner or later, after the war, so now is the time . . . if we do not organize Muslim League here we cannot make propaganda here, and propaganda in this country, it carries a good worth, because the whole world hears your voice. So you had better think about it, Mr Jinnah is trying his hardest to organize the Indian people.'

Assam was Muslim League . . . Assam and Bengal. Punjab at that time didn't come to the Muslim League, they had a Unionist Government under Sir Sikkender Hayat Khan, a great character, maybe English born. After him was Nawab Jeddar Saad Mohammedkizir Hayat Khan Tihana, he was from the Unionist Government they didn't support the Muslim League. They came in the fold of Muslim League later on. So Mr. Abbas was proposing to me, 'Look, everybody is coming, now they are opening their eyes. In a united India, we will be nowhere, we will always be in a minority. So they will pass all kinds of laws against us and against our religion, and we will be in a helpless situation, under majority Hindu rule.' So after some thinking, I joined Abbas Ali, and we formed the London Muslim League. I became the first General Secretary, and Abbas Ali was the President.

I was with Abbas Ali all along, we were doing various activities, receiving all the Muslim League people, but I missed Jinnah – I left this country in September 1946, and Jinnah came later, just before Partition of India and Pakistan at Independence in 1947. During the Partition time I was at home . . . working day and night. During the Sylhet referendum, I used to have no time for eating even, I had to make speeches here and there, and convince people why we want Pakistan. And since Pakistan is already established question was only Sylhet – whether we join rest of Bengal in India, or whether we join Pakistan – that was the point on which I had to speak. After Sylhet declared for Pakistan, I was unwell for some time because of all this activity. Voting was in every village, every town, every *bazar* . . . we used to have our mikes, and everything. The people of Sylhet never had any quarrel with the Hindus, but the Hindus knew that they couldn't fight it, because it will go to Pakistan – they knew, though a section of Muslims were with them, still they couldn't hold it.

In my early days in London, mostly I used to be with Hindu people. They were the cultured society – the student community . . . in Gower Street, Belsize Park, Indian clubs and all that. I used to go and mix with them, they were the people who were studying law and philosophy and medicine and all that. And journalists . . . I had a few journalists who were my bosom friends, and they were all Hindus. I never had any ill feeling, or any thought that they are Hindus and I am Muslim – I was far above these things because I used to love them and they were broadminded too, just like me. Abbas, he was a bit communal . . . as he was a business man he couldn't show his feelings outwardly . . . but inwardly he had that feeling, that Hindus are different. But me I didn't feel any difference because I felt that everyone – Hindu, Muslim, or English – created by the same Creator, and I didn't feel any ill feeling against anybody.

After – Sir Syed Ahmed Khan opened the Aligarh University, and preached to the Muslim people, that, 'You will be a slave nation very soon, you have still got time, co-operate with the British, they are the masters now'. Then he came to London and pleaded in the House of Commons, then got permission to open this University. And then through this Muslim University the Muslim scholars increased – otherwise Muslims today would have been in a hopeless situation, just like slaves. At that time the British also did a little favour to the Hindus because they were doing, what do you call that thing – 'Divide and Rule'? So they gave more preference to Hindus in Government Service and all that and some Muslims co-operated and some didn't want to co-operate and they were left behind.

I was for some time associating with Hindus and all different people. I used to go to Hyde Park . . . sometimes used to speak in favour of Russia and all that, I was turning into a Socialist, more or less – through the Hindu people, and the Labour Movement as well . . . one day, just before I became General Secretary and Organizing Secretary of the Muslim League, I was sitting among my Hindu friends, and they were all educated people. One fellow was a big hefty fellow, with a big chest, and so strong. We were discussing many things, and politics also . . . at that time whenever Indian people met, politics used to come up. That strong and stout fellow was denouncing Jinnah . . . he said Jinnah is the blighter who is keeping us down, and all that. I said . . . I won't tell you name . . . I shouldn't . . . He said, 'What! You support Jinnah?' I said, 'It's not that I am supporting him, I am a Congress man, I am with Anio – Subhash Bose's nephew.' Anio Bose, he was the General Secretary and I was the Joint Secretary. 'I was all along supporting Congress, but that doesn't mean Jinnah is not a leader. He is a leader of the Muslim community, it is a fact, and he has got a following of people behind him, don't forget that. He has got already three provinces, Muslim League provinces – that means people support him, and he is the leader of the Muslim community.' Then he said, 'How dare you support that blighter Jinnah?' and he was about to punch me on my nose. God almighty knows that I am not telling a word of a lie, and if I tell a word of a lie, may God punish me . . . I looked at my other friends, and nobody said a word. I found that they were sharing his views, sitting there so quiet . . . nobody said, 'Hey! Mister, what are you doing? We are friendly talking and discussing and you are going to punch him, what is that?' Nobody said a word, I suddenly got up, and got hold of his tie.

I am a fellow that if he wants to hit me, he could throw me about twelve yards, he was such a giant fellow and yet, how I got the strength I don't know – I got up, held his tie, and started threatening him. 'You coward, how dare you? Don't you know, I am the son of a Muslim?' This very word I repeated. It acted like a miracle . . . I don't know, if it was Act of God or not, but that fellow was shivering. And everybody was pleading . . . all those Hindu friends, 'Mr. Qureshi, Mr. Qureshi, don't get annoyed.' They thought that I am going to hit him, or I am going to finish him. I said, 'I understand you now', and since that day I had a different belief, and then I joined with Abbas Ali.

So at that time I changed my attitude – I bought the religious book, my Koran. I have got the Koran today – Maulana Mohammed Ali's interpretation, English translation and commentary – I started reading Koran . . . I started regular prayer, and even today I do . . . I became a proper Muslim. I had had a time when I didn't bother so much – I believed in God, but as regards religion, I was not so strict – I took it like this, that Islam, and Hinduism – all the teachers are different, but God is God. At that time I had a dream of my Prophet. I saw my Prophet in my dream, and I was asking him does everybody call you Prophet? Are you a real Prophet? He said, 'Well, I don't know, but if anybody call me Prophet, then they ought to know'. That was my first dream of my Holy Prophet, in whom I believe next to God. So I was a bit influenced by the Socialism and all that, but since that day, I changed. And the more I read my Koran, and the more I think of it, I think that Islam is a hundred per cent correct, and I have strong faith. In my mind I am a socialist too – if I see a Hindu, or Englishman, or Jew . . . anybody who is in need of any help, and I am in a position to help him, I will do it.

I got married when I first went back, after nine or ten years, in 1946 – 10th October. At that time at home I didn't have any money. All my life I lost money for different reasons, so I went home empty handed . . . of course I managed to take some little things, but not much. Of course they were surprised – my people expected that I would be able to give them a lot of money, but I couldn't. So my father was worried, how to get a wife for me . . . then her father was approached. They lived only four miles distant, they were landowning people, they had about three or four villages of their own – tenants. My father-in-law liked me – he picked me out and said, ' I would like to have this young boy as my son-in-law, because although he is poor I can see that he has some personality, and I think in future he has got a lot of good qualities. Money is not everything, and he is quite suitable for my daughter.' My wife didn't have much education . . . she didn't have any . . . if I say not much, it will be incorrect . . . her father was a schoolteacher, and her brothers, and also her sisters had some education . . . After the death of her mother, she lived with her mother's mother and there she avoided going to school. Since my marriage I have found her very obliging, and very faithful, and she is proud to have a husband like me.

I have to tell you the story of how I first became known, when I went back to India – as it was then. As I was politically minded, and the General Secretary of the Muslim League here and all that, whenever I used to go to Sylhet Town or Sunamganj I used to go to the college to see the students, and all the various political leaders and workers.

I used to make speeches and tell people to be more active, and that I am fully convinced about our demand for Pakistan, and I think we are going to get Pakistan very soon – but unless we are united it will be very difficult. So I used to go to different towns, and I was always busy for this business, organizing the referendum. I remember when I first went back to India through my activities all the intelligensia knew me, that I am already a leader, and they took me as a leader . . . Now and then I used to visit the *thana* headquarters. There were different offices, and the market there on Sundays and Wednesdays – so for good food or good fishes I used to go there. By going there I came in contact with different officials, they seemed to respect me, and they knew about me. Most of the Muslim people used to regard me with respect.

When I went back to Pakistan for the third time my sister died, as I told you. It was a very pathetic scene for me, because I loved my sister very dearly . . . because when my mother died, we used to always look after her very specially.

After the death of my sister, it came that there had to be *sarpanch* (local leader) elections . . . the people unanimously elected me. I was planning to come back to London, but they made me stay at home. Not only the people of my circle, but the people of the whole Jaganathpur . . . when anybody is in trouble, they don't bother to go to their own *sarpanch*, they used to come and tell me that 'you are our *sarpanch*'. While one is *sarpanch*, or headman it sometimes happens that one's area is affected with flood, and the Government gives relief, so you have to go and see how the relief is distributed. With most of the *sarpanchs* there is some corruption – they try to give their own people more than the really deserving persons, but my principle is different. I used to go early and I used to see that everything was fairly distributed, and every needy person got it.

While I was *sarpanch* for those four or five years, the Military took the food because of the corruption. The Military controlled the food of the whole district of Sylhet . . . not only

Sylhet, but other places also. The military people, who were Punjabis mostly, were in some respects better than our Bengali people – they were not usually very involved in corruption. In Bengal there was corruption in all the offices – without giving them something on the quiet, under the counter, they won't do your job. Where people are poor corruption exists – everywhere in the world, and not only because they are poor, but it has become a disease in their blood they are so habituated . . . from their environment, from their childhood. They go to schools and colleges, they read and write, they study philosophy and all that, they come here or go to America, get different degrees and diplomas but when they go back to India, or Bangladesh, or Pakistan, they forget all that and they are the same as all the rest. It is very sad. It must change one day.

When there was a famine, the military would put the food in the hands of the poor people themselves, instead of letting the Local Government people have it . . . all the officials were frightened to death of them . . . Jaganathpur was worst affected by famine, and most of the poor people were suffering. The military were coming to Jaganathpur – to visit the affected area, and distribute more food. The officers of Jaganathpur all consulted together and they said, 'He is the only fellow. We must put him before all those military people so he can control the situation, otherwise we will be in a mess.' So one day about four in the morning an orderly came to my house and said, 'There is a letter for you, from all the officers. You must come early, because you are going to represent whole Jaganathpur.'

I went very early. They told the orderly to tell me to bring my suit and everything and come as a posh man – as the spokesman of the whole area. When I went there I found about ten or fifteen thousand people, it was rainy season, and they came by boat. People were there with big ties and all – posh people, educated people, highly educated people, M.Sc.'s – in our area there are a lot of educated people – but nobody dared to go in front of the military. I was used to them – during the war I was entertaining them in my restaurant and I knew a lot of them – Captains, Majors . . . and anyway I had nothing to worry about or be frightened about . . . I was on the

right path. So when they came they asked me whatever
questions they wanted, and I answered them, in English or
Urdu. They were very pleased, and at last they said, 'Yes, the
area is really seriously affected, and we suggest that there
should be some food distributed – but at the same time as
giving the food, you should give them some work.' The work
was this, that it was rainy season, and in the rivers there was
some rubbish floating – water hyacinth – that must be
cleared. And also the roads and all that must be cleared . . .
and then the food would be distributed.

Somehow, I challenged them. I said, 'Since I am the spokesman, I must tell you and request you, that these people who
have come here to see you, and hoping to get some help from
you – some of them are starving for one, two or three days. So

first give them food, and then allot them their work – that will be better.' The officials agreed that my suggestion was correct – because they were hungry they were weak, and they couldn't work – so it was better to first give them food. I wasn't wearing a suit – I just had a *lungi* – or even shoes on my feet, because it was raining, and thousands of people came without shoes. Just I had a shirt and *lungi* – that's all. The officers said, 'Oh, goodness, why did you come like that? Today you are representing the whole *thana* – you should have come with tie and good suit.' I said, 'No! today is not the day for good suits. The people of the whole area are starving, and if I come here as a posh man, I cannot tolerate it. If I could have helped them to get food by wearing a suit, that would be different, but while I know that the people are starving, and some are ill clad, I am not going to come here as a posh man.'

Somehow these big bugs – Generals and all – they took it differently . . . I am trying to organize for the people, and I am one of them, and I can speak English and Urdu, and how can a fellow in my position come in these sort of clothes – that is beyond their expectation. So one of the officers got up enough courage to speak to them, and told them, 'He is a very religious man, he hates Communism, but he believes in real Islam – he thinks that while the whole country is starving and hasn't got proper clothing, he should dress like this.'

Sometimes I used to meet people from different villages and they used to say, 'You must come back, we will support you, and you will not need to spend anything out of your own pocket.' During the election campaigns nowadays for chairmanship people will spend a million – they know how much they can make out of it. But in my case they said that you need not spend a penny, because we know that you will not make a penny. It has been the same in my London life – I was the head of quite a number of organizations but there was no election and no voting – the people chose me unanimously and that is the way I wanted it. If anybody said that they had no faith in me I wouldn't have done it, so the people always requested me unanimously. Some villagers told me that, 'During the day of Resurrection, we will ask you the question in front of God, that you had the capacity to do some good work but you failed to do it.' I said that, 'Well, I am a poor man, I wish that I could afford to do it, but I can't.'

I can tell you, in my *elakha* (constituency), after I left the *sarpanch* people used to pray to me to resume it, they said things are different now, but I couldn't. I gave up the *sarpanch* because I am not a wealthy man – I have got my family to look after – and those other people could afford to be in that position, who would have to spend something out of my pocket, and sometimes I can't afford it.

Even now we are not rich, though we are not quite so poor as when I first came to London . . . my life has gone on political work and all that – if I wanted to sum up I should say I have been a failure, in a material sense at least.

When the Bangladesh struggle started, I had gone back to Pakistan again. I have been all along associated with the Hindus – I never made any difference between Hindus or Muslims, or any nationality, or any religious faith. I myself was not so religious . . . at one time I became quite irreligious, but . . . I changed . . . and then Abbas Ali convinced me that we must establish Pakistan. I lost my second restaurant because of my Pakistani activities. So I am a fellow who made some sacrifices for the establishment of Pakistan. Why? Because if we had a majority Muslim state, at least we would be free to perform our religious duties, and one day we might be able to establish a *real* Islamic state – there is no Islamic state existing in the world today, though Saudi Arabia in name of Islamic state cuts the hands off thieves, and makes a few attempts to show that it is real – but that is not Islam. While people are poor they build so many palaces. We who supported Pakistan . . . we had in mind that in the future, one day we would make a real Islamic state. One who sacrifices himself for a principle, it is very difficult for him to change overnight.

When I sold my restaurant in 1967, I went back to Pakistan with the idea of becoming an M.P. – that was my lifelong aim. But when I went to Pakistan, I saw that the situation was quite different . . . the people of East Pakistan had turned quite differently, they didn't think of Pakistan any more . . . and there was some justification, I wouldn't deny that. I have seen here with my own eyes the treatment of Bengalis by the West Pakistani officers, in the Pakistan Embassy itself . . .

The Pakistanis were all the *burra sahibs* (big shots), and they had Bengalis to serve them only in clerical jobs. But the big posts were all held by West Pakistani people. In the Military, in all the Government posts, there was some unfairness. It was a sad thing, not only due to the Pakistanis' fault, Bengalis were at fault as well. This separation business came, but we never hoped for that, and never sacrificed for that, and never worked for that.

When we were building Pakistan, Awami League were not the only party, there were also other Muslim organizations – Muslim League, Jamaat Islami, Nizami Islam, and others. They all had for their demand in the election that we must have East Pakistan self sufficient, and that there should be two commands – one in East, and one in West . . . It is my firm belief that it was not Mujib who framed his constitution. That constitution of six points was framed in India, and they tried to incite the people of East Pakistan that we must separate from the rest of Pakistan, because we have been ill-treated – we have been robbed of our things – Pakistan is the gainer. I know in some respects we had been the losers, but still, separation business is a dead dog. Somehow if we could have kept Pakistan intact it would have been better.

I am sorry to say that the whole world – not only India and Russia, but some sections of Britain, America, Israel – they didn't look at Pakistan very sympathetically. They liked to see Pakistan crushed, because Pakistan had taken a different way, and wanted to make an Islamic state. Before Pakistan came into existence the people of Turkey and Saudi Arabia were enemies. The Turks hated the Arabs because they thought of them as slave people, you know. The Ottoman Empire – they lost it because of the treachery of the Arab states, so they wouldn't sit with them – they thought it beneath their dignity. Muslims are poor throughout the world, but once you are united, you have got some strength and Pakistani leaders – Ayub Khan, Bhutto and others, they worked hard for that.

Russia had some grievance as well, because Pakistan used to co-operate with America. They used to call Pakistan their 'younger brother', until after a time Pakistan wouldn't obey when they wanted to establish a zone in Pakistan . . . because the Americans never take anybody for a friend unless they have got some interest. Otherwise, although it was a big country, India would never have dared to attack Pakistan – because they had a fight in 1965, and they saw the strength of Pakistan – but it was Russia and every other country who gave much help against Pakistan, and that is why India managed.

As I have told you, in the early days it was only single men who were here. People have brought their families quite recently, but one lady came along before . . . I think this fellow is no more, but his wife is still in London . . . He was a soldier in the Second World War, and the Government gave him opportunity – they gave him free ticket, and he brought his wife. At that time, Ayub Ali had a restaurant, *Shahjalal Restaurant*, in Commercial Street, and the fellow brought his wife there first after he arrived in London. She was looking to hide somewhere, where there were other women, and she asked, 'Where is the kitchen?'. So she went to the kitchen, and she found that also full of men . . . Later other people began to bring their families . . . first the business people. It was very strange for those ladies – the atmosphere was very different. But now there are hundreds of women here, and they don't feel so lonely – they can go to each other's houses and pass the time, and don't feel so much homesick – and a lot of them want to come to London.

I applied to bring my wife and children over here in 1964 or '66, and immediately they saw my family, they never asked any questions – they just looked at me and the children, and they gave it. I obtained an entry visa, but at that time my wife was pregnant with my daughter, so she hesitated and said, 'I don't feel like going now', so due to her disinclination I decided to leave it for a while. That entry was granted to me in the time of Pakistan, but then everything was changed, so in 1975 I had to apply again, and we had to appear before the immigration officer . . . but we didn't have much difficulty, and they came here in 1976.

My children – for their future – they must establish business here, because in this country business is more permanent than there and to think of establishing in Bangladesh there is always corruption and crookedness . . . so those who survive must be more crafty and have long experience. And the other business men, out of jealousy, always try to do down the fellow who comes from London with some money and establishes a business overnight – so he finds more difficulty. Of course not everyone – there are some people who gain experience and open very good business in Dhaka, Chittagong, where the people have more money. But

Mr. Qureshi   *Tom Learmonth*

ordinary people like my children have to struggle – and as they are brought up here in this country, in a straightforward way – they cannot cope with the Bangladesh business people. They say one thing and mean another thing inside their heart, and simple people like our children who are brought up here will face more difficulties there to establish themselves. So it is better that they do business here, and go to Bangladesh to enjoy for six months or a year.

When I first came here, I never imagined that I would spend most of my life here, and bring up my children here – in those days nobody thought like this.

Among those who came to England early were some of the educated people who liked to see the world, and thought that they could earn money if they came to England or America . . . what could they earn in India? Say a graduate, maximum he could earn was one hundred rupees at that time, and that hundred rupees for his whole family – it's nothing. So some of the adventurous people, like me, wanted to see the world at the same time as seeking their fortune. Later . . . during Surrawardy's time, when the Queen went there . . . they gave free vouchers. The Queen gave a promise to Surrawardy that these people are down and out, and they need to go some-where else to work, to other country to earn some money, and that is how the vouchers started. Anybody who applied for a voucher would get it. Later it was stopped, because the whole country was about to come. The vouchers had no connection with Navy service, so some people came who had nobody here. They saw that the early people – those who were in the Navy and settled before and after the war – whatever work they did, they sent some money . . . and it was quite good money . . . a little money here is a great deal there.

Then after the war, when Pakistan was established, we or-ganized the Caterers' Association, and through the Caterers' Association we managed to bring thousands of people – they used to give vouchers only to those who are to be employed by a Pakistani restaurant. I was general secretary of the P.C.A.

Sylhet has been altered in every respect by the people coming to London. The only way in which they have gone down is educationally, because probably some of the students, on whom we had counted for great things, have been more at-tracted by money. After passing M.A or B.A, they don't get a job where they can earn more than five hundred rupees a month, but here they can earn a thousand or more in a week, so very many of them have left Bangladesh and come to London – for work rather than education. Of course there is the college in Sylhet, and it is full – but still a good number of the boys left Bangladesh to come to London, and they do make money.

The people have gained from coming to London, and for those who have got good business here, and can go to Bangladesh every year for a few weeks' holiday, it is very

PAKISTAN CATERERS' ASSOCIATION
IN GREAT BRITAIN

OUR REF. _____

YOUR REF. _____

28, GOODGE STREET,
LONDON, W.1.

TO WHOM IT MAY CONCERN

Mr S. A. M. Qureshi, General Secretary of the Pakistan
Caterers' Association and Mr Jorif A. Hussain, Assistant
Secretary, have been authorised, by a resolution of the
National Executive Council of the Association, to represent
the Association in all related affairs as its official
spokesmen and to negotiate with proper authorities in
Pakistan with a view to secure support in favour of the
various demands of the Pakistani Catering community in
Great Britain.

For & on behalf of the
NATIONAL EXECUTIVE COUNCIL

Israil Meah
Israil Meah
President

London,
30th Jan.1961

good. But for those who have not been successful it is very hard – leaving their wives and children, and struggling here . . . in a way they are missing many things which they would have enjoyed at home . . . but how could they enjoy? If they had remained in Bangladesh, whatever money they are earning now – at least their wives and children and other people are able to have a better standard of life, which they could never imagine to give them if they remained in Bangladesh and never came to this country . . . It is a very hard life – sometimes their parents die and they can't see them . . . it is the same problem in all poor countries, it is not their fault.

The country I have always admired and preferred . . . England is the best country in God's Creation. It was not so before, you know. It was after the Second World War that people got all these opportunities, and these opportunities were all created by the sacrifices of the Labour Movement. Those fellows like George Lansbury and all, they sacrificed, and people are always enjoying the fruits today . . . if there is any Welfare State in the world, it is here. They are trying to cut it now, but still, will you find these benefits anywhere else in the world? No! I have got two cousins in America, and what they write to me . . . anything . . . medicine . . . My cousin's wife was in hospital for the delivery of her son and they had to pay for everything. For education you have to pay everything, but here the Government provides everything for the people . . . what more could one expect? America may be rich, but what people of this country have gained, the world in general would never get.

Mr. Syed Rasul

Mr. Rasul's home in Mirpur is far from Sylhet. But his account echoes the experiences of seamen from all over the sub-continent.

I was born in Mirpur (Pakistan) 1914 . . . joined the Navy in 1933 . . . came to Birmingham 1944. I can't tell you much history because I don't speak good English – if I make mistakes please correct them when you write it.

I come from a village in Mirpur. When I grew up – about sixteen or eighteen years old – I came down to Bombay to start work in the ships. You have seen our country – you know that village people are very poor. I had only enough land to grow a little food – not enough for next season food. When I first came to Bombay I went alone, on the train. I was young, I wanted to go somewhere, for adventure. I said to my friends, 'I am fed up with working on the land and having no money – I want to go somewhere.' My friend said, 'best go to Bombay and get a job in a ship.' so I said, 'Alright – I will go.'
   That time I didn't have enough money to go so I asked my mother, but she only had eight or ten rupees – so I said, 'Alright, give me that.' At that time the fare was twenty-one rupees, the journey took three nights and two days. When I saw the train I thought, 'How marvellous!' I didn't take a full ticket to Bombay – when I passed Delhi my ticket was finished, but nobody came and checked, and I got to Bombay. When I passed through the gate, the gate-man asked for my ticket. I said, 'I won't lie to you – I have come from Jhelum.' He said, 'Oh, God, you have come from Jhelum to Bombay?' I said, 'Yes'. He said, 'That is twenty-one rupees, and you have only paid six rupees and something.' I said, 'Well, I haven't got any more money.' He looked in my pockets and every-where, then he said, 'Alright – I will keep you on the station for three days and you do some work, and after I will let you

go.' I said, 'Yes, that's alright, but you will have to give me something, because I haven't had food or drink for three days!' He laughed, and he said, 'Alright, go – but don't do it again!' Then I went.

I had never seen a city before – different from village . . . different from town. I knew where my people lived, and I asked someone how to go there. When I got there I saw my people, and I was happy . . . I think I lived in Bombay about one year. I lived in a lodging house – didn't pay anything then . . . the lodging house people used to say, 'When you get a ship, you come back and pay.' It was not a good place – twenty men lived there together.

I used to get little jobs around the town – carrying some-thing at the station. Then at last, someone got me a job on the

. . . then at last . . . a job on the ship .   PLA Collection, Museum in Docklands

ship. He gave me twenty-one rupees for the month. Oh my God, I was so glad to get that money! I felt very happy inside, because I had a lot of money. They took me down, down inside the ship – such a strange place. I was frightened, because I never seen anything like that before. Then the sea started to go . . . up and down . . . *OH MY GOD*! I think for six or seven days I didn't have a cup of tea or food or anything – still I had

... loading and unloading ...   PLA Collection, Museum in Docklands

to work. I swore to God – 'When I get back to Bombay, I am
never going to leave my home and family again!' The other
men looked after me – they said, 'Don't worry, after a few
days the sea will go smooth.' It was true – I was alright when I
got used to it.

I came to England. My God – first time I see these people, it
was marvellous! People were very polite, they asked me,
'Where do you come from?' Very sweet talk, I can't explain,
it was different from the way we speak – very respectful.
I stayed around England a month. From London the ship
went to Liverpool – then to Glasgow – loading and unloading
cargo.

Then we went to Africa – it took a month to go there. When
I saw the African people I was surprised! I never saw people
like that before. I had a feeling inside that I really believed in
God. Looking at my own skin I see one thing, then in England
I see different, then in Africa different again. Honestly I sat
by myself for ten or twelve hours, not speaking – like, you
know, meditation. One bloke said to me, 'What are you
thinking?' I said, 'I have been thinking of God, and what He

had made.' That bloke just laughed and said, 'What are you talking about?' I explained to him, how all the people are made different, different skin, different hair.

It was good in Africa, the fruit was very cheap – orange, mango, banana, Most of the shops were run by Indian people, African people didn't have shops. We stayed there fifteen or sixteen weeks, going to different ports: Johannesburg, Mombasa, Capetown.

Then we went to Liverpool, then straight back to Bombay. Then I thought I would go home, so I asked my *serang* to let me go. He said, 'You would be silly to go now – you have only been away six months – you haven't earned enough money yet. The ship is going for another year – to America, then England, then back to India – you better go again and earn some more money, then go home. I still said I didn't want it, but he told me to think about it for two days and then I decided to stay with the ship.

The next cargo was from Bombay to New York . . . My goodness, it was a long route, and a very dangerous sea! Then I saw the American people, very good people. From New York I came to Baltimore, then to England – Newcastle – then back to Bombay . . . whole journey took one year and three months. It was Lister line. When I got to Bombay, I felt very rich, plenty of money – I spent some of it for clothes. I felt very happy – thought it would be very good when I saw my family. When I saw my father and mother, my mother was crying – I said, 'Why are you crying? I been to Bombay and brought plenty of money.' I stayed in the village for one or two years – I was very happy because I had money to buy more food.

The first time I had a cup of tea was when I came to Bombay. In the village we used to drink only milk, and water. Only if somebody was ill they would give . . . something like a cup of tea – it was like a medicine. In Kashmir they make it with salt – they don't use much sugar there. Then I needed money again so I went to Bombay, to a ship called the *City of Calcutta*. By that time the war had started – no light in the ship, no smoking on deck, if anybody saw a light they were to tell the bridge. After we had been in Port Said three days, there came at night a siren . . . 'Woowooowooowoo . . . !' I think at that time you weren't born, you haven't heard it. Then fire and light, one ship went down, then another – I think three people dead from that ship – two people died in my ship because something blew up.

We stayed there eleven days to take on cargo, then we came to Malta – very dangerous place Malta – seven ships altogether. Four days we didn't see anything, then on the fifth night about five in the morning I saw an aeroplane, coming nearer – very dangerous. I put on my life jacket. Then – oh my God, the bombing started – three ships hit – all the men lost. We had to leave our ship and go in small boats because there was a cargo of cement, and there was some damage and the ship went low in the water, but then we got it in the dock, slowly . . . slowly. That place is called Tobruk. We were in our dark ship for two nights – all night *'Bomb! Bomb! Bomb!'* – one ship after another going down. Then somebody came and examined our ship and said, 'Alright – not much damage, better move from there' . . . very big ship, the Calcutta. I went then to Alexandria – very slowly – I think it took six or seven days to get there. When I got there I was very glad to be in safety. One bloke from my district came on the ship. He asked me where I came from, and when I said, 'Mirpur' he was very glad. He was in the Army, he had been at the Front, and I went back to Bombay, and I thought I would not go in another ship until the war finished.

SS City of Calcutta, Capetown. 1946   *National Maritime Museum*

But when I went home my father said, 'How long will you stay here?' and I said, 'Until the war finished.' He said 'No – no good – now the British need everybody for the war. Although you are my son, I will be glad if you are killed over there.' So I understood very well what war was like.

When I went back to Bombay I got a job very quickly, on a Polish ship – Polish men. Of course I couldn't understand their language. We went to Africa. All the ships from different countries gathered in one place, a hundred and eighty of them, and all sailed together on one night. For sixteen days we sailed very peacefully, no trouble. Then came some submarines at four o'clock in the morning, on the seventeenth day. I came upstairs, listening '. . . *Whooooo . . . BOOOOOM* . . . !' it was light so I could see . . . the front of the ship went up, the back went down. All the men were saved – after two or three hours in the boats a Navy ship came and picked us up. About ten or twelve ships were sunk in the convoy.

Some ships were going to Glasgow, some to Newcastle – mine came to Liverpool. After three days I left the ship and went to Birmingham. A lot of people were doing that then. It was weekend, so we were allowed on shore. I went to the station and took a ticket for Birmingham.

When I came there, I had nowhere to go – no address, nothing. I was sitting in the train – very quiet and miserable. One lady and gentleman were there with their child, and the child said, 'Look Mummy, there is a black man! Black man!' You know, little kiddies – they say whatever comes into their minds. The mother kept saying, 'Stop it, he is a gentleman!' Then he would stop for a while, then again start. Then I said, 'I don't mind, he is only a little kiddie, and after all my skin is black.' She said, 'Oh – thank you very much.' The father gave me a cigarette, and asked me where I was going, and I said, 'Birmingham.' After get out in Birmingham, they ask me if I got address, I say, 'Yes.'

And show address. They say, 'You wait here in front of the station, while I take my wife home, then I come back.' He came . . . he bought a tram fare . . . he took me to house where I got address – one of my village men. One English lady opened the door and said, 'You want Karamat? Come on in.' Then I sat down and that gentleman gave me ten shillings, said, 'Here you are – buy cigarettes.' Then he went. When night-time is coming and everybody came home from work, I see my own people, and I very glad. My village man bought me some clothes, and took me to the Labour Exchange. I had to report to the Police Station too, and they gave me a card and said that I would get an identity card after two years. Everything was rationed.

Well sometimes these days, I think to myself that I would like to go back to Pakistan. Sometimes I feel I have lived half in this country, half in my own country. I am sixty-seven years old now, and when I was nineteen or twenty I started working in this country's ships – now if I have finished with my own country, and this country doesn't want me, where could I go? It's marvellous, isn't it!

I have been back three or four times since I have been in England, but not for long – only a few months. I married twice – the first wife was the same age as me, second was younger. The second one I married in 1957 after the first one died. She is here now. I don't remember when the first marriage was – I was very young then, about twelve years old. I tell you true – because very poor people live over there, some people got too many daughters – not happy. I think she was the same age – we used to play together at home and not think of each other as husband and wife – later of course it was different. When I married in 1957, I had gone home for the first time after twelve years in England. My mother said, 'You may be away a long time – you'd better take your wife with you.' So my wife came in 1957, and my daughter was born, August 12th, 1958, in Marston Green Hospital. My wife was one of the first Pakistani ladies to come here. She stayed here three years, then her father wrote and asked her to come back. Her father died, and she stayed to look after her mother. She stayed there sixteen or seventeen years. I made them passports, and they came back here three years ago.

I still have my land over there – it is still my own country. I think I am fifty-fifty, half Pakistani, half British. My wife asks me sometimes what I want to do, and I say, 'I don't know.' I like it there, but it is very difficult to live. I had a

farm but the Government took the land to make a reservoir –
a dam. They didn't give me compensation. Things are different in my country – some people are good but a lot are corrupt.
If you are a quiet person you won't get compensation – you got
to make a lot of fuss, go to court. It is different in this country
– things are properly organised. The children of my second
marriage are here in England – those of my first marriage are
in Pakistan, they are alright.

Oh yes, I am very glad I came to England, because . . .
although it's different from how it used to be, still . . . better
than my country. I think that for every one thousands people
who don't like us, there are a million who do. I love this
country, and I would like my children to stay here. The young
generation is too different. I still think of my own country –
my mother and father – because I was born in a different life,
lived in a different life but my children don't know any of
that. I still think of all my family, my mother's family,
father's family, everybody . . . my family is so big . . . My
brother lives over here – I say to my son, 'You must go to your
uncle's house.' He says, 'Who is my uncle?' I say, 'He is my
brother.' 'Well, he's your brother, not mine.' I say, 'Don't be
silly.' but he doesn't want to know . . . these days it's all
different. He says, 'Daddy, you are my family, I am your
family, that's all.' I say, 'Alright, if that's what you want.'
     Only my mother is in Pakistan now. I think she is a
hundred years old. I saw her three years ago when I went for a
holiday. She was sewing . . . she had a needle and cotton – I
thought she was too old – couldn't see. I said, 'Mother, give it
to me, I will thread it for you.' I tried for four or five minutes,
but I couldn't see well enough to do it. She said, 'Come on, give
it to me!' I said, 'How come your eyes are still good?' She
laughed! After she said like this – 'When I was born in this
country, it was a poor country, very hard living, but I never
worried. Still, at the end of my life, I never worry. What I get,
I eat and I am happy. If I don't get it . . . still, I am happy. You
make money – you say, "Oh I want nice furniture. Nice
furniture," You say, "Oh, I buy television, I buy radio, I buy
this, I buy that . . ." Don't think anything, don't think
building, furniture, nothing. When the water comes too deep
one side, move to the other side.'

I started in a factory making aeroplanes – I was just a sweeper – they gave me about five pounds a week. I stayed there for a year, and then the war finished. There were a lot of Indians working there, as labourers. Most of the workers were ladies because it wasn't heavy work. Everybody was very good to me, they used to say, 'Hello Charlie! You want a sweet? You want a cigarette?' At that time I had no girl-friend. They used to ask me to go to the shops for them, to buy cigarettes or sweets – they would write down what they wanted because I said I wouldn't be able to tell the shop-keeper. When I brought the cigarettes or sweets, they would give me some. At lunch break, at ten o'clock, they would ask me 'Do you want something?' I said, 'No.'

At that time people were very good, but at this time . . . I think myself the reason for the change is like this. At that time the British ruled India – people felt that we were all one family. They knew that we were poor people living over there, and they wanted to be good to us. Now people say that we are dirty people, who have come to rob this country – they feel differently about us. It changed about ten years ago – bit by bit, it started to get worse. People don't remember that India was part of Britain. In those days there were many people who had been in India – as rulers or in the Army . . .

After the war, the aircraft factory closed – we were only four men left. That time I couldn't speak English, I said, 'Everybody finish, why me no finish?' He said, 'You good man – you do good work.' I am like that – if I start something, I don't stop – I must finish it. When all the work was nearly finished there was just one foreman – he said, 'You come at eight o'clock, I come at seven o'clock.' Then after two or three months the work there was really finished, and he sent me to another factory making car parts. I worked there about nine months, working on the machine.

Those times were very different – not much money, but you got everything and you were very happy. I got five pounds a week, enough for food, clothes, drinks, pictures, and still I saved three pounds – sent it to Pakistan. Before I retired, I was getting about a hundred and twenty gross – food, electricity, rates, gas, clothes – before the war you could buy a best suit for ten pounds, now you pay a hundred pounds for rubbish! I couldn't save any money – couldn't even live. I bought my house in 1953. I think that even if the world isn't finished by war, people are finished. All over the world, people are fighting. In the old days, I could walk on the street at twelve or one at night – if you met anybody on the street, say 'Hello, John!' These days, when it gets dark at seven o'clock, I don't go out. If my wife wants some tea or sugar, I say, 'No – leave it 'til the morning.' I rather save my life than get the shopping! It's miserable. I have a pension now – if I went to Pakistan I could get it sent. It's alright – not bad living, not good – I eat twice a day anyway.

If you look at the outside of anything, you can't see what the inside is like, and it's the same with people. Some people are bad – stealing and killing because they haven't got money – others, if they haven't got money, well they haven't got it. People should think of the next life – this life is not long. When they are young, people don't understand, what is life. Then they come to fifty or sixty, and they understand a lot, then come to eighty, and they go round again – like a child . . . very short life. People don't understand. Sometimes my daughter says, 'Daddy, you think in such a different way.' I say, 'My life is different, my age is different. I can't go worrying, what I am going to get – whatever I get is good. If bread, then bread is good, if *chapatti*, then *chapatti* is good.' I spend my time now thinking. I got nobody who understands my thinking – this life now is too different. I don't say that I am good – when I was young I did a lot of bad things. My bible says that when you are dead, everything you did is there, in front of you. I still believe that everything will be there – what I did, what I said. When I go to anybody's house – my friend or my relative – I like to sit and talk a little – what is life about, what is death. But when they see me coming they say, 'Bloody hell, here comes that old fool again!' So I have stopped going now.

I can tell you what changed me. When I came to England, for about four years I didn't do anything wrong, just went to work, nothing against religion. Then after four years, one bloke – Pakistani man – said to me, 'Come on, let's go out.' He took me to the picture house – I think the ticket was two shillings and sixpence.

Then when we came out he said, 'Where are you going?' and I said, 'Well, I'm going home.' He said, 'Oh, don't be silly, let's go to the pub.' So that was the first time I went to a pub. I waited at the door. He said, 'Why don't you come in?' I said, 'What do you want to go in for?' 'Oh, only to buy some cigarettes, and maybe a lemon drink.'

So I went in with him, and he asked for some drink – I didn't know what it was, and when it came it was too bitter. I said, 'I thought this was lemon.' He said, 'Oh, it is, but there's something mixed with it.' So I had that drink, then another one, then I started to feel something. He bought me four or five and then we came out, and I couldn't walk properly – and when I started talking . . . couldn't stop yapping.

Then next day, oh my head! Then that night, he said, 'Do you want to go out?' I said, 'Oh no, not that place!' Then after that I used to go sometimes – then I did a lot of bad things . . . I was like a gangster – for ten years sometimes good, sometimes very bad.

Then I met Frances . . . she had been married to a Bengali, but she left him and she went back to her mother's house. One time I went to the General Hospital because I got a fishbone stuck in my finger. When I went to the Casualty Department at Fiveways Hospital, she was there – sitting on the bench. She said, 'Where are you from?' I told her and said, 'Why do you ask me?' So she told me that she had been married to a Bengali man. When she had finished seeing the doctor, she waited for me . . . I said to her, 'What about your husband?' and she said, 'Oh – he wasn't really my husband, I was only living with him, and now he's gone back to Calcutta.' And so after a few weeks we started living together . . .

She lived with me for six or seven years, but then she told me she was still married. When she told me that, I really cried. She said, 'What's the matter with you? In all these years we have lived together, I never saw you cry before.' After that I was not happy about us living together, and things weren't right between us. And then she started to get sick in her mind – sometimes alright, sometimes not. After nine months, she was much worse, and they put her in the hospital, and then she got even worse – she wouldn't wash herself or brush her hair. One day, I went to see her, and she recognised me. I said, 'Listen Frances, I'll ask the lady to give you a bath and brush your hair, and then I'll take you home with me.' I took a dress, and everything. She said. 'You wait outside while I bath – talk to me through the door.' I took her home – when we came to the street I said, 'What number do you live at?' and she said, two hundred and ten. She was very happy to be home. That time there was no television. I got a radiogram, and played it for her. But then after one night, she got very upset again, and I had to take her back to the hospital. I used to see her nearly every day . . . she is still there – I see her sometimes still.

After that, I started to think, and I changed my way of living. Everybody makes mistakes, and their life goes up and down, that is God's idea.

Well, that's my story – I expect you think I'm a barmy old man!

The Hooghly River, Calcutta   *Sandy Hedderwick*

Mr. Attar Ullah

First thing . . . I was born in Sylhet. My post office called Unagaon . . . in the countryside, far from Sylhet . . . Habiganj, near Chittagong side – nice area. If I go home, I go to Dhaka, stay a night – go to Sylhet, stay a night . . . take a coach . . . then at last a boat to go to my village . . . it's a very long journey.

I first came to the ship in 1939. I was very young – I came to Calcutta about seven times and the Shipping Master said I was too young, so I would go back home again, but I was longing to get in the ship. I wanted to go for money – other people worked there before me – my father worked in the ships. They all got nice things – clothes, a little bit of money. My father came to England in the First War. When I was a little boy he used to talk to me in German – they kept him in Germany for six months as a prisoner.

Bengali people worked very hard on the ships. There were no Indians at all before – all Bengali people – all from Sylhet. The British liked them because they worked hard – people from other districts didn't want this kind of job. My people like to do a hard job and get money for it . . . they were hungry. Indian people lend money with interest. My people – Muslim people never do like that – no good. Some people over there in India – you borrow one rupee, got to give two rupees back – that's the kind of business they live on. My dad told me that Muslim people can't do that kind of thing, that's why my father . . . my grandfather all going away to work . . . When I came to this country, Britain owned all India.

I got a ship by a lottery, four or five young boys put their names in a ball of paper, I picked up right one – got the job. The English people did it like that in the Shipping Office. All the young boys came wanting jobs, just they wrote all their names on paper, and some plain, and making little balls of paper, just put it on the table, 'You pick it up, and you, and see which one the winner.' Only me and another boy got paper with cross and we win. That time I was maybe twelve or thirteen years old. When I came to this country, my age was no more than sixteen – of course I told them I was older. My moustache wouldn't come – I kept shaving . . . this way, that way – now I'm getting old I can't believe what I used to do when I was a young boy!

PLA Collection, Museum in Docklands

First ship came to Tilbury, then back to Calcutta. Then I went back to the village, to see my mother and everybody and take them some money. My father had died when I was eight or nine, and I had younger brothers and sisters. My mother couldn't stop me going again – when somebody been out in the world, you can't stop them. My next ship was sunk. We were not allowed to show a light – the weather was very bad, there was another passenger ship coming out and our ship bumped into it, and my one sunk completely within quarter of an hour. Too many people died . . . how can I forget it? two hundred soldiers, eighteen English ammunition people, Captain and all . . . my crew, about eighty people lost – only thirteen left alive, and one of the captains – not one soldier or anybody – all dead.

I was in the water, swimming around and holding onto a piece of wood. I was in the water twelve hours before somebody came and picked us up. They brought me back to Bombay. My mother had heard that this ship had gone down, my uncle had told her everybody was dead. I saw one fellow from my village, my relation, at the Shipping Office in Calcutta. We thirteen survivors were all sitting there together no clothes hardly, just the company had given us trousers and singlets in Bombay, to travel to Calcutta and my skin was all black from the sun and the salty water. This fellow was eating *betel* nut. I called him by the relationship name. He looked at me and he said, 'Oh your uncle's here.' He went and found him outside and said, 'Your sister's son has come!' When my uncle saw me, he started bloody crying! And he cried this much! Everybody thought I was dead . . . I can see it now . . . on the ship, and too many people going in the boat and the Captain talking in Hindustani, saying *'Pani pagro, Pani pagro, . . . jump in the water! No time to put out the boats or the ropes!'* But they didn't listen to him. I jumped into the water, about twenty or fifteen yards down, then came up drinking salty water . . . ugh! . . . and very cold. That was the sort of life I had in the ships. When I went home, somebody told my mother I was coming and she jumped in the water! And cry, cry, cry! I said, 'Don't cry, I'm alright – God giving me long life. Don't worry that I'll die. I'll only die if God takes me out – nobody else can kill me.' Then my mother said, 'I'm not giving you again to go back to the ships.' I sad, 'Yes mother – I'm going back to the ship.'

I went back, and signed in the Shipping Office for a ship to Glasgow. The ship went to Alexandria – so many ships torpedoed. I have seen many people die in wartime – some with no head, some with no leg, some ships blown in half. In Liverpool Docks you would see half a ship lying in the water, and people lying on the rail, with no head or no leg you know, where a bomb had dropped. I never forget in my life what

. . . skin all black from sun and salt water . . .

happened in wartime . . . My mother's brother died in a ship,
they never knew where his ship went. When you went in a
ship, you could write a *bata*, with the name of your wife, or
mother or father, to send them ten or twenty rupees from
your wages every month, they didn't give big money if somebody was killed. Even I have still got two thousand rupees
owing in Calcutta, after I came to England – I wasn't going to
go back just to get that!

I was supposed to pick up another ship in Glasgow to come
back to India, but instead I took a train to Cardiff, where I had
the address of one of my countrymen who was working under
English articles. We were three together on the train. When I
got to Cardiff I went to my countryman, and I was shivering.
There was a fellow there I'd been together with in Calcutta,
and he said, 'Wait a minute – I'll bring you some clothes.'
He brought me a sweater and everything. It was snowing.
Oooh, this much snowing! I sat right down by the fire in the
coffee bar. My countryman had the coffee bar – he said, 'You
sit down by the fire.' There weren't many of my countrymen
in Cardiff then.

I stayed there for a couple of weeks, and then people said, 'Do you want to go in an English ship?' I said, 'No, I don't want to go on the water any more – I'm finished with the water' I'll stay in this country and get some work.' So these two fellows said, 'You better go to London.' I said, 'How can I go to London, I don't know anything about London.' They said, 'Alright, don't worry.' They put me in a train – too many soldiers going to London. These fellows talked to the soldiers in English, and one of them said, 'Don't worry I'm going to Aldgate, I'll take him over there.' They looked after me in the train and brought me biscuit and everything, but I was frightened, because I couldn't understand them when they said anything. Just took biscuit and ate. When we got to London it was night-time. This soldier took us and said to the landlord. 'Here you are, this is your man, I've brought him from Cardiff,' I remember the house – number 13, but I can't remember the name of the road – somewhere off Brick Lane.

I went into that house, and I stayed in London six months, and then this fellow said, 'Don't stay in London, you should go to Birmingham, I know two or three of our countrymen there, I'll send you to them.' So I came here, and started looking for a job.

When I came to Birmingham, there were two houses in Bath Road, one house in Saltley, two houses in Belgrave Road, two in another road – that was all the Bengali houses. I was walking down the road, and an English girl, maybe eight or nine years old, kept turning round and saying, 'Mum, Mum, look at the black man! Look at the black man!' I laughed – after all I am a coloured man. The mum didn't take any notice, and the girl kept pulling her mother's arm. 'Mum! mum! Look at the black man!' I just couldn't help hearing! The lady looked at me, and her face was so red, and she gave a wallop to the girl. I said 'Don't hit her – she's only a baby and she can't understand – please don't hit her!' Then she laughed too, and I said to the little girl, 'Yes, that's right, I have got dark skin.' That sort of thing used to happen then, but not any more. You never used to see a black man then.

I started work in a factory – very hard work. A man came to Birmingham and said, 'Do you want to go to the ship?' I said, 'I'm not going in the ship. I'd rather go to jail.' He said, 'What about your company?' I said, 'I've finished with my company, they don't want me.' Then, this Police Sergeant writing to my company in Glasgow, and they answered – 'We can't do anything with this fellow, it is the Indian High Commissioner's business.'... that was the Clan Company. Then the Sergeant, Sergeant Low, he said, 'Bloody hell, nobody wants you! You're an Englishman now!' The next year I got an identity card and everything, ration book and everything... Sergeant Low got it all for me.

After, when I got a house, lots of people left the ship and came to me, and the Police used to come and say, 'Is this man in your house?' I would say, 'No.' I had a registration book, but I didn't put these people's names on. One fellow came with his *Nollie* and everything, and he was shaking in front of the Police, and I put my arm round him, and told him to sit down ... That Sergeant, he liked me too much, he wanted me to marry into his family! I said, 'No, I come from very poor people. I don't want to marry here.' Afterwards when the other Police had gone out to the car, he said, 'Attar, I know that fellow is here, but I won't say anything, but you better be very careful, in case somebody reports him!' That fellow has got plenty of money now, he's a restaurant owner, he saved twenty-five thousand pounds and bought a restaurant. He never gave anything to me.

So then I got my identity card, and I could get a job. The card was to prove you were British, not Spanish or something. When you went to a factory, you got a gate pass with your name and your check number – you had to show it to the Policeman on the gate every morning. One morning they caught five spies at the rubber factory where I was working. One time I took my identity card to the insurance for proof of my identity, and after three weeks they didn't give it back, so I said, 'what have you done with it?' and they said, 'Can't find it, must be somebody hide it or something.' I said, 'Well, I can't do anything without it.' Now I got a British passport, and I don't need that card any more. My passport got my name, my father's name – all that.

In that first factory, I had a job with the furnaces – had to get something out of the fire, and punch it. Very hard job, nothing in the ship was ever as hard as that. I said, 'Give me my cards,

I can't stand this job.' They said, 'You won't get your cards unless you make a case.' I said, 'Case?' They said, 'Yes'. So I left, and told some lies and got a new card – I said I lost that one!

Then I went to another place in Birmingham – very bad – the foreman was a very bad man. Any hard job, he always gave it to me. There was an English fellow called 'Ginger' – because he had ginger hair. We used to cut plates together, sixteen thousand in one day – him on the front of the machine and me on the back, and we had too many iron plates still left to do. Next morning another hard job came, some very heavy plates to cut.

The foreman came and said to me, 'You go on that machine.' I said, 'No, I'm not going, I haven't finished this job yet.' Ginger didn't say anything, he just put his thumbs up. Then the foreman pushed me, and I said, 'Why you done that?' And I got very temper and I swore at him, 'You bastard, you wait!' His brothers and nephews were all there on the machines. I got a crowbar, and the foreman ran into the office, and I ran after him and called out, come out and fight! His brothers were all looking, but I wasn't frightened. I said, 'You're the foreman, why do you push me? I want to know.'

Then he rang the head office, and two men came, and said, 'Come on now son, what's the matter? Why are you so angry?' and I said, 'You ask this fellow, yesterday I cut sixteen thousand plates and I haven't finished, but the foreman wants to give me another job. Why not give it to somebody else? I refused to do it, and the foreman pushed me.' I said, 'Give me my cards please, I don't want to work here any more.' It was Fisher Ludlow, a big company. They said, 'Alright, you go to another side,' I said, 'No, I can't work here, I want my cards, or I want that foreman to come out and explain why he pushed me.' Then they said, 'Come on, in the wages office.' I said, 'Alright', but before I went, I said to the foreman, 'if I don't get my cards, I'll be back to see you.' Went in, sat down, got my cards.

Then I got a job in a nice place in Coventry. Gaffer and manager – everybody liked me. They said, 'Don't let the foreman bother you, you're the foreman of your work.' My job

was to look after the fire. They let me bring another man too –
they said, 'You bring somebody you can understand and work
with.' I worked there eight years.

For sixteen years I worked on the night shift for nine
pounds or ten pounds a week, forty-eight hours on a machine,
power press operator, piece work, five pounds ten shillings.
That was before you were born! Cor, you could live well for
that money! Get a big chicken, eight or ten pounds, for two
shillings, and for ten bob (fifty pence) you got a carrier bag
full of more food than you could carry. Ten Woodbines, fourpence ha'penny, with a box of matches. Then seven pounds
ten shillings was one hundred rupees, now it's nearly four
hundred rupees. Money's changed everywhere, England,
Bangladesh, everywhere, people don't worry for money now.
Before, if somebody had one hundred pounds that was too
much money – now one hundred pounds, even one thousand
pounds no good – just like a penny. Everybody says, money's
no good now – we can't live on money.

Too many girls in the factory, and everywhere I went they
used to say, 'Hello,' this and that. I would say, 'No, don't
bother me!' I suppose I was nice looking. I never went out with
any of them. I left two factories because of girls.

In Coventry I worked in an American rubber factory, with
about two thousand girls, and only me, one Bengali man.
There were two sisters, one in the canteen, and one in the
factory, making planes . . . every day one fighting plane went
out from there. She loved me, but I said, 'No, I don't want it.'
I was a little bit shy. Every morning she used to give me cake,
biscuit . . . apple, orange, banana, or something. I said to my
foreman, 'Do something for me!' He said, 'What can I do?'
I said, 'Just get a cardboard box and put my name on it, and
write that please if anybody wants to give me anything, they
can put it in that box!' They used to fill it up, and the English
people used to eat it.

Then one morning I was going into the factory on my
pushbike, and a car came right in front of me, and I thought,
'What the bloody hell is that?' Then I saw this girl, she had
brought her father and mother, brother and all, in a car. The
mother said, 'My daughter has been talking about you, she
loves you too much' . . . and this and that. I said, 'Alright!'

I went into the factory, and I was thinking, 'Bloody hell!' She brought me tea, and I said, 'Why did you tell your family about me and bring them to the factory?' She said, 'They wanted to see you.' Then I went to the boss, and said, 'I've got to go to London, I had a telegram.' . . . Liar talk, you know! He said, 'Alright, you can go on Friday.' I never said anything to anybody.

On the Friday, I got my pay, and I got out. Then some other people said, 'That girl is looking for you everywhere.' I didn't like her – one night she kept me out till two o'clock in Coventry Park. She was crying, I never touched her body or anything. I said, 'Why are you crying?' You know, she loved me this much, inside, and I didn't love her this much.

After I left there, another girl used to come in the house where I lived, and tell people. . . . 'I want Attur!' She was very young – a nice looking girl. One day I was with her and she said, 'You take me wherever you want to go.' I said, 'No, I'm not going anywhere . . . staying here.' Then I left Coventry and came to Birmingham. This girl had only a mother. One Bengali man came and gave his wages to her mother, because he wanted to marry this girl, but she didn't want him. I didn't know why she liked me and I thought maybe after a few months she would stop liking me and go to somebody else. I didn't want any of that, so I came to Birmingham.

Here I lived with my friend, and he said, 'There is one girl Joyce who never talks to Bengalis. Her sister is married to a Bengali, but never talks to anyone. If anyone talks to her, she turns her head away and says, 'Don't talk to me, I don't want to listen to anyone.' This fellow said, 'I'm going to put you to this house.' I said, 'No, I'm not going.' He said, 'Yes, you are.' Then we went to his best friend – her sister's husband and said, 'There's a nice young boy living in my house.' The sister's husband came and said, 'I like you – you are my younger brother – you come and live in my house, there is one room for you.' So I said, 'Alright – I will come.'

So I lived in Banner Road, Belgrave Road side, in her sister's house. She never spoke to me, she never even looked at me. I looked at her sometimes – she was very nice looking. Sometimes I would go in the back yard . . . see her in the window. But when she saw me she would move away. I thought inside, 'Alright, you can bloody well come to me slowly – not yet.'

Then a big fair came to Aston – Lakey Hill. Everybody was going, the sister and her kiddies were crying to go to the fair, but her husband said, 'No, I'm not going, take Attur with you.' Then all the kiddies called, 'Uncle, Uncle!' I said, 'What?' 'Uncle going to the fair.' I said, 'No, not me, your father can take you.' 'No, Father won't go, you got to take us' – they were cheeky you know. Then their mother came, her name was Gladdy. She said, 'Attur', I said, 'What?' 'Take me and the kids to the fair.' I said, 'No, why can't Ali go?' Then Jawid Ali came, and said, 'You are my younger brother, you take them.' He got no bloody money, gambler man, so I had to spend my bloody money! . . . He was such a gambler man – he still owes some money to me! So I said, 'Alright, don't cry kiddies.'

There was a restaurant there at the fair, and a few of our Bengali people were there, and wives and kiddies, you know – English mothers, half-caste kiddies. This family had brought sandwiches from home, and were sitting at the table eating them, nice table, white tablecloth and everything. The waitress came, and I said to the sister . . . I said, 'Come on Glad, you give the order – order what you want to eat.' All these other people had brought their sandwiches and cup of tea from home, but I ordered food there. After we finished, the waitress brought the bill on a saucer – five pounds. I got a five pound note, put it on the plate, and another two shillings tip. The sister was worried, but I said, 'Never mind, only once coming.'

When we got home, Gladdy said, 'Go on, take her to the pictures, and take my little girl too.' 'Her daughter's name was Julie, she's grown up now, over thirty.' Joyce said, 'Oh, I'm shy, don't want to go.' Gladdy said, 'Go on, he spent so much money, why not go with him?' So we went. She was clever, she put her niece in the middle – she on one side, me on the other, I thought, 'Oh, well, that's alright.' Picture finished, we go home.

Next morning I'm going to work, had an accident with a truck, my finger in a terrible mess, blood everywhere. Foreman came running, 'Oh quick, come in the surgery!' I went in the surgery, they dressed it and everything, but oh, so much pain, you know!

In the night I was crying from the pain, fever and so dry, I wanted a glass of water. She came . . . bare feet – nobody could hear her, and she said, 'Why are you crying?' I said, 'I've got a very bad fever and I want a glass of water.' She put her hand on my head, and said, 'Oh dear, your head's like a fire.' She brought the water, and I drank it, and she said, 'Is there anything else you want?' I said, 'No, nothing' and she pinched one of my cigarettes and smoked it, but I never said anything.

I went to the hospital with my arm, and they said, 'It's very bad, you can't work.' She had just started work – at that time you left school at fourteen. One day I was in the backyard with my arm in a sling and she laughed. I said, 'Don't you bloody laugh!' . . . and then she started to talk sometimes.

She was going to work in the morning, and I went to a Greek cafe. The owner was a Greek fellow, he had a wife and five kids – they liked me too much. They wanted me to go and live with them, and I could have anything I wanted in the restaurant, no charge. As I couldn't work with my bad arm, I would go down to the restaurant about ten a.m. and sit there, and have a cup of tea.

Rain! This much rain, oh it was pouring down! I sat there all day. She finished work . . . went home . . . did something wrong, I don't know what. Then her sister's husband shouted at her, and I think he smacked her . . . I don't know. Anyway she didn't eat anything, just ran outside in all the rain. Looking for me. She ran in the Greek cafe, all wet. She had long hair, hanging down . . . all wet. She had water pouring off her. I said, 'What is this?' I took her in the back room – the Greek fellow gave me a towel, and I rubbed her dry, sat her by the fire, took her coat and hung it up. I said, 'Have you eaten anything?' She said, 'No.' I told the Greek fellow, he gave her and she ate it.

Talk, talk, talk! Everything was in her sister's house – my identity card, my ration book, my case, my clothes – everything . . . Ten o'clock, I said, 'Hey, come on, aren't you going to work tomorrow?' She said, 'No, I'm not going to work.' I said, 'Come on, let's go home.' She said, 'No, I'm not going back there.' About eleven o'clock we went for a walk . . . she said, 'Come on , let's go in the park' . . . one o'clock, in the night. I said, 'Come on – won't you go back to your sister?' She said, 'No – you take me anywhere you go.' I said, 'I can't take you just like that.'

Then I thought of another house, Bengali man married to English lady, so I said, 'Let's go to Mary's house.' She said, 'No – I'm not going to Mary's house.' So we walked across Birmingham to my relation's house in Saltley, arrived at two o'clock in the night – woke up my cousin. He said, 'Come on, what happened?' . . . Snowing, this much . . . I said, 'I'll explain later, let's get warm first.' He gave the fire and we got warm, and then he cooked some food. Then he said, 'There's a double bed in my room. You two go there together, and I'll sleep down here – explain in the morning.' I said to her, 'Joyce – you're making a big mistake.' 'No –' She said, 'Wherever you go, I will go.' I said, 'You're too young, your sister and mother will make a case against me.'

Next morning, I left her to sleep and went out to find out what was happening. Found out sister looking for me, and sister's husband – looking for me to kill me and so on. Next morning I found her mother has made a case against me, and all going to police. I and another two fellows going to sister's house, and police came. Police ask me, 'Why you take a young girl?' I say, 'What do you mean?' He say, 'You know you take her too young, and get a court case against you, you might get six months' jail.' I said, 'You won't give me any jail.' He said, 'Oh?' Sister said, 'Look, he's not frightened of you!' I said, 'Look here, policeman, you look after your street, and don't bother about me. If anything happens to me, the Police Court will see about it. Whatever happens, I'm satisfied, you can't do anything.' Then the sister said again to the policeman, 'Look, how he talks to you – he's not frightened.'

Next morning, I said to Joyce, 'Look, your sister's making a case. Do you want to go back to her, or what do you want to do?' She said, 'No, you take me wherever you want to go.' I said, 'Come on then, let's go to the Police Station.' Going to see the Sergeant, my friend. When we got there, I said to her, 'Now you sit down here, and I'm going to see someone.' When I went in the office he was on the telephone and told me to sit down. As soon as he finished on the 'phone he came and said, 'What's wrong Attar? Something happen to you? Don't worry about anything! While I'm still here in the Police Station, nothing going to happen to you.' I told him all about this case coming through, and how I left everything in her sister's house – my ration book, identity card – everything.

He said, 'Where is this young lady?' I said, 'I brought her here.' He said, 'Bring her in then.' He took us in one room all three together, and he said, 'Please – go to your sister, go to your mother, leave Attar alone. He comes from a different country – he is a poor man, don't bother him, go to your family.' She said, 'No – I am not going to anybody. I would rather cut my throat than go back to my family. I don't want anybody, only him.' So many questions he asked her – she didn't take any notice. After he said, 'Alright Attar, take her home, and tomorrow morning you come here yourself, and bring another fellow with you – your countryman.'

So next day I went, taking my cousin with me. When I got there he gave me a typewritten letter, and said, 'Go to Banner Road Police Station, leave this on the desk and come out. Don't wait there, just leave the letter and come out.' So I did what he said.

Her sister's husband was looking for me, to fight . . . and another fellow, Mary's husband, said, 'Listen! Attar's got relations here, if you hurt Attar his relations will kill you. Everybody will be on Attar's side, only you and your wife on your side – I'm going to Attar's side.' Then he calmed down a bit.

Next morning her sister saw me in the street and she held my neck and cried in the road. I said, 'Bloody don't cry in the road! What's the matter? Tell me what's happened?' She said, 'Come on in my house, Attar please.' I said, 'Alright – if you want me to come, I'll come.' She gave me a cup of tea and said, 'Please, bring my sister back and live together in my house.' I said, 'Your sister won't come – I would, but she never would.' She said, 'If you come, my sister will come.' Like this, she cry, cry, cry – she said, 'My sister with me all the time seven or eight years – where I going, she going with me, and I love my sister.' So I said, 'Well – I'll ask her if you like.'

After, I went back to the house, and said, 'Joyce – your sister wants you to go back' She said, 'No, I won't go back.' I said, 'What do you mean, you won't go back – it's your family.' She said, 'No, I won't go – you go.' I said, 'Are you sure? . . . Alright then, I'll go.' So I start packing, she keeps looking – I said, 'What are you looking at?' She said, 'Well if you're going, I have to go too.' I said, 'Yes, I know!' So we called a taxi, and I took her home.

We lived at her sister's house for a few months, I worked in a new factory – night shift. Then I bought a house for sixty-eight pounds from an old Pakistani man – a private landlord's house – I bought the lease. My first daughter was born in her aunty's house. Her name is Subiya, she was born in 1944. We lived together for twenty-five years, and then she left me and went to live with somebody else. That case went to the High Court – I got all the High Court papers to say it was finished. She is still in Birmingham. Oh yes – we were married. Her mother and father and sister wouldn't give permission, but Sergeant Low brought two ladies off the road, to sign as witnesses.

We had seven boys and three girls. She left them all with me, and I looked after them. All the kiddies are big now, bigger than me. One boy works as an electrician in the factory where I used to work. The big son lives with his mother, and the older daughter. They all got good jobs – good places to live. They all come to see me. Sometimes I see their mother at the kiddies' houses, but I don't bother. I went home in 1972, for the first time and married there – my wife and two kids are coming here soon – Raquib Ali at the Advice Centre has arranged their entry and everything – the Immigration Office have been very difficult.

I still like Birmingham, but it's changed too much – much worse. Before, everything was nice – people talked really friendly – now very rude, very dangerous. When I came first, there were no buses, only trams and trolley-buses. Now they knocked down so many houses, so there's room for the buses to move around. The roads are better but the people are worse. I don't want to go to Bangladesh, I have spent all my life here.

Mr. Hasmat Ullah

Just don't say anything, and I will count from one to a hundred for you in German, and Greek. Ein, zwei, drei, vier, funf . . . acht und neunzig, neun und neunzig, hundert! Now Greek . . . ena, dio, tria, tessera . . . I learn it in six months in Greece.

My first ship, Calcutta to London, 1939. From London, going to Africa – Australia, come back again, come to troop-ship. Thousands of people from our villages that time in the war for the British. That time, of you want to buy a good horse, two hundred pounds, if you want a man to kill, you paid him eighteen rupees a month! British people didn't like the heat, but our people would work in the heat. Indian people win the war for the British. We were stuck in Greece for six months, refitting, then in April 1941 the ship was sunk by a torpedo, and we were taken prisoner, to Germany.

. . . refitting . . .   *P&O Group*

I was in the camp nearly four years . . . I show you what we used to do all day, marching up and down, exercise. Counting every twenty-five men. Digging with shovels, hungry, no good, no water. Dinnertime, everybody queue, with small small cup. Soup comes out of the pot. All water, hot water . . . two hundred pounds water, and two pounds meat . . . maybe one bath water, one pound *dal.* Oh . . . very hungry . . . fifteen days, fourteen days, two days, seven days, no eat anything. Fleas, nits, cockroaches . . . six months, no wash, no bath, no anything. After six months, going in a boiler, getting good wash. I was all bones, no meat . . . people would fight for potato skins! . . . There was nobody looking after the conditions in the camps. I was lucky . . . long life . . . I went home again. My friend Afsur Miah, living round the corner now, we were together in the same ship, and Punjabi men escaped. They dug a hole with screwdrivers and hammers, like from Aston to Saltley. For punishment, we had to stand outside all day, for six days. They used bloodhounds to hunt them . . . plenty trouble . . . You had to help yourself in the camp, nobody look after you. After a few days you might manage a bit of food, another week manage a bit of water to wash.

This was the letter the Company sent me, in the camp.

Clan Line Steamers, 1 Clive Street, Calcutta. Air mail, p.o.w post. Hasmat Ullah, son of Shohor Ullah, coal trimmer, ex S.S. Clan Cumming p.o.w no 7332, Lager Bezeichnung M Stammlager 4D 2W, Germany . . .

We are pleased to advise having received a letter written by your father Shohor Ullah to you, details of which are as follows . . . 'We are all well here, by the grace of God, your sister of Sinajpur gave birth to a male child in the last Agrahayen. All your relatives and villagers are well. We have received 4 or 5 letters from you after your detention, but for the last 7 or 8 months, we are not getting any letters from you. We wrote a letter to you on the last Churcha, on receipt of a letter from the shipping office. We have received a letter from the shipping office this day, to write to you again. We applied for allowance last year, and received a lump sum of rupees 282, last Baishak. This year's allowance for 23 months and 15 days. I wrote 15 or 16 letters to you, but I do not know whether you have received them or not. I am maintaining the family. They wish to get good news from you. Signed, Shohor Ullah, Village Keshabpur . . . '

We shall be glad to render you all the assistance we can to keep you in touch with your relatives and friends in India. Meanwhile, we trust you are well. pro. James Finlay and Company.

After the war the bombing planes came and took us out – brought us to England – a military airfield, don't know where . . . no people there. Then we went to the ship, want to go home see father, mother, if they alive or dead . . . if we want to, we could stay in England. British Government then was good, but now, with this government . . . When we got back to Calcutta, the government gave us this paper:

It says, 'Message of welcome, from the honourable Sir M. Azizul Hoque, C.I.M., D. LIT, Member of the Governor General's Executive Council, in charge of Commerce Industry, and Civil Supplies Department, on the occasion of the return to India of Indian seamen, ex-prisoners of war . . . to all of you who are returning to your home country, after years of trials, tribulations, and privations, I extend a most hearty welcome on behalf of the Government and people of India, and I rejoice to see you back again. By your sufferings and by your sacrifices, you have not only served the cause of this great war, but you have also served the millions in your country and the Commonwealth who are working in the same cause, namely to win this war. Indian seamen have a most proud record of their achievements and glory for centuries past. In this war they have again proved that they are second to none in their patience, in their enduring power, in their valour, and in their heroism. You have earned your good name and fame, as also the good name and fame of our country. On this day of your most happy return to the shore of your land, I welcome you most heartily, and I pray to God that you may have good health and prosperity in your lives.

You will now return to your families and children, and be happy in their midst. As in the period of your stay in the enemy land, so in your life's journey and career, may providence protect you from all difficulties and evils . . . M. Azizul Hoque, 28th June, 1945.'

After the war they gave me a thousand rupees, from the Indian government. That time the world was poor, the war left the government very poor. You have been to our country, not much food, but food is fresh, plenty of vitamins. Our country very bad weather, hot and wet . . . My father is a hundred and two years old . . . when he starts talking about his life . . . we think he's dreaming . . . penny for this, penny for that . . . he just thinks, my God, where I was before – and where I am now! . . . You see these days . . . very hard, America and everywhere – waste money, throw away money but not give to the poor people . . .

After the war I stayed at home for a few years, then made a passport, when Mr Macmillan was Prime Minister and our President was Ayub Khan, they made a case to Mr Macmillan, 'Do you need any labourers? We have unemployed too many.' That time many many people took vouchers and came to this country.

So then I came to Leeds, because I had a friend there. It was there that I had an accident in a factory and lost my arm. Three times . . . first time two fingers . . . second time three fingers, . . . third time half my arm. It was a leather factory. That was in 1970. Since then, I can't work. I got my compensation . . . but still we are poor.

Mr. Abdul Wahab

My home is in Sylhet, Chhatok *thana,* village Hohirpur. I was born in 1914. I went to school in the village, up to class five. My father died when I was very small, my elder brother looked after me, and I had lots of uncles and aunts – many people to love me.

When I was young there were English people in Sylhet, in the tea gardens. I have never seen a tea garden, only from the train going to Calcutta. It was never necessary to go to the tea garden. . . coming to London was necessary.

I went to the ship because I was very poor – no work, no money in my village, or in Sylhet district. There were many Sylhetti men in Calcutta, Kidderpore. I went to Number Nine Dock. Calcutta was very big – many people. I saw Aftab Ali in Calcutta, very good man. His home was somewhere in Ballaganj.

I have been in many ships . . . first ship before Hitler's war – Calcutta to Hamburg – Clan Line . . . I was a fireman. All Sylhetti people in engine-room crew. Hamburg, New York, London. The work was terribly hard – many men died of heat. That time see London . . . not stay.

We had to fight for the British in the war because otherwise England would be finished. No – I wasn't afraid in the war.

In the war I went to many places in the ship . . . Africa, Arabia . . . so many places. In Africa I saw wonderful fruit.

When I ran away from the ship in London, we were seven men . . . the police caught the others. It was night time. God helped me, and I got away.

First job in London in restaurant, then come to Birmingham, working factory – British Tincan . . . then other factories . . . now I am retired . . . I am very sick now. My wife came only a few months ago.

Before 1947, I was Indian . . . that time India alright, then after I was Pakistani . . . Pakistan alright, then after 1972 I was Bangladeshi . . . now Bangladesh alright. I never made British passport – not like. I don't think I could get one now.

I have three sons and three daughters in Bangladesh, and two sons here, they are at school. I have made enough money in all these years abroad to buy a little land in Chhatok. When I am better I am going home, and my sons will stay here.

Ten men from my village work abroad. When I go home I say that it is good here – there is money, and work and – *maya* _ yes, *maya* . . . everything is good here. London is better than Birmingham. Why? Raj-rani London (Royal London!)! I came here because there was more work, in London there were few factories, few jobs . . . this was the industrial centre.

England used to be much better than it is now. In those days people were very friendly, but now Bengali people get attacked – not so much here, but in London. One reason is because there are too many Sylhetti people, and they don't know English. I went to Brick Lane for the demonstration after Altab Ali was killed. We marched to Hyde Park. He came from Chhatok, he was a very good man.

My pension is ten pounds forty-one pence a week. We live in one room in this rented house. If I went home, and I got my pension, I would be quite rich with ten pounds forty-one pence – that is four hundred *takas* – but here I am not rich. I can't afford to go home now. My son is going to school, then he will work here.

I have had a good life, I am happy, but my son will have a better life.

'*Those nameless thousands have no memorial,*
they are perished as though they have never been . . .'

We were called from a distant land,
Counting the waves of
Thirteen rivers and seven seas
With hopes for a better life.

'*Trades Union*' by Abdus Salique

Notes

Books and other written sources are given here in full for the first reference, usually with title (in *italic*), author or editor (with surname or family name in **bold**) and publisher, followed whenever possible with place and date of publication (in brackets).

A number of quotations from seamen have been included in these first chapters. Some of these quotations are from the life stories but others are from the transcripts of taped conversations which have not been published. These remain in the possession of the Author.

(Home)

References for pp 1-14:

1   **Shah Abdul Majid Qureshi.**
2   *The Background of Assamese Culture,* Raj Mohan **Nath.** Dutton (Gauhati).
3,4   **Nath,** op. cit.
5   **Shah Abdul Majid Qureshi.**
6   **Haji Taslim Ali,** (unpublished transcript).
7   *A History of Sufism in Bengal,* Prof. Md. Enamul **Haq.** Asiatic Society of Bangladesh (Dacca, 1975).
8   *The Annals of Rural Bengal,* Sir William **Hunter.** Smith (London, 1868).
9   *Anecdotes of an Indian Life,* the Hon. Robert **Lindsay.** From Lives of the Lindsays vol.III, ed. Alexander **Crawford** also in *Oriental Miscellanies,* various authors. Wigan (1840).
10-28   **Lindsay,** op. cit.
29   *History of the Indian Tea Industry,* Sir Percival Joseph **Griffiths.** Weidenfeld (London, 1967). For an up to date report on the British Tea Estates of Bangladesh, with a short historical background to the conditions for tea-workers see also *Tea and Justice,* Dan **Jones**. Bangladesh International Action Group (London, 1986).
30   *A Tea Planter's Life in Assam,* G. M. **Barker.** Thacker (London, 1884).
31   **Mr Ashraf Hussein,** (unpublished transcript).
32, 33   **Shah Abdul Majid Qureshi.**
34, 35   **Haji Kona Miah.**
36, 37   **Shah Abdul Majid Qureshi.**
38   **Haji Taslim Ali,** (unpublished transcript).

(Going to the Ship)
References for pp 15-30:

1 **Mr Nawab Ali.**
2 *An Essay on the Diseases Incident to Indian Seamen or Lascars on Long Voyages,* William **Hunter** M. D. Press of the Honourable East India Company (Calcutta, 1804).
3 **Hunter** (William, M. D.), op. cit.
4 *The Muscles of Empire: Indian Seamen and the Raj.* Prof. Frank **Broeze.** International Commission on Maritime History (Bucharest, 1980).
5 *Lascars, the Forgotten Seamen,* Conrad **Dixon** (in *Working Men Who Got Wet,* ed. R. **Ommer** and G. **Panting** – *Proceedings of the Fourth Conference of the Atlantic Shipping Project*). Maritime History Group, Univ. of Newfoundland (St. Johns, 1980).
6 **Dixon,** op. cit.
7 *The Asiatic in England: Sketches of Sixteen Years Work Among Asiatics,* Joseph **Salter.** Seely, Jackson & Halliday (London, 1873).
8-11 **Salter,** op. cit.
12 **Dixon,** op. cit.
13 *A Victorian Shipowner,* Augustus **Muir** and Mair **Davies**. Cayzer Irvine & Co. (London, 1978).
14 **Shah Abdul Majid Qureshi.**
15 *Our Merchant Seamen,* Govt. of India (1947)
16 *Our Asian Crews,* M. **Watkins Thomas.** From *About Ourselves* (P&O company magazine). P&O Group (London, 1955)
17 *A Sea Affair,* Capt. D. G. **Baillie**
18 **Baille,** op. cit.
19 **Broezé,** op. cit.
20 **Dixon,** op. cit.
21 **Muir** and **Davies,** op. cit.
22 **Haji Kona Miah**.
23 **Shah Abdul Majid Qureshi.**
24 **Mr Ashraf Hussein,** (unpublished transcript).
25 **Haji Taslim Ali,** (unpublished transcript).
26, 27 **Shah Abdul Majid Qureshi.**
28, 29 **Haji Taslim Ali** (unpublished transcript).
30 **Mr Syed Rasul.**
31 **Mr Kamal Ahmed,** (unpublished transcript).
32 *History of Pakistanis in Britain,* Kathleen **Hunter.** Pakistan House (London, 1962).
33 **Haji Taslim Ali,** (unpublished transcript).

(The War at Sea)
References for pp 31-38:

1   Anon.
2   **Haji Nesar Ali.**
3   *The Clan Line in the Great War,* Archibald **Hurd.** Clan Line Steamers Ltd.
4   *Merchant Shipping and the Demands of War,* C. B. A. **Behrens.** HMSO (London, 1955).
5   *In Danger's Hour,* Gordon **Holman.** Hodder & Stoughton (London).
6   **Mr Attar Ullah.**
7   *The Cruel Sea,* Nicholas **Monsarrat.** Penguin (London, 1970).
8, 9   **Mr Attar Ullah.**
10   **Behrens,** op. cit.
11   **Mr Hasmat Ullah.**
12   **Mr Abdul Malik.**
13   **Mr Nawab Ali.**
14   **Haji Kona Miah**
15   **Holman,** op. cit.

(London)
References for pp 39-58:

1   Anon.
2   Anon.
3   Anon.
4   **Shah Abdul Majid Qureshi.**
5   **Mr Sona Miah.**
6   **Mr Nawab Ali.**
7   **Shah Abdul Majid Qureshi.**
8   **Haji Kona Miah.**
9   **Mr Ashraf Hussein,** (unpublished transcript).
10   **Haji Kona Miah.**
11, 12   **Mr Ashraf Hussein,** (unpublished transcript).
13   **Mr Nawab Ali.**
14-16   **Shah Abdul Majid Qureshi.**
17   **Mr Nawab Ali.**
18   **Hunter** (Kathleen), op. cit.
19, 20   **Mr Nawab Ali.**
21   **Haji Kona Miah.**
22-24   **Mr Nawab Ali.**
25   **Haji Nesar Ali,** (unpublished transcript).
26   **Haji Kona Miah.**

27   Anon.
28, 29   **Mr Israel Miah,** (unpublished transcript).
30   **Mr Abdul Malik.**
31   **Mr Israel Miah,** (unpublished transcript).
32   **Hunter** (Kathleen), op. cit.
33-36   **Shah Abdul Majid Qureshi**.
37   **Mr Israel Miah,** (unpublished transcript).
38   **Shah Abdul Majid Qureshi**.
39   Quoted in **Hunter** (Kathleen), op. cit.
40   **Shah Abdul Majid Qureshi**.
41   **Haji Nesar Ali,** (unpublished transcript).

(The Next Generation)

References for pp 59-65:

1   **Haji Nesar Ali,** (unpublished transcript).
2   *Address to the Bengal Cabinet,* Aftab **Ali.** Indian Seamen's Union (1937).
3   *Report on Seafarers Conditions in India and Pakistan,* International Labour Organisation (1949).
4   **Mr Abdul Manan.**
5   **Mr Nawab Ali**.

Suggestions for further reading

The written sources of references quoted in this book,
together with other relevant reading, have been included in a
short booklist. Some of the older titles listed in the booklist are
now long out of print but many of these may be found in
appropriate libraries, particularly those of the India Office in
Blackfriars Road (London SE1) and of the School of Oriental
and African Studies, University of London, in Malet Street,
WC1.

Adams, C. E. *They Sell Cheaper and They Live Very Odd.*
British Council of Churches (London, 1977)
Ali, Aftab. *Address to Bengal Cabinet.* Indian Seamen's Union
(Calcutta, 1937)
Ali, Mohsin. *The Bengali Muslim.* Pakistan Publication
(Karachi, 1971)
Anand, Mulk Raj. *Two Leaves and a Bud.* Orient Paperbacks
(Delhi, 1937)
Asian Women (various authors) *Breaking the Silence:
Writing by Asian Women.* Centerprise (London, 1984)
Baillie, Capt. D.G.O. *A Sea Affair*
Bangladesh, Govt. of. *Sylhet District Gazetteer.* Govt. of
Bangladesh (Sylhet)
Banton, Michael. *The Coloured Quarter.*
Barker, G.M. *A Tea Planter's Life in Assam.* Thacker
(London, 1884)
Behrens, C.B.A. *Merchant Shipping and the Demands of War.*
HMSO (London, 1955)
Berger, John & **Mohr,** Jean. *A Seventh Man.* Penguin
(London, 1975)
Bethnal Green & Stepney Trades Council (various
authors). *Blood on the Streets: A Report by Bethnal Green and
Stepney Trades Council on Racial Attacks in East London.*
(London, 1978)
Bhattasali, Nalini Kanta. *Coins and Chronology of the Early
Independent Sultans of Bengal.* Heffer (Cambridge, 1922)
Bradley, Birt. *'Sylhet' Thackeray.*
Broeze, Prof. Frank. *The Muscles of Empire: Indian Seamen
and the Raj, 1919-1939.* International Commission of
Maritime History (Bucharest, 1980)
Burke, Thomas. *Limehouse Nights.* Grant Richards (London)
Chaudhuri, K.C. *History and Economics of the Land System
in Bengal.*

Chisolm, Nick; **Kabeer,** Dr Naila; **Mitter,** Dr Swasti; **Howard,** Stuart. *Linked by the Same Thread: The Multi-Fibre Arrangement and the Labour Movement.* Tower Hamlets International Solidarity & Tower Hamlets Trade Union Council (London, 1986)

Collins, Larry & **Lapierre,** Dominique. *Freedom at Midnight.* Panther (London, 1982)

Deakin, Nicholas. *The Vitality of Tradition.*

Dhondy, Farukh. *East End At Your Feet.* Macmillan Educational. (London, 1976)

Dhondy, Farukh. *Come to MeccA.* Armada Books (London, 1978)

Dixon, Conrad. *Lascars, the Forgotten Seamen (Working Men Who Got Wet — Proceedings of the Fourth Conference on the Atlantic Shipping Project.* ed. R. **Ommer** and G. **Panting**). Maritime History Group, Univ. of Newfoundland (St. Johns, 1980)

File, Nigel & **Power,** Chris. *Black Settlers in Britain, 1555-1958.* Heinemann Educational Books. (London, 1981)

Finlay & Co. *Seamen of Bangladesh.* Finlay & Co. (company magazine)

Firminger, Walter Kelly. *Bengal District Records, 1770-85.*

Fryer, Peter. *Staying Power: The History of Black People in Britain.* Pluto Press (London, 1984)

Gait, Edward Albert. *History of Assam.* Thacker, Spink & Co. (Calcutta & Simla, 1926)

Gordon, P.R. *The Khasis.* United Publishers (Gauhati, 1907)

Gordon, Leonard A. *Divided Bengal: Problems of Nationalism and Identity in the 1947 Partition.* (Journal of Commonwealth and Comparative Politics Vol.16 No.2, July 1978). Cass. (London, 1978)

Griffiths, Sir Percival Joseph. *History of the Indian Tea Industry.* Weidenfeld (London, 1967)

Hartmann, Betsy & **Boyce,** James. *Needless Hunger: Voices from a Bangladesh Village.* Institute for Food and Development Policy (San Francisco, 1979)

Hartmann, Betsy & **Boyce,** James. *A Quiet Violence: View From a Bangladesh Village.* Zed Press/Institute for Food and Development Policy. (London/San Francisco. 1983)

Haq, Prof. Md. Enamul. *A History of Sufism in Bengal.* Asiatic Society of Bangladesh (Dacca, 1975)

Hayat, Abdul. *Mussalmans of Bengal.* Zahed Ali (Calcutta, 1966)

Holmes, Colin. *Immigrants and Minorities in British Society.* (in *Britons Old and New,* V.G **Kiernan**)

Holman, Gordon. *In Danger's Hour.* Hodder & Stoughton

Hunter, Kathleen. *History of Pakistanis in Britain.* Pakistan House (London, 1962)

Hunter, William (M.D). *An Essay on the Diseases Incident to Indian Seamen or Lascars on Long Voyages.* Honourable East India Co. Press (Calcutta, 1804)

Hunter, Sir William. *The Annals of Rural Bengal Vol.I.* Smith (London, 1868)

Hunter, Sir William. *The Thackerays in India, and Some Calcutta Graves (London, 1897)*

Hurd, Archibald. *The Clan Line in the Great War.* Clan Line Steamers Ltd.

India, Govt. of. *Our Merchant Seamen.* Govt. of India. (1947)

International Labour Organisation. *Report on Seafarer's Conditions in India and Pakistan.* ILO (1949)

Jones, Dan. *Tea and Justice.* Bangladesh International Action Group. (London, 1986)

Labour Research Dept. *Black Workers, Trade Unions and the Law: A Negotiator's Guide.* LRD Publications (London, 1985)

Leech, Kenneth. *Brick Lane 1978: The Events and Their Signifcance.* AFFOR (London, 1980) (Stepney Books 1994)

Lees, William Nassau. *A Memoir Written After a Tour Through the Tea Districts of Eastern Bengal in 1864-65.* (Shillong, 1948)

Lees, William Nassau. *On the Cultivation of Tea in India. Allen (1863)*

Lindsay, The Hon. Robert. *Anecdotes of an Indian Life.* from *Lives of the Lindsays,* ed. Alexander **Crawford,** and in *Oriental Miscellanies.* Wigan Publishers (1840)

Little, K.L *Negroes in Britain: A Study of Racial Relations in English Society.* Kegan Paul, Trench, Trubner & Co. (London, 1947)

Mason, Philip. *A Matter of Honour: An Account of the Indian Army, its Officers and Men.* Macmillan. (London, 1986)

Middlesbrook, Martin. *Convoy.* Allen Lane (London, 1976)

Monsarrat, Nicholas. *The Cruel Sea.* Penguin (London, 1970)

Muir, Augustus & **Davies,** Mair. *A Victorian Shipowner.* Cayzer Irvine & Co. (1978)

MacInnes, Colin. *City of Spades.* Alison & Busby (London, 1957)

Nath, Raj Mohan. *The Background of Assamese Culture.* M.N. Dutton (Gauhati)

Peninsular and Oriental Steam Navigation Company. *Men of the Ships.* P&O Company (London, 1960)

Race Today Collective. *The Arrivants: A Pictorial Essay on Blacks in Britain.* Race Today Collective. (London, 1987)

Race Today Collective. *The Struggle of Asian Workers in Britain.* Race Today Collective. (London, 1983)

Rajkhowa, Benudhar. *Notes on the Sylhetee Dialect.* (Sylhet, 1913)

Reid, Sir Robert. *History of the Frontier Areas Bordering on Assam 1883-1941.* Assam Government Press (Shillong, 1942)

Reid, Sir Robert. *Years of Change in Bengal and Assam.* Benn (London, 1966)

Salter, Joseph. *The Asiatic in England: Sketches of Sixteen Years Work Among Asiatics.* Seely, Jackson & Halliday (London, 1873)

Salter, Joseph. *The East in the West: or Work Among the Asiatics and Africans in London.* S.W Partridge & Co. (London, l896)

Sen. *Indian Land System and Land Reform.*

Shyllon. *Black Slaves in Britain.*

Taylor, James. *Ellermans:A Wealth of Shipping.* (1976)

Tinker, Prof. Hugh. *The Banyan Tree: Overseas Emigrants from India Pakistan and Bangladesh. Oxford Univ. Press. (Oxford, 1977)*

Visram, Rozina. *Ayahs Lascars and Princes.* Pluto Press (London, 1986)

Visram, Rozina. *Indians in Britain. (Peoples on the Move* series). Batsford (London, 1987)

Watkins Thomas, M. *Our Asian Crews.* (in *About Ourselves.* P&0 Magazine) P&0 Company (London, 1955)

Wilson, Amrit. *Finding a Voice: Asian Women in Britain.* Virago (London, 1978)

Yule, Sir Henry. *Cathay and the Way Thither: Being a Collection of Medieval Notices of China.* Hakluyt Society, 2nd series. (London, 1915)

Yule, Sir Henry. *Hobson Jobson: Being a Glossary of Anglo-Indian Colloquial Words and Phrases.* (London, 1886)

Glossary

Ag-wallah: Fireman (on board ship).

Andakha: Area of Land.

Backshish: Tip or gratuity.

Barriwallah: Landlord of a lodging house.

Bettiwallah: A 'ladies man'.

Bhai-sahib: Older brother (term of respect).

Bhakti: Religious devotions (Hindu).

Bicchu: Group cooking or mess.

Bilait: Abroad.

Chunam: Lime extracted from limestone.

Coal(a) Wallah: Engineer responsible for supplying ship's firemen with coal.

Commis: Apprentice waiter, steward or chef (French).

Dal: Lentils.

Daroga: Hermitage of a Saint.

Donkey-wallah (or *'Donkeyman'*): Engineer in charge of the 'Donkey' (small auxiliary) engines on board ship.

Eid: Muslim festival marking the end of Ramzan or the sacrifice of Abraham.

Elakha: Area of land.

Fakir: Religious mendicant (Muslim).

Ghat-serang: Recruiter and foreman of a crew of dock workers (also a money-lender and lodging-house keeper).

Ghoosh: Bribe.

Haji: One who has been on the pilgrimage to Mecca.

Halal: Pure and acceptable for a Moslem (e.g. religious dietary requirements).

Haram: Forbidden to Muslims.

Imam: Leader of a Muslim congregation.

Kaffir: Infidel, non-Muslim.

Kashi: Tribal people of Meghalaya (North East India).

Kobiraj: Herbal healer.

Kuki Nagas: Tribal people of Nagaland (North East India).

Kuta: Cottage.

Lascari-bat: Simple form of Hindustani used in merchant ships and armed forces between (white) British officers and Indian men.

Maidan: Parade ground (particularly in Calcutta) now large public open space.

Maripathi: Spiritual practices (Sufism).

Maulana: Charismatic religious leader (Muslim).

Mazar: Tomb (of a religious figure).

Miah-sahib: Teacher.

Moghul: Muslim dynasty which ruled much of India. From 1526 (Babur) to 1739 (Badhur Shah).

Nadi: River

Namaz: Muslim prayers

Nana: Grandfather.

Navadingas: Decorated ceremonial boats.

Nolly (also Nollie): Merchant seamen's continuous discharge papers.

Paan: Leaf used for chewing Betel nut.

Pathans: People from Afghanistan and the North West Frontier (Pakistan).

Peon: Servant, orderly.

Pir: Muslim saint or holy man.

Pirzada: Descendant of a saint.

Ryot (also *Raiyat*): Peasant cultivator.

Ryotwari: System of land tenure.

Ramzan: Fasting month (Muslim).

Sahib: Term of respect.

Sarpanch: Local Government elected leader.

Sepoy: Indian soldier.

Serang: Bosun, foreman or recruiter of ship crews.

Shadiwallah: Married man.

Sirdar: Jobber or recruiter.

Sufi: Muslim mystic, dedicated to achieving union with the Divine through devotion, love and song.

Sunderbans: Jungle on river delta – South Bangladesh.

Tel-wallah: Engine-room greaser, responsible for checking engine performance and temperature.

Thana: Police district (administrative boundary).

Tindal: Bosun's mate.

Vishnu: Hindu deity whose incarnations include Sri Krishna and Sri Rama.

Vishnaivite: Devotional Hindu worshipper.

Zemindar: Landholder, collector of Revenue.

The index includes proper and place-names when given more than a passing mention. An exception is made to this rule when such references might be of special historical or social interest, or where people and places are of particular importance for the story teller.

In the entry *'Ports of Call'* have been included those numerous lists of stopping-off places which these cosmopolitan seafarers visited on their travels around the world.

Normal indexing practice has been followed for sub-headings and cross-references – using *'see'* and *'see also'* for alternative and additional entries respectively.

Index